Feminist Posthumanisms, New Materialisms and Education

This edited collection is a careful assemblage of papers that have contributed to the maturing field within education studies that works with the feminist implications of the theories and methodologies of posthumanism and new materialism – what we have also called elsewhere 'PhEmaterialism'.

The generative questions for this collection are: what if we locate education in doing and becoming rather than being? And, how does associating education with matter, multiplicity and relationality change how we think about agency, ontology and epistemology? This collection foregrounds cutting-edge educational research that works to trouble the binaries between theory and methodology. It demonstrates new forms of feminist ethics and response-ability in research practices, and offers some coherence to this new area of research. This volume will provide a vital reference text for educational researchers and scholars interested in this burgeoning area of theoretically informed methodology and methodologically informed theory.

The chapters in this book were originally published as articles in Taylor & Francis journals.

Jessica Ringrose is Professor of Sociology of Gender and Education at the UCL Institute of Education, UK. Her work develops innovative feminist approaches to understanding subjectivity, affectivity and assembled power relations. Her books include *Post-Feminist Education?* (2013); *Deleuze and Research Methodologies* (2013) and *Children, Sexuality and Sexualisation* (2015).

Katie Warfield is a faculty member in the Department of Journalism and Communication at Kwantlen Polytechnic University, Canada. She is the Director of the Visual Media Workshop, a centre for research and learning into digital visual culture. Her recent writings have appeared in *Social Media + Society*, *Feminist Media Studies* and *Feminist Issues, 6th ed.* (2016).

Shiva Zarabadi is a PhD candidate at the UCL Institute of Education, UK. Her work explores subjectivity in relation to assemblages of matter and meaning, humans and more-than-humans, and affect, taking a New Materialist and Posthumanist approach. Her PhD research focuses on the becomings of Muslim girls under the structure of Prevent policy in London secondary schools.

Education and Social Theory
Series Editor: Stephen J. Ball, Institute of Education, University College London, UK

Social theory can help us to make sense of many aspects of contemporary education by providing analytic concepts and insights. Social theories are tools of analysis and interpretation for educational researchers that enable us to make sense of the processes, effects, and outcomes of educational experiences and institutions.

Drawing together selections from the best work previously published in Taylor and Francis journals to create powerful and effective collections, this series highlights and explores the social theories critical to educational writers, researchers and scholars. Each book focuses a different key writer or field of theory, with the overarching aim of providing an overview of the social theories important to education research, but also of showing how these theories can be applied in a practical manner in the current education landscape.

Books in the Series:

Foucault and Education
Edited by Stephen J. Ball

Marxisms and Education
Edited by Noah De Lissovoy

Actor Network Theory and Education
Edited by Tara Fenwick and Richard Edwards

Feminist Posthumanisms, New Materialisms and Education
Edited by Jessica Ringrose, Katie Warfield and Shiva Zarabadi

Feminist Posthumanisms, New Materialisms and Education

Edited by
Jessica Ringrose, Katie Warfield and Shiva Zarabadi

Routledge
Taylor & Francis Group
LONDON AND NEW YORK

First published 2019
by Routledge
2 Park Square, Milton Park, Abingdon, Oxon, OX14 4RN, UK

and by Routledge
52 Vanderbilt Avenue, New York, NY 10017, USA

First issued in paperback 2020

Routledge is an imprint of the Taylor & Francis Group, an informa business

Chapter 2, 4–7, and 10 © 2019 Taylor and Francis
Chapters 1, 3 and 8 © 2016 Philosophy of Education Society of Australasia
Chapter 9 © 2015 Pedagogy, Culture & Society

British Library Cataloguing in Publication Data
A catalogue record for this book is available from the British Library

ISBN 13: 978-0-367-58591-4 (pbk)
ISBN 13: 978-0-8153-9413-6 (hbk)

Typeset in Times New Roman
by RefineCatch Limited, Bungay, Suffolk

Publisher's Note
The publisher accepts responsibility for any inconsistencies that may have
arisen during the conversion of this book from journal articles to book chapters,
namely the possible inclusion of journal terminology.

Disclaimer
Every effort has been made to contact copyright holders for their permission to
reprint material in this book. The publishers would be grateful to hear from any
copyright holder who is not here acknowledged and will undertake to rectify
any errors or omissions in future editions of this book.

Contents

Citation Information

The chapters in this book were originally published in a variety of Taylor & Francis journals. When citing this material, please use the original page numbering for each article, as follows:

Chapter 1

Voice in the agentic assemblage
Lisa A. Mazzei and Alecia Y. Jackson
Educational Philosophy and Theory, volume 49, issue 11 (October 2017), pp. 1090–1098

Chapter 2

Images of thinking in feminist materialisms: ontological divergences and the production of researcher subjectivities
Hillevi Lenz Taguchi
International Journal of Qualitative Studies in Education, volume 26, issue 6 (November 2013), pp. 706–716

Chapter 3

Learning to be affected: Matters of pedagogy in the artists' soup kitchen
Stephanie Springgay and Zofia Zaliwska
Educational Philosophy and Theory, volume 49, issue 3 (March 2017), pp. 273–283

Chapter 4

Objects, bodies and space: gender and embodied practices of mattering in the classroom
Carol A. Taylor
Gender and Education, volume 25, issue 6 (October 2013), pp. 688–703

Chapter 5

Gettin' a little crafty: Teachers Pay Teachers©, Pinterest© and neo-liberalism in new materialist feminist research
Elizabeth A. Pittard
Gender and Education, volume 29, issue 1 (January 2017), pp. 28–47

Chapter 6

Dexter time: the space, time, and matterings of school absence registration
Linnea Bodén
Discourse: Studies in the Cultural Politics of Education, volume 37, issue 2 (April 2016), pp. 245–255

Chapter 7

Diffractive pedagogies: dancing across new materialist imaginaries
Anna Hickey-Moody, Helen Palmer and Esther Sayers
Gender and Education, volume 28, issue 2 (March 2016), pp. 213–229

Chapter 8

Selfies, relfies and phallic tagging: posthuman part-icipations in teen digital sexuality assemblages
Emma Renold and Jessica Ringrose
Educational Philosophy and Theory, volume 49, issue 11 (October 2017), pp. 1066–1079

Chapter 9

Learning with children, ants, and worms in the Anthropocene: towards a common world pedagogy of multispecies vulnerability
Affrica Taylor and Veronica Pacini-Ketchabaw
Pedagogy, Culture & Society, volume 23, issue 4 (December 2015), pp. 507–529

Chapter 10

A Walk in the Park: Considering Practice for Outdoor Environmental Education Through an Immanent Take on the Material Turn
Jamie Mcphie and David Andrew George Clarke
The Journal of Environmental Education, volume 46, issue 4 (September 2015), pp. 230–250

For any permission-related enquiries please visit:
http://www.tandfonline.com/page/help/permissions

Notes on Contributors

Linnea Bodén is a Postdoctoral Researcher in Early Childhood Education at Stockholm University, Sweden. She has a background in gender studies, sociology and pedagogy; and her current research focuses on children's perspectives on research and on being part of a research project.

David Andrew George Clarke is a PhD candidate at the University of Edinburgh, UK. His research focuses on confluences in environmental humanities, environmental education and contemporary (post)qualitative research methods.

Anna Hickey-Moody is Professor of Media and Communication at RMIT University, Melbourne, Australia. She is known for her methodological expertise with affect theory, qualitative and practice research. She has developed a philosophically informed, cultural studies approach to youth arts as a subcultural form of humanities education.

Alecia Y. Jackson is Associate Professor of Educational Research at Appalachian State University, USA. Her research brings feminist and poststructural theories of power, knowledge, language and subjectivity to bear on a range of overlapping topics: deconstructions of narrative and voice, cultural studies of schooling (with an emphasis on the rural) and qualitative method in the postmodern.

Hillevi Lenz Taguchi is Professor and co-Director of the Section for Early Childhood Education at Stockholm University, Sweden. She has experience of trans- and interdisciplinary research, specifically focusing on feminist theories and continental philosophy in her studies of higher education, teacher education and early childhood practices.

Lisa A. Mazzei is Associate Professor of Education Studies at the University of Oregon, USA. Her teaching and research include qualitative research methodology and curriculum theory, and her research is focused on a study of racial identity and awareness among white teachers and implications for curriculum.

Jamie Mcphie is Lecturer in Cultural Landscapes and Aesthetics in the Outdoors at Cumbria University, UK. His research is interested in how mental health and well-being is distributed in the environment, including the influence of perceptions of environments on behaviour.

Veronica Pacini-Ketchabaw is Professor of Early Childhood Education at Western University in Ontario, Canada. Her research contributes to the Common World Childhoods Research Collective (tracing children's relations with places, materials and other species), and the Early Childhood Pedagogies Collaboratory (experimenting with the contours, conditions and complexities of 21st century pedagogies).

Helen Palmer is Senior Lecturer in English Literature and Creative Writing at Kingston University, UK, working at the intersections of philosophy, speculative writing and critical theory. Her research interests include the avant-garde, queer performance, critical theory, gender, the body, synaesthesia, intersectional feminism, utopias/dystopias, afrofuturism and new materialism.

Elizabeth A. Pittard is Clinical Assistant Professor of Early Childhood and Elementary Education at Georgia State University, USA. Her research interests include investigating the working lives of women elementary school teachers and the manifestations of neoliberalism in P-12 and teacher education.

Emma Renold is Professor of Childhood Studies at the School of Social Sciences, Cardiff University, UK. Working with feminist, queer and post-humanist approaches, her research explores gendered and sexual subjectivities across diverse institutional sites and public spaces across the young life course.

Jessica Ringrose is Professor of Sociology of Gender and Education at the UCL Institute of Education, UK. Her work develops innovative feminist approaches to understanding subjectivity, affectivity and assembled power relations. Her books include *Post-Feminist Education?* (2013); *Deleuze and Research Methodologies* (2013) and *Children, Sexuality and Sexualisation* (2015).

Esther Sayers is Lecturer in Education at Goldsmiths, University of London, UK. Her research interests centre on arts participation, in particular the pedagogies that enable the production of knowledge locally, where equality and emancipation are foregrounded.

Stephanie Springgay is Associate Professor at the Ontario Institute for Studies in Education, University of Toronto, Canada. Her research interests include feminist new materialism, queer theory and the inhuman, research-creation, methodologies and affect theory.

Affrica Taylor is Associate Professor in the Faculty of Education, Science, Technology and Mathematics at the University of Canberra, Australia. Her research is interested in the interdependent and mutually-constitutive relations between people, places and other species; informed by her work in cultural geography and teaching in remote desert and urban Australian Aboriginal communities.

Carol A. Taylor is Professor of Gender and Higher Education in the Institute of Education, Sheffield Hallam University, UK. Her research utilises feminist, neo-materialist, and posthumanist theories and frameworks to explore gendered inequalities, spatial practices and students' participation in a range of higher education sites.

Katie Warfield is a faculty member in the Department of Journalism and Communication at Kwantlen Polytechnic University, Canada. She is the Director of the Visual Media Workshop, a centre for research and learning into digital visual culture. Her recent writings have appeared in *Social Media + Society*, *Feminist Media Studies* and *Feminist Issues, 6ᵗʰ ed.* (2016).

Zofia Zaliwska is a PhD candidate in the Curriculum Studies and Teacher Development program at the University of Toronto, Canada. Her current research explores experimental methods and an ethics of agency within qualitative research methodologies, with a focus on developing radical processes of representing the relational experiences in the academic work of reading and writing.

Shiva Zarabadi is a PhD candidate at the UCL Institute of Education, UK. Her work explores subjectivity in relation to assemblages of matter and meaning, humans and more-than-humans, and affect, taking a New Materialist and Posthumanist approach. Her PhD research focuses on the becomings of Muslim girls under the structure of Prevent policy in London secondary schools.

Introducing Feminist Posthumanisms/New Materialisms & Educational Research: Response-able Theory-Practice-Methodology

Introduction

"Not only subjects but also objects are permeated through and through with their entangled kin; the *other* is not just in one's skin, but in one's bones, in one's belly, in one's heart, in one's nucleus, in one's past and future. This is as true for electrons as it is for brittlestars as it is for the differentially constituted human . . ."

Karen Barad, Meeting the Universe Halfway

This edited collection is a careful assemblage of some of the foundational publications in Taylor & Francis journals that have contributed to the maturing field in education studies that works with the *feminist capacities and possibilities* of the theories and methodologies of posthumanisms and new materialisms (note the plural to capture the multiplicities of these approaches and the slash to capture the entanglement of these approaches in our conceptualization). We have elsewhere called this movement PhEmaterialism where the *Ph* refers to posthuman, the *Fem* from feminisms, and materialism from the new materialist movement (see Ringrose, Renold, Hickey-Moody and Osgood, 2015 PhEmaterialism Conference, PhEmaterialism Facebook page and Twitter page; Renold, 2017; Renold and Ringrose, 2018; Niccolini and Ringrose, forthcoming). In this introduction, we unfold and 'infold' (Manning, 2016) a PhEmaterialism process of remixing important contributions to this new area of educational, theoretical and methodological research doings.

After many embodied and existential collective threads of thought, many marker-ridden paper balls in trash cans, glitchy skype calls, and rainbow marked-up shared digital documents across oceans and time zones, after temporal stretches and contractions of concern and then conviction over those we are citing and not, and those who may cite us, we believe that a shift into feminist new materialist thinking requires a re-turn of some of the ontological re-imaginings of habitual relationalities of data, theory, methods, analysis, writing, and researcher responsibility which are represented in all the publications in this collection. We begin our introduction with what we think of as a "remixed" edited collection (Massumi, 2015; Coleman and Ringrose, 2013; Kanai, 2015). We are bringing together previously published work that we feel moves the field of educational research somewhere different than before. Through putting to work the lenses of feminist Posthuman and New Materialism thinking and doing in educational research these pieces are brought together in a new assemblage of possible entry points into this territory of research productions.

In invoking territory here, we are very aware of the entangled power plays and force relations that shape new modalities of thinking and doing in academia, and are aware that in the shaping of this volume we are *infolded* (Manning, 2016) in the research assemblage of this collection and the generative genealogy of knowledge of feminist posthumanisms and new materialisms as an emergent field. Moreover, some research was cut in and made to *matter* while other work was either not published in Taylor & Francis journals, was unknown to us, neglected or passed over. We recognize publication and citation as great matters of feminist ethics, and so take our privileged roles to make such agential cuts (Barad, 2007) as curators of this collection, an assemblage of thinking and doing, with great response-ability, as Barad, would say. It was our active agential scissors that have marked the theoretical distinguishing lines wherein we've cut away the inherent disciplinary complexity in order to tell only a few of the many possible stories. And so we begin by marking this very process as a *storying*. Far from being a flat fixed and structured mapping of articles, our open-ended and very much incomplete narrating here seeks to actualize *some (but definitely not all)* the layers of the various plateaus of education, feminist posthumanism and new materialism. Each article is not a unit but rather a knot or a partial exploration, which unearths a unique entanglement to their own field of research. This collection has movement and rhythm where we map connections and intra-actions—from the knot to new sensations and movements and objects. Working across dancing, art and crafts, to playing and walking as part of immanent forms of environmental education. This edited collection is an impartial partiality that opens up the possibilities to move across and along various plateaus in this field. Like any, this collection is incomplete. It is an opening, a becoming, and a place for debate. We openly waft the flames of dialogue concerning the cuts we've made herein and those we've left out. In the posthumanist tradition of vibrant matter (Bennett, 2010), we conceive of this document as a living one and encourage it to become a lively one.

Core conceptual starting points in Feminist Posthumanisms and New Materialisms

Taking all of this into account, the generative questions for this collection are:

What if we locate education in doing, becoming and making rather than being?

How does associating education with matter, multiplicity and relationality change how we think about agency, ontology and epistemology?

Perhaps most importantly, what happens to materially-laden educational assemblages when we purposefully in-fold them back into one another, as Donna Haraway (2016) would say, or plug into one another in different combinations as Jackson and Mazzei (2012) might ask, to generate our attentiveness to gender as it manifests materially, discursively, and affectively?

In keeping with the material threads of feminist genealogy (Van der Tuin, 2014) we highlight throughout this collection those who we call the "fem-inal" theorists and themes at the heart of feminist new materialism. Our selection of fem-inal, as opposed to semin-al texts, trouble masculine citation practices and genealogies. In this spirit, we mark the key conceptual terrains of a series of central queer kinshipping (Freeman, 2008; Haraway, 2016) partnerships and feminist fore-mothers and we view as underpinning some key moves in the traditions of feminist new materialism. We ground our discussion in the queer partnership of **Deleuze and Guattari**, who worked at the intersections of psychiatry and philosophy to offer important new concepts for rethinking the individual, society and power. To us their partnership evokes collaborative tensions key to PhEmaterialism, to embrace and enliven hybridity, multiplicity and entanglement in our research, as they noted: "The two of us wrote *Anti-Oedipus* together. Since each of us was several, there was already quite a crowd." (Deleuze and Guattari, 1987). Deleuze and Guattari's queer theories of affect take form through concepts such as re/de/territorialization, rhizomatics, becoming, lines of flight, assemblage and more and are critically important to many philosophers and researchers cited in this volume and to the research articles chosen for this remixed edited volume who deploy these thinking/doing tools; such as elaborating the material vitality of objects (Bennet, 2010; 2012 in Jackson and Mazzei) or in attending to everyday affects (Massumi, 2015 in Springgay and Zaliwska). **Rosi Braidotti**, whose work is shaped by Deleuze and Guattari and Spinoza, has offered key insights into the post-human perspective that charts new ways of thinking and doing outside of rational humanist man and the anthropocene via concepts like figuration and nomadic thinking. **Donna Haraway**, who emerges from feminist science studies, dissolves the nature/culture and nature/technology divide through her work on cyborgs, human-animal relations and new planetary ethics for staying with the trouble. **Karen Barad**, a theoretical physicist, helps us to rethink the relationship between researcher, research design and research production through underscoring the profoundly relational nature of being and knowing and mattering: ethico-onto-epistemology. This has influenced a paradigmatic shift and development from post-structural discourse analysis (Butler) to a form of posthuman performativity, that sees the inseparable entanglement of discourse and materiality in both our phenomena of research and our processes for research and data production; it also is a yoking of ethical reponse-ability of researchers to be aware of these relationalities of knowing and being to doing, with her hyphenated mash up.

We purposefully meld together these key theorists for two key reasons: to invoke a new territory of immanence that of *feminist* new materialism and posthumanism—joining up what are sometimes taken as distinct spheres of educational research. We also meld these scholars together to build a PhEmaterialism assemblage of scholars who we feel collectively offer shared and overlapping theoretical and methodological lenses and tools for a feminist reimagining of the boundaries of the self, the researcher and the researched.

Although we foreground these key scholars as the queer feminist philosophical backbone of this emergent field, we equally acknowledge and work within and through, in creative ways, the power dynamics that remain at play when we mark them as philosophical/theoretical 'masters' informing educational research. We trouble this mastery by using intersectional feminist Audre Lorde's (1979) pressing message that the master's tools cannot dismantle the master's house. Indeed, New Materialism approaches have been criticized for ignoring intersectional power struggles by reifying materialism as "new" while turning away from the long-held place of materiality as a source of deep epistemological value within indigenous ways of knowing (Tallbear, 2013). We also want to break away from a tendency to cite masters without citing our emerging feminist peers. Thus, our curation herein reaches back and forward in time, seeking to purposefully entangle intersectional diversity in terms of authors, citations, and geographic locations of case studies and participants. Therefore, we present the work selected in this volume as a complex entanglement of post-phallic generative, rhizomatic doings and tentacular thinkings, that is branching out—feral—not bound to the arborescent lineages (Deleuze and Guattari, 1987) found in conventional text book accounts that map back to masculinist, humanist, western, white, masters. Our feminist politics and response-ability weave through and wrap around every article chosen, and every word typed, here.

Our feminist politics, however, remain constrained and we must acknowledge, make visible, and take ownership of the limits of those constraints. Restricted to only articles published by Taylor & Francis, we are indebted to and have drawn extensively upon recent special issues devoted to the themes of *either* new materialism and posthumanism in education. Although not an exhaustive list, some of these important collections include a special issue in *Gender and Education* on new materialism (Ivinson and Taylor, 2013) as well as a methodological special issues that explore moving beyond conventional qualitative research strategies and analysis (Lather and St. Pierre, 2013) such as rethinking and redoing coding practices (Jackson and St. Pierre, 2014) and finding 'new empiricisms and new materialisms' which challenge what is and how we encounter 'data' (St. Pierre et al., 2013). We also drew on an important book *Posthuman Research Practices in Education* (Taylor and Hughes, 2016) a special issue of *Educational Philosophy and Theory* on more-than-human research practices (Pederson and Pini, 2017) and recent overviews of posthuman research in education (Ulmer, 2017; Snaza et al., 2014), which challenge humanism, the humanities and associated research conventions. Challenging humanist conventions in educational theory, methodology and practice.

We were also constrained by the number of articles to include while also displaying a breadth of scholarship that adhered to our feminist politics listed above. Had we the space we would narrate the story of the breathy expansion and contraction of our table of contents from twenty articles to fifteen, to ten, back to twelve, to eight, to (oh!) three more, to two more sliced out, to sleep-interrupted nights marred by the weighty responsibility of this list curated through recognition of discursive power dynamics and poked and prodded by affectively agonizing discussions and debates.

We also acknowledge that in selecting these articles we purposefully chose those that named "feminist new materialism" or "feminist posthumanism" as their disciplinary positionality. Many articles we read, and worked through, but did not include here performed what we ourselves would name as feminist new materialist theoretical or methodological contributions, but we negotiated the relational power dynamics at play were we to ascribe names involuntarily and non-consensually (a discursive and likely affective act) and therefore classify these studies as such if the authors themselves did not located themselves there first.

Guided by our fem-inal fore-mothers and queer partnerships, our feminist intersectional politics, our anti-mastery desires to respect genealogies while actively and critically questioning their authority, we have divided the articles in this book into three distinct thematic yet diffractive sections: (1.) Affect, attunement, entanglement: research assemblages, (2.) Space-Time-Matterings: agency, intra-action, diffraction, and (3.) Posthuman participations, micro-ontologies and immanence. The following sections detail the common themes in these sections and summarize the articles that are grouped under each.

Affect, attunement, entanglement: research assemblages

In the first section of the book we foreground the significant contributions Deleuze and Guattari make to theorizing prepersonal, more-than-human affects by returning to Spinoza to rethink bodily capacities to affect and be affected.

> . . . we know nothing of a body until we know what it can do, in other words, what its affects are, how they can or cannot enter into composition with other affects, with the affects of another body, either to destroy that body or be destroyed by it, either to exchange actions and passions with it or to join with it in composing a more powerful body. (Deleuze and Guattari, 1987, p. 284)

Deleuze and Guattari argue "affect is not a personal feeling, nor is it a characteristic, it is the *effectuation of a power* shifting from an ontology of being and fixity to an ontology of 'effectuation' and affective process in constant motion . . . 'an ability to affect and be affected' . . . a pre-personal *intensity* . . . implying an augmentation or diminution of that body's capacity to act" (Massumi, 2004, p. xvii). This concept of affect thus helps us to analyze power relations between bodies in relation to another concept: that of assemblages or configurations of connections in any decidable unit. Assemblages as units, however, are never singular and naturally bound but rather are ontologically wild and rhizomatic grouped in a given moment but always living and in flux. It is these sorts of fluctuating "units" our articles examine and explore. The assemblage, which relates to the notion of agencement in French, references the agential relations between the connections of the assemblage. Educational research can use these theories to map these affective assemblages and think about bodily capacities to affect and be affected (at various scales and intensities) (Ringrose, 2011, pp. 601–602; Fox and Alldred, 2014)

We start off this remix collection with Mazzei and Jackson as they draw on Deleuze, Guattari, Barad, and Jane Bennet's theories of vibrant matter, to, importantly, move us away from a consideration of a singular human "I" to distributed networks of agency in order to rethink conventional units of research data such as the 'voices' in empirical qualitative research. *Voice in the agentic assemblage* builds on Mazzei's (2008) earlier important work, which has re-theorized the meanings of voice and silence in research, and the importance put on the voice in transcript materials as part of the normative conventions of qualitative research. Jackson and Mazzei (2012) have also posited silence as an important force of desire and implication in qualitative research challenging researchers to take seriously the refusal or inability to speak around issues such as racism in relation to how research subjects deal with, for instance, white privilege. To counter humanist notions of individualized, agentic self-identity and voice, they use Barad's notion of intra-action and agential realism to think about a range of forces at work in the materialisation of voice in research; and they think about the distributed agency of objects and inanimate things to reconsider a range of elements in the production of research 'findings'. The article is useful in mapping out how they understand and map posthuman voice as "an assemblage of heterogeneous elements—objects, signs, utterances, bodies— existing on different temporal and spatial scales: a kitchen table and chairs, gendered bodies, discourses of patriarchy and institutionalized religion, enunciations of critique, a garage door, histories, communities, childhoods . . ." (2016, p. 4). A key contribution to this article is that it troubles uni-dimensional qualitative research about interview data and encourages a multisensory approach to thinking about the multiplicities of a moment that are taking place to create the research encounter.

Relatedly in her article *Images of thinking in feminist materialisms: ontological divergences and the production of researcher subjectivities*, Hillevi Lenz Taguchi works to use new directions in posthumanist, anti-anthropocentric and material feminism research to move away from the assumed humanist "I" of the researcher in qualitative inquiry. In this article Lenz Taguchi works with Deleuze to try to trouble representational thinking and the I/eye of the researcher rooted in representational interpretation from a core site of researcher subjectivity. Through working, collaborating, and engaging with and among the research analyses of 10 student-researchers, a multiplicity of meanings grew up "wildly like weeds." Rather than singular stories about a research participant named Fataneh, what emerged were multiple stories—and thus multiple participant subjectivities—that intermesh and entangled to create new imagined possibilities. And further, multiplicity in the collaborative analyses lent itself to the construction of a 'collective-body-assemblage research subjectivity." Taguchi (p. 714) calls for a sort of rhizomatic thinking which aims to 'acentre' and 'asubjectify' and subsequently create a new multiple researcher reality. This is a profound and significant interruption of the traditional of a singular agentic anthropocentric I/eye in research who authoritatively interprets and presents research findings.

Pedagogical attunements: eating as art

In *Learning to be affected: Matters of pedagogy in the artists' soup kitchen*, Springgay and Zaliwska explore affect and rhythm as two important matters of pedagogy that are at work in research and need to be activated although with unpredictable results. Rhythm here is what we call capacity—in its flow and potentiality—on the move (Niccolini and Pindyck, 2015; Renold and Ringrose, 2016; Hickey-Moody et al., 2016). They invite us to think about pedagogy as politics of attunement and responsibility, which is never determined prior to the event of pedagogy. This forces us to pay attention to 'live mapping of the process under transition' (Massumi, 2015). Springgay and Zaliwska problematize the traditional standards of learning as a process of transmitting knowledge and challenge representational thinking, causation, linear time and theory as inventive. They propose: "Learning to be affected, to reside and co-invent on the refrain, necessitates a particular politicality, a differentiated ethics that demands a particular attunement to the matters at play." (p. 280). They posit that in their artist soup kitchen they create as part of their research, or any other field such as classroom or pedagogy, individuals do not hold predetermined fixed identities prior to their entry and entanglement to the field rather the field 'braces them into a kind of differential attunemnet with others'. In a sense, our differences in the field are our different ongoing attunements, 'we're all in on the event together, but we're in it together differently'. The soup kitchen as an affective event 'carries subjectivities elsewhere, to new territories and a dismantling of the old, ever toward the infinite possibilities and power contained within our bodies, our friends (and our foes), and their ecological contexts' (Guattari quoted in Bertelsen and Murphie, 2010, p. 153). Springgay and Zaliwska propose 'affective intensity is literally the life of territorial processes' (Bertelsen and Murphie, 2010) noting the becoming-art of eating, and other mundane affective events such as pedagogy and becoming-student/teacher carry with them the potential for something different to materialize in space and time.

Space-Time-Matterings: agency, intra-action, diffraction

In the second section of the book we explore Karen Barad, whose work straddles posthumanism and new materialism through her theories of posthuman performativity and her (and, and, and hyphenated) ethico-onto-epistemology of *agential realism*. Drawing upon Niels Bohr's quantum theory, which refuses the notion of *separation* as the *a priori* starting point of existence, she advocates ontological starting points of *entanglement, connection and touch*. Barad argues that previous ontological frameworks that have dominated Western thought, like Cartesianism which are premised on separation and distinction are apparatuses of thought that ignore the natural intimacy and proximity of the universe. The ontology of agential realism, and thus entanglement and intra (not inter-action), implicitly requires attention to—and an ethics towards—the power dynamics at play behind the *cuts* that discursively and materially separate concepts and objects from one another. Barad argues agential cuts, although entrenched, are not immutable and that "iterative reconfigurings of *topological manifolds of spacetimesmatter relations*" (Barad, 2007, p. 178), or the sometimes small and sometimes significant departures from discursive and material habits can work to reshape patterning structures of existence. Importantly Barad is interested in the privileged and powerful role of the researcher in research and the material and discursive cuts made in the production of authoritative knowledge, and it's these contributions that perhaps most deeply have influenced feminist educational research most broadly.

A second major contribution of Barad's is her push to go beyond Butler's concern for the materialisation of discourse upon the subject. Instead Barad works to enfold matter as an equally entangled potential starting point of data and analysis, which expands and brings forward Butler's ideas of discursive resignification—offering new tools for educational research (Ringrose and Rawlings, 2015)—where typically the question of how a resignification of language through embodied resistance has been suggested but *not* mapped through. New materialism does not suggest that the discursive turn never acknowledged the material nor does it forgo discourse for analyses of materiality, rather the material gives increasing weight to material-semiotic-affective entanglements.

Agential realism and discursive-material intra-action: mattering the classroom space?

In *Objects, bodies and space: gender and embodied practices of mattering in the classroom* (2013), Carol Taylor foregrounds the gendered materiality of the classroom to argue that human and non-human actants bear equal importance in educational settings and practices and especially in research practices involving observational research. Taylor combines theory from three distinct fields: posthumanism, via mainly Karen Barad, material culture theory (Miller, 1997), and spatial understandings (Massey, 2013) to re-read the data she collected from an ethnographic case study of a UK A-level classroom. Rather than examining only the discursive events, she *agentially cuts* her complex data to reveal the "vital materialism" (p. 692) of a series of objects, which act as players in the production of classroom learning. She narrates, for instance, the teacher, Malky, and his "magisterial chair" forming a material assemblage that both displays, via performance and spatial occupation, "adult hegemonic masculine nonchalance" and the binary mechanisms of control that dictate, as the teacher wheels around the room, who is free to move and who is not. Taylor further shows the gendered material agency of objects like: a flipchart, he at once dramatically man-handles and jokingly refers to as "Sheila", a stack of papers which "memorializes credentialism" (p. 696) of the A level meritocratic educational system, and pens noting how a student's use of a pen as a whistle was seen to challenge the auditory and spatial authority of the teacher.

Throughout the article Taylor also uses various posthuman methodological approaches in her own writing. She draws on theorists not via logic and deduction but via, intuition and a process of collage. She actively narrates the choices she made in *cutting out* the materiality from the natural complexity of the case study in order to take response-ability for the ethico-onto-epistemological focus on materiality in order to help researchers think about agency not as singular and exclusively the privy of humans, but rather to "get down and dirty in the empirical details" (p. 701) in order to see the classroom as a "co-constitutive enactment of human and non-human" (p. 701) agents and forces.

Intra-acting social media and digital curricula

In *Gettin' a little crafty: Teachers Pay Teachers©, Pinterest© and neo-liberalism in new materialist feminist research*, Elizabeth Pittard draws upon Barad's key concept of intra-action to explore how women teachers navigate the conditions of neoliberal subjectivity required in contemporary schooling environments; and how they produce "good enough" teacher subjectivities in conditions where they are to perform to high assessment standards but lack curricular materials (resources) provided by the state. Pittard explores the creative neo-liberal economy of DIY teaching curricula that are developed for teachers, by teachers and bought and sold on Pinterest. The curriculum themselves are positioned as discursive-material-digital actants that come into the classroom through the attachments and desires of the teachers to be "good enough" in conditions of impossibility in contemporary performative and audit driven neo-liberal education systems. Importantly Pittard's article is a hybrid that draws upon Foucauldian theories of technologies of disciplinary power constituting neoliberal subjects; but it also tries to move beyond simply understanding these power relations as acting *upon* teachers to consider how a range of actors, things and technological affordances entangle to constantly produce new conditions to be navigated. Pittard debates whether these new openings to buy and sell curriculum are empowering or regulating because they create a new market of engagement, through which women teachers must evaluate themselves. Ultimately a binary driven argument is resisted through the new materialism frame, which insists that we look at the complex relationships being enacted between the material classrooms and lesson plans, the digital marketplace and the subjective experience of becoming a "good enough teacher."

Technology, actants, thick temporality

As noted in the discussion of networked educational environments explored by Pittard, we need to pay greater attention to the importance of technologies like social media platforms and how they reshape educational experiences around space but also importantly around time. Feminist new materialist 'thick temporality' begins not from the point of subject/object relations (or human/inhuman, nature/culture or cause/effect, for that matter), but from the position of being always already entangled in a vital materiality. Instead of relying on chronology or the progressive construction of the politics of the subject formed around key dates and events and self-actualization, feminist new materialist re-imagining of time is a kind of emergent feminist 'living present' (Walker, 2014, p. 46) that is always a stretching between a past full of intra-active materialities and a realm of future possibility to which we are accountable, but not bound. Living present demands attention to a 'dynamic specificity' (Barad, 2006, p. 377) and it is also to become a time maker (Walker, 2014, p. 58) who is ethically response-able to the complex processes of making and unmaking habits, memories and chances in the world around us.

In *Dexter time: the space, time and matterings of school absence registration*, Linnea Bodén explores how a computer attendance software is radically reconfiguring how school absence is produced and understood. This software operates through text alerts and computer software, which come to constitute the reality of who is present and absent at school.

This article adopts a posthumanism frame to rethink the production of human subjectivity via this computer software. This is an important application of posthuman theory, since it is not simply a decentring of the human but a rethinking of the relations through which a human is made possible. The article takes a Baradian approach to temporality exploring how space, time and matter are intra-actively produced. The chapter diverges from understanding Dexter software effects as just a system of control and resistance, and instead sees it as creating new affective-material embedded practices like anxiety, fear and alarm technologically produced through the software register of lateness and presence or non-presence. Dexter also changes material practices during school and in the classroom, such as the coupled material-disciplinary practice of closing the door to make students wait outside until a later time so as to avoid stragglers who would be identifiable and documented as late. In "Dexter time," Dexter is producing educational spaces and temporalities as before/in/after the presence of the present.

Diffractive pedagogy and micro-movement

In *Diffractive pedagogies: dancing across new materialist imaginaries*, Anna Hickey-Moody, Helen Palmer and Esther Sayers harness the new onto-epistemological shifts of Barad, Braidotti (2011) and others to question several paradigmatic and humanist assumptions in higher education, like how the body is largely ignored in lecture and seminar style environments. The authors work through the design of a university course from theoretical foundations to specific classroom creativity exercises to suggest that traditional forms of arts-based learning do not foster a student's sense of expression and becoming. They recount their experiences developing a university course that is premised on a Baradian-informed diffractive pedagogy. This article is important for moving beyond simply modelling posthuman and new materialism *analysis* to showing how new materialism works—like the Baradian concept intra-activity, diffraction is a key concept that is about mashing together a range of seemingly unrelated components into a research assemblage (Barad, 2007). For Barad diffraction expresses "a self-accountable feminist type of intellectual critique and textual engagement . . . employing different texts, theories and strands of through against one another, diffractively engaging with texts and intellectual traditions means they are read dialogically through one another to engender creative and unexpected outcomes" (Geerts and Van der Tuin, 2014, np). Hickey-Moody, Palmer and Sayers argue a multiplicitous diffractive pedagogy allows students to learn through multimodal engagement (film, photography, object use), and movement (dance, gesture, movement), to explore different modalities forged through intersectional elements of one's identity. A diffractive pedagogy, therefore, brings together different affective waves, and bodily capabilities and senses outside normal classroom learning. Such engagement requires a degree of unlearning on the part of the students and teachers, and recognition that students are at once affectively connected to their surroundings and embedded within complex materially laden learning environments. What is important about this piece is that these authors are able to demonstrate is that by creating spaces for embodied intra-action through valuing embodiment differently in the classroom, changes can happen through micro-shifts in attention and sensibility, for instance a reorientation of a dance move from a reductive expression of sexualized/racialized and religioned femininity to creating new cartographies of bodies— "a practice of live theorisation: the thinking in action that takes place as students come to understand concepts about which they have read and then formulate (or materialize) their own" (p. 225). The authors argue that movement, materiality, and especially the body are key to learning, and are therefore "legitimate knowledge" (p. 215) rather than feminized, abject, and outside the realm of scholarly learning.

Posthuman participations, micro-ontologies and immanence

In the final section of the book we consider the contributions to feminist posthuman thinking of two more of our founding fem-inal figures: Donna Haraway and Rosi Braidotti. Rosi Braidotti's scholarship is heavily inspired by Deleuze and Guattari's queer partnership productions: *Anti-oedipus* and *A Thousand Plateaus*. Braidotti's posthuman or anti-human approach provides a genealogy of the discursive and material historical power structures that have led to the rootedness of humanist values that permeate society today. She maps a posthuman ethics that decenters the humanist masculinist Eurocentric subject of Western history. Braidotti proposes nomadic, or wild and wandering thinking, as a counterpoint to monadic singular and teleological thought through new figurations that challenge binary and oppositional epistemologies in favour of complexity capable of grasping the chaotic multiplicities of advanced capitalism, and more recently, 'cognitive capitalism' (Moulier-Boutang, 2012). Perhaps less adopted to date by feminist educational researchers, Braidotti's work forms the foundation for Renold and Ringrose's article and other joint work (2008; 2011) exploring how figurations of Western girlhood are caught up in 'schizoid' Oedipal and phallic regulatory formations which proscribe, for instance, hyper sexualization and innocence at the same time. Schizo-feminist cartographies are offered as a methodology to micro-map these contradictory formations (Ringrose, 2015).

Post-phallocentric posthuman bodily part-icipations

In Renold and Ringrose's article *Selfies, relfies and phallic tagging: posthuman part-icipations in teen digital sexuality assemblages*, they begin by rejecting a psychoanalytic approach where desire is explained through lack and elaborate Deleuzoguattarian framework where desire is productive, makes connections, and activates real dynamic socio-material assemblages. They draw on Braidotti's (2013) reversal of Deleuze and Guattari's body without organs to organs without bodies to foreground a sexualized technocultural environment prioritizing phallic-oriented desire and objectified body parts like breasts and penises. They suggest that in digital and virtual spaces, concepts of affect and feeling incorporate indeterminate assemblages of human and non-human entities like interfaces, computers, flesh and feeling. Through this reasoning, Renold and Ringrose suggest that the digital affordance of tagging in Facebook images can be a form of phallic touch and coercion. Attaching oneself non-consensually to an image via name, comment, or reblogging "operate[s] as a vector of posthuman digital touch" (p. 3). Renold and Ringrose trace examples of boys tagging themselves onto sexy images that girls post of themselves that can be seen as "forming a non-consensual digital union." Coercive phallic tagging also occurs when old relfies (relationship selfies) are shared and re-distributed by boys once a relationship has terminated in order to phallically reattach status of ownership over others. Selfies also have agentic potential as material actants, however, as a selfie of a girl's breasts posted on a boy's Facebook wall holds the potential to destabilize a teen boys' performance of sexually predatory masculinity, given his friends intra-act with the digital image as a joke upon him. The manner in which Renold and Ringrose view the research data—the image, the Facebook comments and the interview 'voice'—connects with Mazzei and Jackson's critique of voice in interview data as singular and individual, and also with Pittard's arguments that digital-material actants are dramatically reshaping our ideas of subjectivity. Importantly this article shows the limitations of a Foucauldian analysis that would create clear and bounded directions and flows of power, in favour of more granular micro-mapping of the complexities of material, discursive and affective entanglements that are situated in online and offline practices of networked youth intimacy.

Posthuman micro-ontologies

Donna Haraway's influence on multiple fields of inquiry has been significant from her early work on cyborg subjectivity (1984/1991) disrupting the nature-culture divides and proposing new hybrid entities, formations and species (2008) to challenge human exceptionalism; like Barad she insists on human response-ability in relationality with all matter: "individual animals, human and nonhuman, are themselves entangled assemblages of relatings knotted at many scales and times with other assemblages, organic and not. Individuated critters matter; they are mortal and fleshly knottings . . . Kinds matter; they are also mortal and fleshly knottings not typological units of being" (Haraway, 2008, p. 88). In her most recent text, *Staying with the trouble* (2016) Haraway works with posthumanism yet prefers her own theorization of com-post, which, instead of going beyond (post), sits in trouble with and troubles humanism:

> staying with the trouble requires making oddkin; that is, we require each other in unexpected collaborations and combinations, in hot compost piles. We become-with each other or not at all. That kind of material semiotics is always situated, someplace and not noplace, entangled and worldly. Alone in our separate kinds of expertise and experience we know both too much and too little and so we succumb to despair or to hope, and neither is a sensible attitude (p. 4).

Haraway also works with and builds upon the notion of the Anthropocene, which describes a new geological epoch in which human activities have fundamentally altered the earth in ways that will lead to mass extinction. Haraway presents us with the science fiction and speculative fiction-informed reworking 'Chthulucene': a kind of 'timeplace for learning to stay with the trouble of living and dying in response-ability on a damaged earth' (2016, p. 2) and that is 'made up of on-going multispecies stories and practices of becoming-with in times' (p. 55). Indebted to indigenous knowledge, Chthulucene must be embraced in order to rethink and revise patriarchal notions of Eurocentric man and kin, articulating strategies for researchers to amass new 'seed bags'; to plant seeds that have a richer 'congress for worlding' that mix and mingle—through tentacular tendrils—outside of normative constructs of fertility, biology and reproduction to sow worlds and tell other worldly 'good stories that don't know how to finish' (2016, p. 120, p. 125).

Taylor and Pacini-Ketchabaw explore the relevance of the Anthropocene for educational research in their article *Learning with children, ants, and worms in the Anthropocene: towards a common world pedagogy of multispecies vulnerability*. They work with Haraway's ideas of multispecies vulnerability as a new pedagogy for enabling learning about 'more-than-human socialities' (Tsing, 2013) while witnessing the real-life encounters among children, ants and worms. They use Hirds (2010) research on bacteria's lively matter and force relations in the planet and the concept of micro-ontologies to explore ways of developing understandings of the ethical entanglements of the micro relations of everyday small things in the 'common world'. For Taylor and Pacini-Ketchabaw our ethical response to Anthropocene (a new era marked my 'man's destruction of the planet') is not only about the geo-sublime proportions of carbon measurements, global warming and melting ice caps (Instone, 2015) but also paying close attention to and learning with what they call tiny earth movers and small things such as worms and ants that industriously work underground, take collective action, and are literally reshaping, shifting and making the earth.

To map the complex minutia of interspecies reciprocities and co-shapings they move beyond education's traditional focus on child development and learning within an exclusively socio/cultural (read: human) context (Rogoff, 2003) and reposition children within the full, heterogeneous and interdependent multispecies common worlds. Taking 'multispecies ethnography' as their methodology, they witness the intense earthy encounters of the touching of bodies of muddy children and slippery worms in the wet forests of British Columbia and the congregation of dusty ants and children in the dry bushlands of the Australian Capital Territory. Making noteworthy such minor earthly encounters not only help us to move away from the dominant individual child-centred early childhood pedagogies but also enable us to focus instead on multispecies and collective modes of learning or 'common world pedagogies'. Drawing upon feminist environmental humanities debates, Taylor and Pacini-Ketchabaw encourage educators to pedagogically engage with the issue of intergenerational environmental justice from the earlier years of learning. They argue pedagogical earthly encounters among ants, worms and children teach us our entanglements and mutual vulnerabilities with other species in these challenging ecological times.

Immanent learning with walking

In *A Walk in the Park: Considering Practice for Outdoor Environmental Education Through an Immanent Take on the Material Turn*, Mcphie and Clarke practice an environmental education by shifting the normative and hierarchal classroom space of learning to the outside environment. With a material turn to environmental education, Mcphie and Clarke, take the reader and the students along on an outdoor learning session in a park, seeking to decolonize, dehierarchize and deterritorialize our understating of the relationships between human and environment. They show us the ways in which the immanent and material turn through environmental education can disrupt the essentialist assumptions of the human mind as disembodied and separate from the world to one of becoming with the world. For them to understand the relationship between human and environment, as being and becoming *of* the world instead of *in* or *on* the world, brings important changes in our learning, pedagogy, conception, perception and behavior. They propose a metaphysics of immanence with a material turn in environmental education, the human-environment are co-constitutional becomings, that challenge the human-centred metaphysics of transcendence and the narratives of the environment as an object we (humans) modify and act upon. According to Mcphie and Clarke, the way we act, behave, value, decide and move are directly influenced by how we conceptualize our relationships to the socio-material world. Full of material and embodied stories and encounters with/ of the plants, trees, wasp-orchids, stones, walking sticks, plastic bags, people, weather and kites, this article shows how students learn *with* the world and *become an emergence* as they go, move forward and intra-act rather than learning about the world as an objective eternal essential object disconnected from human becoming.

Conclusion: What can response-able feminist posthumanisms and new materialisms research do?

Taken together these articles demonstrate that posthuman and new materialism framings are not simply about new ways of theorizing or philosophising but more importantly they offer new ways of *doing* educational research; research which is generating material changes in the wider social sphere (Zarabadi and Ringrose, 2018). As Renold (2017) has recently articulated in her research using posthuman and new material ethics to design and enact participatory methodologies with young people to counter gender and sexual violence; whilst we are engaging with these new research practices to create change we are also faced with the difficult task of slowing down and taking stock of our practices in order to "illuminate and theorize the micro-processes of how change and transformation might occur, or expose and theorize the more-than-human 'politics of affect' (Massumi, 2015) in our research-activisms (De Cauter, De Roo and Vanhaesebrouck, 2012; Meissner, 2014)" (Renold, 2017, p. 37).

Whilst we have worked with a somewhat linear mapping to showcase the articles in our remix we want to finish with a more mashed up bricolage that summarizes the main onto-epistemological shifts and moves being made by feminist posthumanism and new materialism in educational research that blend and bend various concepts and tools. Taken together we locate three main shifts that characterize this approach: First: a decentring of human subjectivity challenging humanist exceptionalism. Second: a reorientation to *becoming* rather than *being* via re-mattering of classical notions of individual agency. Third: an expansion of the units of analysis in educational research to foreground *complex discursive, material and affective force relations*.

First, what is key across all of the articles we have remixed together is a rejecting of the essential, unified, singular, humanist subject. The subject, according to Deleuze and Guattari, Barad, Braidotti and Haraway is prism-like—a temporary and situated momentary juncture point through which material, discursive and affective forces meet and flow. At the heart of feminist posthumanism and new materialism is a rethinking of anthropocentrism—or the Renaissance celebration and reification of the liberal human man-subject. As Juanita Sundberg explains, posthumanism "refuses to treat the human as (1) ontologically given, [and] not the only actor of consequence, and (2) disembodied and autonomous, separate from the world of nature and animality" (Sundberg, 2013, p. 34). The human, for the feminist posthuman new material researcher no longer has priority as the knowing subject or the single organizer of the knowledge production. In this sense the question of education with feminist new materialist lens has shifted from *who* participates in knowledge production to *what and how* in the forms of agential objects and force relations as we saw with Taylor, dance/motion with Hickey-Moody et al., walking with Mcphie and Clarke; art/activism/eating with Springgay and Zaliwska, and ants and worms with Taylor and Pacini-Ketchabaw. Several of our articles rewrite subjectivity along posthumanist lines such as Bodén who shows how the school attendance software reconfigures time-space-matter, Pittard who explains the complex digitization/collectivization and monetization of teachers via Pinterest, and Renold and Ringrose who work to decenter the humanist subject and digital touch and relocate it in "becoming and fields of composition" (p. 2).

Thus, second, feminist posthuman new materialism repositions research away from first person anthropocentric humanist queries of *being*, towards posthuman processes and complex entanglements of *becoming* in our research practices. Karen Barad's ethico-onto-epistemology of agential realism fundamentally rejects the concept of an *a priori being* arguing that the starting point of all entities is a state of unbounded material-discursive-affective entanglement. Rather than preexisting and distinct entities interacting in the world, agential realism argues entities are agentially *cut* from their original state of entanglement via research processes in order to see and understand them. Agential realism, for Barad, therefore is at once an ontology, an epistemology, and an ethical proceeding—an inseparable onto-ethico-epistemology. The ontological starting point of entanglement, requires self-reflective forms of epistemologies that question the micro ethical agentic actions of the researcher and their practices of cutting objects into or out of their natural complexity via processes of research inquiry. Researchers can either cut along familiar and habitual lines—thus upholding dominant systems of power that determined these agential cut lines historically—or cut them anew in ways that produce topographical reconfigurations (Barad) or lines of flight (Deleuze and Guattari) that create positive *difference* in becoming with the world—perhaps creating new knowledges. As Mazzei and Jackson pointed out in their discussion of the agentic assemblage drawing on Bennett, it is the relations amongst things in the research assemblage that need to be accounted for: "agential cuts that are made, in the assemblage . . . force[s] an attentiveness on the part of researchers." Carol Taylor similarly showed how the analytical cuts in her research assemblage "make it apparent that in an entangled materialist ontology 'knowing does not come from standing at a distance and representing but rather from a direct material engagement with the world'" (Barad, 2007, p. 49) (Taylor, 2013, p. 692). Lenz Taguchi demonstrated a decentring of the humanist I/eye through non-representational and non-interpretive readings of data and building up collaborative analyses in the research assemblage; that troubled the authorization of the singular, knowing researcher and enabled multiplicity and difference to emerge.

Feminist posthumanism and new materialism therefore, moves far away from a classical sociological notion of human agency set in dialectical relationship with social structures. Rather we have thinking tools to grasp complexity of force relations—rhizomatic offshoots and assemblages (Deleuze and Guattari, 1984), entanglements and *phenomena*, what Karen Barad describes as "the ontological inseparability of agentially intra-acting components" (p. 33). This approach then forces us to revise our understandings of the types of actors and forms of agency participating in the research environment.

Third, and perhaps most importantly, this approach prioritizes the diverse multi-modalities of discourse, materiality and affect expanding our theoretical and methodological educational research toolkits. Building from the discursive turn, the *material* element of feminist new *materialism* considers the manifold material forces we encounter, be it the ominous stack of hierarchically-graded papers on a teacher's desk, as Carol Taylor describes in her article, or ways that non-human sounds and objects can be reconfigured to remake the 'voice' that matters in the research encounter in Mazzei and Jackson; the way that eating as art and pedagogy offers the attunements to the agency of all manner of artistic performances in Springgay and Zaliwska; the way dancing may restage embodiment through a diffractive pedagogy of difference generating multi-modal re-learningin Hickey-Moody, Palmer and Sayers; or likewise how re-learning with environments; grass, stones, walking sticks, plastic bags, and weather can deterritorialize traditional subject/object binaries in an immanent material methodological turn in Mcphie and Clarke. Matter doesn't replace discourse in any of these accounts; rather matter and discourse intra-act and we gather more tools to understand and revalue material objects and relations and happenings. These forces are also affective; and although affect is given hardly any attention in some posthuman accounts such as Barad and Haraway (see Niccolini et al., 2018) our selection seeks to realign affect as a critical tri-partite dimension of thinking in the posthuman and new material terrain. Reprioritizing the conceptual lexicon of Deleuze and Guattari in our remix, affect and capacities to affect and be affected are absolutely central to many of our selections, such as how the physical and emotional influences of dance upon the body are documented by Hickey-Moody, Palmer and Sayers or how the affective, material and discursive dimensions of digital affordances create new forms of coercive touch as explored by Renold and Ringrose. The attunement to affect is a critical aspect of educational inquiry as argued powerfully by Springgay and Zaliwska. As Margaret Sommerville (2016) argues, affect "profoundly unsettles any conception of method as being in the control of human agency or human consciousness inhering in the human subject" because researchers, educators and students must admit to the elasticity of affective forces on their decision-making processes in the conduct of research, or for educators in their pedagogical practices.

A discursive, material and affective orientation can help in reconsidering the micro-macro and paying attention to various multiple scales and units of analysis making visible the sensory and temporal rhythms of research encounter. For instance it 'reanimates' (Chen, 2012) the micro-level and every day mundane politics of education such as the whiteboard in Carol Taylor's accounting of an everyday classroom as well as the 'macro' notions of neoliberalism, power and identity as is seen in Elizabeth Pittard's discussion of how teacher's use Pinterest to negotiate ever increasing demands to self-tailor inadequate curriculum, which further responsibilizes teachers—extending their work day and making them entrepreneurs selling their lesson plans online to potentially gain economically from their digital forays into the edu-marketplace. In other words, the "units" of analysis of feminist posthumanisms and new materialisms practices are at once material, discursive and affective, they may be smaller micro forces or larger power relations; but they are always complex rather than singular entities; they are relational, rather than inter-acting they are intra-acting, rather than *a priori* in existence they are unfolding and becoming through research encounters, rather than linear, logical, thematic and classifiable they may be diffractive waves that generate new analytical spaces for mashing up and putting together unlikely 'data'. This approach therefore enables us to attend to the on-going generation of complex relations and flows, and changing capacities and multiplicities between matter and meaning, epistemology and ontology, along with the human and non-human (Hinton et al., 2015). These processes of complex and entangled becomings, which could be inclusive of human, non-human (e.g. technologies, material objects), and/or more-than-human forces (Whatmore, 2002), mean "the bodily enjoins the technologies of life and ecology, on the one hand, and of prehension and feeling, on the other" (Whatmore, 2006, p. 602) where the material, discursive and affective are now considered inseparable and entangled forces. Through this new "ethico-onto- epistemology" we attune to the relational attitude of "response-ability" towards all of our fellow beings and things (Haraway, 2008, p. 88, and Barad, 2012, p. 208, in Geerts, 2016). What we hope to have shown here are how these re-assembled response-able theory, method and practice of the ever expanding PhEmaterialism tool kit are alchemizing new research imaginaries, makings, and doings (see Ringrose and Zarabadi, 2018).

References

Barad, K. (2007). *Meeting the universe halfway*. Durham, N.C.: Duke University Press.

Bennett, J. (2010). *Vibrant matter*. Durham, N.C.: Duke University Press.

Bertelsen, L. & Murphie, A. (2010). An ethics of everyday infinities and powers: Félix Guattari on affect and refrain. In M. Gregg & G. J. Seigworth (Eds.), *The affect theory reader* (pp. 138–161). Durham, NC: Duke University Press.

Bodén, L. (2015). Dexter time: the space, time, and matterings of school absence registration. *Discourse: Studies in the Cultural Politics Of Education, 37*(2), 245–255. http://dx.doi.org/10.1080/01596306.2015.1010073

Braidotti, R. (2011). *Nomadic subjects*. New York, NY: Columbia University Press.

Braidotti, R. (2013). *The posthuman*. Polity.

Chen, M. (2012). *Animacies*. Durham, N.C.: Duke University Press.

Coleman, B. & Ringrose, J. (2013). Introduction: Deleuze and Research Methodologies. In B. Coleman and J. Ringrose (Eds.), *Deleuze and research methodologies*. Edinburgh: Edinburgh University Press.

De Cauter, L., De Roo, R., & Vanhaesebrouck, K. (Eds.). (2012). *Art and activism in the age of globalization*. Rotterdam: NAi Publishers.

Deleuze, G. & Guattari, F. (1987). *A thousand plateaus*. Minneapolis: University of Minnesota Press.

Fox, N. & Alldred, P. (2014). New materialist social inquiry: designs, methods and the research-assemblage. *International Journal of Social Research Methodology, 18*(4), 399–414.

Freeman, E. (2008). Queer Belongings: Kinship Theory and Queer Theory. In G. E. Haggerty and M. McGarry (Eds.), *A Companion to Lesbian, Gay, Bisexual, Transgender, and Queer Studies*. Oxford: Wiley Blackwell.

Geerts, E. (2014). Ethico-onto-epistem-ology. *New Materialism: How matter comes to Matter.* http://newmaterialism.eu/almanac/e/ethico-onto-epistem-ology

Geerts, E. & Van der Tuin, I. (2016). Diffraction and Reading Diffractively. *New Materialism, How matter comes to matter.* http://newmaterialism.eu/almanac/d/diffraction

Haraway, D. (1984/1991). A Cyborg Manifesto: Science, Technology, and Socialist-Feminism in the Late Twentieth Century. *Simians, cyborgs and women: the reinvention of nature*. Oxford: Routledge.

Haraway, D. (2008). *When species meet.* Minneapolis: University of Minnesota Press.

Haraway, D. (2016). *Staying with the trouble: making kin with chthulecene.* Durham, N.C.: Duke University Press.

Hickey-Moody, A., Palmer, H., & Sayers, E. (2016). Diffractive pedagogies: dancing across new materialist imaginaries. *Gender and Education, 28*(2), 213–229. http://dx.doi.org/10.1080/09540253.2016.1140723

Hinton, P., Treusch, P., Tuin, I., Dolphijn, R., & Sauzet, S. (2015). *Teaching with feminist materialisms.* Utrecht: ATGENDER.

Ivinson, G. & Taylor, C. (2013). Introduction to Special Issue Feminist Materialisms and Education. *Gender and Education, 25*(6), 665–670.

Jackson, A. Y. & Mazzei, L. A. (2012). *Thinking with theory in qualitative research, viewing data across multiple perspectives.* London and New York: Routledge.

Kanai, A. (2015). Jennifer Lawrence, remixed: Approaching celebrity through DIY digital culture. *Celebrity Studies, 6*(3), 322–340.

Lather, P. & St. Pierre, E. A. (2013). Post-qualitative research. *International Journal of Qualitative Studies in Education, 26*(6), 629–633. DOI: 10.1080/09518398.2013.788752

Lenz Taguchi, H. (2013). Images of thinking in feminist materialisms: ontological divergences and the production of researcher subjectivities. *International Journal of Qualitative Studies In Education, 26*(6), 706–716. http://dx.doi.org/10.1080/09518398.2013.788759

Manning, E. (2016). *The minor gesture.* Durham and London: Duke University Press.

Massey, D. (2013). *Space, Place and Gender.* Hoboken: Wiley.

Massumi, B. (2004). Notes on the Translation and Acknowledgments. In Deleuze, G. & F. Guattari (Eds.), *A Thousand Plateaus: Capitalism and Schizophrenia.* London: Continuum.

Massumi, B. (2015). *Politics of affect.* Malden, MA: Polity.

Mazzei, L. A. (2008). Silence speaks: Whiteness revealed in the absence of voice. *Teaching and Teacher Education,* 24, 1125–1136. DOI:10.1016/j.tate.2007.02.009

Mazzei, L. & Jackson, A. Y. (2017). Voice in the agentic assemblage. *Educational Philosophy and Theory, 49*(11), 1090–1098. http://dx.doi.org/10.1080/00131857.2016.1159176 49:11

Mcphie, J. & Clarke, D. (2015). A Walk in the Park: Considering Practice for Outdoor Environmental Education Through an Immanent Take on the Material Turn. *The Journal of Environmental Education, 46*(4), 230–250. http://dx.doi.org/10.1080/00958964.2015.1069250

Meissner, H. (2014). Politics as encounter and response-ability. Learning to converse with enigmatic others. In B. Revelles Benavente, A. M. G. Ramos, & K. Nardini (coord.). New feminist materialism: Engendering an ethic-onto-epistemological methodology. *Artnodes, 14,* 35–41.

Miller, D. (1997). *Material Culture: Why some things matter.* Hoboken: Taylor & Francis.

Moulier-Boutang, Y. (2012). *Cognitive capitalism.* Cambridge: Polity Press.

Niccolini, A. & Ringrose, J. (forthcoming). Feminist Posthumanism: Practices and Methodologies. In P. Atkinson & S. Delamont (Eds.) *SAGE Encyclopaedia of Research Methods.* London: SAGE.

Niccolini, A., Zarabadi, S., & Ringrose, J. (2018). *Spinning yarns: Affective kinshipping as posthuman pedagogy.* Parallax.

Niccolini, D. & Pindyck, M. (2015). Classroom acts: New materialisms and haptic encounters in an urban classroom. *Reconceptualizing Educational Research Methodologies, 6*(2), 1–23.

Pedersen, H. & Pini, B. (2016). Educational epistemologies and methods in a more-than-human world. *Educational Philosophy and Theory, 49*(11), 1051–1054. http://dx.doi.org/10.1080/00131857.2016.1199925

PhEmaterialism Facebook https://www.facebook.com/groups/403539713163770/?ref=bookmarks

PhEmaterialism Twitter: @phematerialism

PhEmaterialism 2 [Conference]: Matter-realising pedagogical and methodological interferences into terror and violence, Conference, UCL Institute of Education and Middlesex University, June 7 & 8, 2018. http://www.ucl.ac.uk/ioe/news-events/events-pub/jun-2018/phematerialism

Pittard, E. A. (2016). Gettin' a little crafty: Teachers Pay Teachers©, Pinterest© and neo-liberalism in new materialist feminist research. *Gender and Education, 29*(1), 28–47. http://dx.doi.org/10.1080/09540253.2016.1197380

Renold, E. (2017). 'Feel what I feel': making da(r)ta with teen girls for creative activisms on how sexual violence matters. *Journal of Gender Studies, 27*(1), 37–55. DOI: 10.1080/09589236.2017.1296352

Renold, E. & Ringrose, J. (2008). Regulation and Rupture: mapping tween and teenage girls' 'resistance' to the heterosexual matrix. *Feminist Theory, 9*(3), 335–360.

Renold, E. & Ringrose, J. (2011). Schizoid subjectivities?: Re-theorising teen-girls' sexual cultures in an era of 'sexualisation'. *Journal of Sociology, 47*(4), 389–409.

Renold, E., & Ringrose, J. (2016). Selfies, relfies and phallic tagging: posthuman part-icipations in teen digital sexuality assemblages. *Educational Philosophy and Theory, 49*(11), 1066–1079. http://dx.doi.org/10.1080/00131857.2016.1185686

Renold, E. & Ringrose, J. (2018). Phematerialism Jarring Methodologies: #GenderMatters and the More-Than of Research, paper presented at American Educational Research Association Conference, New York City, April 17, 2018.

Ringrose, J. (2011). Beyond Discourse? Using Deleuze and Guattari's schizoanalysis to explore affective assemblages, heterosexually striated space, and lines of flight online and at school. *Educational Philosophy & Theory*, *43*(6), 598–618.

Ringrose, J. (2015). Schizo-Feminist Educational Research Cartographies. *Deleuze Studies*, 9(3), 393–409. DOI: 10.3366/dls.2015.0194

Ringrose, J. & Rawlings, V. (2015). Posthuman performativity, gender and 'school bullying': Exploring the material-discursive intra-actions of skirts, hair, sluts, and poofs. *Confero: Essays on Education, Philosophy and Politics*, *3(2)*, 80–119. DOI: 10.3384/confero.2001 4562.150626

Ringrose, J., Renold, E., Hickey-Moody, A., & Osgood, J. (2015). "Feminist Posthuman and New Materialism Research Methodologies in Education: Capturing Affect. UCL IOE & Middlesex University HEIF Funded Experts workshop London, May 2015.

Ringrose, J. & Zarabadi, S. (2018). Deleuzo-Guattarian decentering the human I/eye: A conversation with Jessica Ringrose and Shiva Zarabadi. In K. Strom, T. Mills, & A. Ovens (Eds.), *Decentering the researcher in intimate scholarship: Posthuman materialist perspectives in educational researc*h. Bingley, UK: Emerald Publishing.

Snaza, N., Appelbaum, P., Bayne, S., Carlson, D., Morris, M., Rotas, N., . . ., & Weaver, J. (2014). Toward a posthumanist education. *Journal of Curriculum Theorizing*, *30*, 39–55.

Springgay, S. & Zaliwska, Z. (2017). Learning to be affected: Matters of pedagogy in the artists' soup kitchen. *Educational Philosophy and Theory*, *49*(3), 273–283. http://dx.doi.org/10.1080/00131857.2016.1216385

St. Pierre, E. (2013). The appearance of data. *Cultural Studies-Critical Methodologies*, *13*(4), 223–227.

St. Pierre, E. & Jackson, A. (2014). Qualitative data analysis after coding. *Qualitative Inquiry*, *20*(6), 715–719.

Sundberg, J. (2013). Decolonizing posthumanist geographies. *Cultural Geographies*, *21*(1), 33–47. http://dx.doi.org/10.1177/1474474013486067

Tallbear, K. (2013). Beyond life/not life: A feminist-indigenous reading of cryopreservation, interspecies thinking, and the new materialisms. Lecture presented at University of California, Los Angeles, Center for the Study of Women. https://www.youtube.com/watch?v=TkUeHCUrQ6E.

Taylor, A. & Pacini-Ketchabaw, V. (2015). Learning with children, ants, and worms in the Anthropocene: towards a common world pedagogy of multispecies vulnerability. *Pedagogy, Culture & Society*, *23*(4), 507–529. http://dx.doi.org/10.1080/14681366.2015.1039050

Taylor, C. (2013). Objects, bodies and space: gender and embodied practices of mattering in the classroom. *Gender and Education*, *25*(6), 688–703. http://dx.doi.org/10.1080/09540253.2013.834864

Taylor, C. & Hughes, C. (2016). *Posthuman research practices in education*. Basingstoke: Palgrave MacMillan.

The Master's Tools Will Never Dismantle the Master's House | Audre Lorde (1979). (2018). *Historyisaweapon. com.* Retrieved 25 April 2018, from http://www.historyisaweapon.com/defcon1/lordedismantle.html

Ulmer, J. B. (2017). Posthumanism as research methodology: inquiry in the Anthropocene. *International Journal of Qualitative Studies in Education*, *30*(9), 832–848. DOI: 10.1080/09518398.2017.1336806

Van Der Tuin, I. (2016). *Generational feminism*. Lanham Boulder, New York, London: Lexington Books.

Walker,R. (2014). The Living Present as a Materialist Feminist Temporality. *Women: A Cultural Review*, 25(1), 46–61. DOI: 10.1080/09574042.2014.901107

Whatmore, S. (2002). *Hybrid Geographies: Natures Cultures Spaces*. London: Sage.

Whatmore, S. (2006). Materialist returns: practising cultural geography in and for a more-than-human world. *Cultural Geographies*, *13*(4), 600–609. DOI:10.1191%2F1474474006cgj377oa

Zarabadi, S. & Ringrose, J. (2018). Pedagogical interferences: Remattering the haptic-optic pre-emptive futurism of terror-thinking and must security culture. In S. Riddle, A. Baroutsis (Eds.), *Education Research and the Media: Challenges and Possibilities*. London: Routledge.

Voice in the agentic assemblage

Lisa A. Mazzei and Alecia Y. Jackson

ABSTRACT

In this article, we explore how a posthumanist stance has enabled us to work a different consideration of the way in which *voice* is constituted and constituting in educational inquiry; that is, we position voice in a posthuman ontology that is understood as attributable to a complex network of human and nonhuman agents that exceed the traditional understanding of an individual. Drawing on the work of Deleuze and Guattari, Barad, and Bennett, we present a research artifact that illustrates how this posthuman voice is productively bound to an *agentic assemblage*. The reconfiguration of a posthuman voice with/in an educational research artifact further enables us to explore various analytic questions: What happens when voice exceeds language and is more than (un)vocalized words emanating from a speaking subject? If the materiality of voice is not limited to sound (i.e. self-present language emitted from a human mouth), how do we account for it? That is, how might the materiality of voice be located in the space of intra-action among human and non-human objects? We conclude with implications for thinking qualitative methodology in education differently.

Introduction

In this article, we think with Bennett's (2010b) concept of the *agentic assemblage* to position the discursive artifacts of qualitative inquiry as always already material and the material as an always already discursive construction. That is, we move toward positing voice in qualitative educational research as a *thing* that is entangled with other *things* in an assemblage (Deleuze & Guattari, 1987) that acts with an agential force (Bennett, 2010b). We do this by (re)configuring voice: we refuse the primacy of voice as simply spoken words emanating from a conscious subject and instead place voice within the material and discursive knots and intensities of the assemblage. Thus, we do not 'calibrate' voice to the human, nor do we attend to voice as 'either pure cause or pure effect' (Barad, 2007, p. 136) via human intentionality. Rather, we account for voice as a material-discursive practice that is inseparable from all elements (human and non-human) in an assemblage.

Like MacLure (2013), we 'argue for research practices that would be capable of engaging the materiality of language [voice] itself—its material force and its entanglements in bodies and matter' (p. 658). To account for these entanglements, we follow Barad's (2007) assertion of posthumanism as critically engaging the 'limits of humanism' (p. 428). By this, we mean that conventional approaches to educational inquiry often privilege the voice of the humanist subject, assuming that voice can speak the truth of consciousness and experience. In such paradigms, voice lingers close to the true and the real, and because of this proximity, has become seen almost as a mirror of the soul, the essence of the self. Educational researchers have been trained to afford authority to voice, to 'free' the authentic voice from whatever restrains it from coming into being, from relating the truth about the conscious self (Jackson & Mazzei, 2009). In this drive to make voices heard and understood, qualitative methodologists have taken up various practices in attempts to 'let voices speak for themselves,' to 'give voice,' or to 'make voices heard' in educational research (see Jackson, 2003, for an epistemological perspective and critique).

Voice as present, stable, authentic, and self-reflective: such a voice is imbued with humanist properties and thus attached to an individual (be that individual theorized as coherent and stable or fragmented and becoming). Voice is still 'there' to search for, retrieve, and liberate. A refusal to seek methodological practices that attempt to retrieve and liberate voice requires a decentering of the humanist voice that 'knows who she is, says what she means and means what she says' (MacLure, 2009, p. 104). An ontological, posthuman consideration of voice moves us from these humanistic practices to emphasize voice as (re)configured in the intra-actions between the material and discursive, as merely one part—and perhaps the least vital component—of an agentic assemblage. As Barad (2007) reminds us, 'Posthumanism doesn't presume the separateness of any-"thing," let alone the alleged spatial, ontological, and epistemological distinction that sets humans apart' (p. 136).

We want to emphasize that our contribution to this special issue on posthuman research practices in education is working within and against a particular methodological 'centrism' that privileges both speaking *and* hearing human subjects; we also attempt to push against the cutting off of a human subject (be it a humanist 'reflecting' one or a poststructural 'contradictory' one) as the prime source of experience, knowledge, and the real (see Snaza & Weaver, 2014). This ontological separation that has permeated educational inquiry has certainly resulted in creating a boundary between 'what *has* a voice' and what doesn't, thus our interest works against this separation to view a posthuman voice not as a possession but as a thing entangled with other things. To experiment methodologically, we rely on the philosophical frameworks and concepts from posthumanism to disrupt normative and normalizing assumptions of voice in educational research. To do so, we take what is typically called an 'interview data excerpt' in qualitative inquiry and rethink it in such a way that the speaking 'subject,' or the 'subject undone' (St. Pierre, 2004) becomes merely one agent in the assemblage. That is, a 'subject undone' is not a pre-existent self-contained individual, but instead, a never fully constituted unfolding produced in social, environmental, technological, and cultural assemblages (St. Pierre, 2004, pp. 288–291).

We will take up a specific example of an entangled voice later in this article, but for now, we turn to the broader ontological, posthuman concepts of assemblage and agency. We begin with Deleuze & Guattari's assemblage and move into Bennett's work on the agentic assemblage and the Baradian concepts of intra-action and distributed agency.

Assemblage and agency in posthumanism: Bennett's *agentic assemblage*

Deleuze and Guattari (1987) wrote that an assemblage

> comprises two segments: one of content, the other of expression. On the one hand it is a *machinic assemblage* of bodies, of actions and passions, an intermingling of bodies reacting to one another; on the other hand, it is a *collective assemblage* of enunciation, of acts and statements, of incorporeal transformations attributed to bodies. (p. 88, emphasis in original)

Deleuze and Guattari's assemblage is a useful figuration for imagining a posthuman voice: voice is one part of an assemblage that includes multiple, heterogenous elements. Objects, discursive signs, utterances, bodies—all exist on different temporal and spatial scales that work collectively to produce a territory. The assemblage offers us traction for our reconfiguration of voice because, as Deleuze and Guattari (1987) explained, words and utterances in an assemblage do not have correspondence (or representational resemblance) to anything *but the whole*; they wrote, 'There is a primacy of the collective assemblage of enunciation over language and words' (p. 90). We will subsequently return to this point, but for now, we want to emphasize that everything in the assemblage works as an aggregate:

the interminglings produce affects, potentialities, desires (see Ringrose, 2011). The *assemblage* is that which creates a territory and the potential for de-territorialization.

We turn to Bennett (2010a) who wrote, 'I experiment with narrating events … in a way that presents nonhuman materialities … as themselves bonafide agents rather than as instrumentalities, techniques of power, recalcitrant objects, or social constructs' (p. 47). These nonhuman materialities are bonafide agents that Bennett bestows with what she terms 'thing-power' (Bennett, 2010b, p. 2). In what she names an 'agentic assemblage,' these 'things' act with a force. It is not just that 'things' in the assemblage act with a force, but the assemblage itself acts, blocks flows, makes cuts, and produces intensities in a theory of distributed agency.

> Assemblages are ad hoc groupings of diverse elements, of vibrant materials of all sorts. Assemblages are living, throbbing confederations that are able to function despite the persistent presence of energies that confound them from within. They have uneven topographies, because some of the points at which the various affects and bodies cross paths are more heavily trafficked than others, and so power is not distributed equally across its surface. (Bennett, 2010b, pp. 23–24)

According to Bennett, 'A lot happens to the concept of agency once nonhuman things are figured less as social constructions and more as actors, and once humans themselves are assessed not as autonoms but as vital materialities' (p. 21). Being faithful to the 'distributive quality of "agency"' (p. 21) is noting that these things, these vital materialities, together in an agentic assemblage, possess agency, not in and of themselves, but in this assemblage, they become an-other body or agent. Thinking voice according to Bennett's framework and her concept of vibrant matter requires an acknowledgment of 'things' as being agential, as functioning as catalysts in producing events. Therefore, we no longer think voice as a discrete representation of experience spoken forth by an individual subject, but as an-other body or agent in the agentic assemblage that acts and confounds from within.

If 'agency is everywhere' (Hekman, 2010, p. 123), and by that we mean that *agents* are everywhere in the artifacts of our research, in the materiality of our educational field sites, in our analyses, and in our knowledge producing practices, then what is to happen to our practices, our researcher selves, and our thinking qualitative data and data analysis differently if we are to think voice as vibrant (Bennett, 2010b), as agentic, as intersectionally linked with/in forces that we refer to as a posthuman voice? To think voice as vibrant and agentic is not to treat voices as something to be mined in the textual artifacts of educational research, nor is it to ascribe meaning by a focus on what people say, but it is to think voice as that which is produced in the intra-action of things—bodies, words, histories—that, as an assemblage, act with a force. As we continue in this article, we will make the argument that it is the assemblage that acts; it is the entanglement that pressures and produces reconfigurings; it is the intra-action of the material and discursive that produces a distributed agency between and among human and nonhuman entities. In doing so, we offer a methodological move to enable a more provocative outcome, a practice that not only pushes against (over) simplified treatments of voice-as-data but also the humanistic analytic strategies that tend to take for granted what voice 'is' and that seek to fix meaning based on one's articulation of 'experience.' As we mentioned earlier, we intend that this methodological experiment will contribute to the practice of theory and research in education.

Voice in the kitchen assemblage

For Bennett (2010b), as for Deleuze and Guattari (1987), bodies and actors in a network, or assemblage, can no longer be thought as subjects and objects. Nor can we any longer think of doers (agents) behind deeds or actions giving "voice" to an experience. There is no hierarchy of primary and secondary agents, nor a deciphering of purpose or intent. Bennett wrote how Coole (as cited in Bennett, 2010b) 'replaces the discrete agent and its "residual individualism" with a "spectrum" of "agentic capacities" housed sometimes in individual persons, sometimes in human physiological processes … and some-times in human social structures' (p. 30). Coole's notion of the spectrum does not imply development from one end to the other. Rather, Coole proposes the idea of a spectrum to suggest the emergence of agency at different levels of (co-)existence (Coole, 2005, p. 128). She further explains that central to her argument with a focus on agentic capacities or properties is an insistence that these capacities or properties are 'only contingently, not ontologically, identified with individual agents' (pp. 124–125). In the same way that agentic properties are only contingently identified with individual agents, so too we imagine voice in a similar fashion.

Next, we present a research artifact to demonstrate how we conceive posthuman voice as not attributable solely to a humanist subject. Rather, we present posthuman voice as a production of a movement of forces in an assemblage. 'Things' with agentic capacities come together with other 'things' in an agentic assemblage to produce this posthuman voice. We position this research artifact as an assemblage of heterogenous elements—objects, signs, utterances, bodies—existing on different temporal and spatial scales: a kitchen table and chairs, gendered bodies, discourses of patriarchy and institutionalized religion, enunciations of critique, a garage door, histories, communities, childhoods ....

Amelia: *We went from Tommy to Steven. I'm not saying that Steven is bad and Tommy is great, but we went from one extreme to another. Tommy was very outgoing and very involved. His kids went to Garner [public schools] and he was always at things. Steven is the complete opposite. His children are home-schooled, and he doesn't go to school events where people from the church would be. He's not visible at all. Outside the church, he's not visible. Our kids need that, especially in the youth department ...*

[As Amelia speaks, the faint sound of the automatic garage door opening is followed by the sounds of a turning door knob, a squeaky opening of a door, a shutting sound, and footsteps. Will, Amelia's husband and deacon at the church, enters the kitchen, interrupting the interview.]

Amelia continues: *Our new preacher Steven is a very godly man. He's very close with God. He is a fine addition to our community.* [Amelia pauses and looks at the interview guide] *Do you want me to talk about what we do after church now?*

We think voice in the agentic assemblage, not to emphasize the individual voice of the speaker in the research artifact—rather, we want to draw attention to the movement, or the agential force, of all sorts of voices (human and otherwise) that attach in an agentic assemblage to mark new territories and to create new becomings and different conceptions of voice. Such marking provides an in-between place for entering the territorial assemblage to see how voices in an assemblage are made, what they make, and what they do.

Amelia contrasted the new preacher, Steven, to the former preacher, Tommy, in her Baptist church when she said,

I'm not saying that Steven is bad and Tommy is great, but we went from one extreme to another. Tommy was very outgoing and very involved. ... Steven is the complete opposite ... He's not visible at all. Outside the church, he's not visible.

When voice is approached as *one* element in an agentic assemblage instead of being spoken by *a* subject, a different conception of voice and purpose is made possible: Amelia shifts her description of Steven in the assemblage as other agents exert forces and pressures, 'Our new preacher Steven is a very godly man ... He is a fine addition to our community.' With this example, we assert that an individual subject, in this case, Amelia, does not merely 'change her mind' about what she is saying but rather such 'dynamism is agency' (Barad, 2007, p. 141). This dynamism is not reduced to Amelia's agency but expanded to include the *distributed agencies* of the church, the community, Steven, the presence of a recording device, a garage door, footsteps—an assemblage that produces an 'ontological performance of the world in its ongoing articulation' (p. 149). According to Bennett (2010b), 'there is not so much a doer (an agent) behind the deed ... as a doing and an effecting *by* a human-nonhuman assemblage' (p. 28, emphasis added).

What, then, is this effecting? What does an assemblage *do,* when it acts as a 'heterogeneous "team" of components'? (Bonta & Protevi, 2004, p. 56). To recall, an assemblage is a *process* of arranging or fitting together, and these arrangements create new ways of functioning:

An assemblage emerges when a function emerges; ideally it is innovative and productive. The result of a productive assemblage is a new means of expression, a new territorial/spatial organisation, a new institution, a new behaviour, or a new realisation. The assemblage is destined to produce a new reality, by making numerous, often unexpected, connections. (Livesey, p. 19, 2010).

Specifically, mapping the function and effects of the assemblage is to see how a territorial field is both made (through repetition) and unmade (deterritorialization) through the rhizomatic connectivity of assemblages. Bonta and Protevi (2004) explain that 'one should look to the openness to novelty of each assemblage, the way it invites new connections with other assemblages' (p. 55).

All agents were on one assemblage and then (re)distributed as other agents from another assemblage, an intra-action to take *everything* elsewhere, to fragment and re-organize to make a new territory. A particular arrangement of bodies, materiality, habits, institutions, and behaviors formed in that moment to enable and claim a territory *of critique*: Amelia, in the domain (assemblage) of domesticity is produced as expert from a working-class education and gendered upbringing, acts with the agents of/in the kitchen assemblage to make a new territory, one of critique. The assemblage produces her as mother who knows what is best for her children, who feeds those bodies, and for that instant, the territory of critique is formed, until the material force of footsteps reclaim the territory of patriarchy. The territory that was claimed in the kitchen assemblage is now fragmented and carried away. The force of Will's footsteps organize to make a new territory, the territory of small-town conservative patriarchy where she is now no longer critic, but docile. Put another way, the function of this assemblage is to re-mark the territory of patriarchy—which also re-territorializes those things in the assemblage: 'ownership' of a house, women's roles in the church and other domestic spaces—even what might be a habitual response to a husband's footsteps. In this other assemblage (of which Amelia's voice is only one element), a new becoming is articulated—articulated not *by* Amelia's voice but articulated *by the agential force of the assemblage*.

A reading of voice from a distributive perspective as described above seeks a reconsideration of how voice is produced that displaces simplistic notions of voice as only 'spoken' by (human) research participants. We do not claim that the garage door 'has' a voice, nor do a husband's footsteps 'have' a voice—anymore than we claim that Amelia 'has' a voice. Certainly, that is one way to think about it. But from a posthuman perspective that necessitates a stance of distributive agency, those *things* are all part of an agentic assemblage that has an ontological force. Voice as emanated from a human subject is not primary here; instead, voice is just one *thing* entangled with other *things* that is becoming in a mutual production of agents, voices, becomings. In the posthuman, 'material and human agencies are mutually and emergently productive [or constitutive] of one another' (Pickering, 1999, p. 373).

Voice in a shifting entanglement of intra-actions

Concomitant with Jane Bennett's agentic assemblage and distributed agency is a concept we take from Barad (2007), that of intra-activity. Intra-activity refers to the ways in which 'discourse and matter are understood to be mutually constituted in the production of knowing' (Lenz Taguchi, 2012, p. 268). Key to Barad's analysis is the agential realist understanding of 'matter as a dynamic and shifting entanglement of relations' (2007, p. 224). For Barad, this understanding of agential realism 'takes into account the fact that the forces at work in the materialization of bodies are not only social and the bodies produced are not all human' (p. 225). We take this then to move from voice as only produced by human bodies, to consider forces at work in the materialization of voice that is a shifting entanglement of relations—of bodies, mores, objects, unspoken thoughts, communities, spacetime, and so on. To open the concept voice to 'an outside whose determinations do not begin and end with the human subject' (Kirby, 2011, p. 15) but emerges in the intra-action (Barad, 2007) with other 'things' in an agentic assemblage.

We recognize how from a posthumanist stance, agency is constituted as an enactment, not something that an individual possesses, nor something that relies on a demarcation between human/non-human. In the research artifact with Amelia, we notated the multiple material and discursive forces (garage doors, gestures, speech, patriarchal discourses) not for the purpose of claiming difference, but for the purposes of, first, troubling those assumed demarcations and second, making transparent how/where/when voice is produced in the assemblage. Voice in the assemblage is continually made and unmade in the fits and starts and interruptions and connections that occur as Amelia is speaking, remembering, being jolted back into the present by the sound of the garage door—taken to a different assemblage, with a different function, and thus being reminded not to push back against the mores of her community. Those forces are drawn and connected from multiple milieus that defy linear, causal, and hierarchical conceptions of space/time/matter. We notice the agentic force of the entanglement of *things* as one assemblage is claimed (that of critique), then another entanglement of *things* organize to mark a different territory with a different function. If we view voice as something materially produced in the agentic assemblage, then we understand Barad's (2007) assertion that intentionality is not the sole purview of humans, but is 'understood as attributable to a complex network of human and nonhuman agents … that exceed the traditional notion of the individual' (p. 23). This excess that is beyond the humanist subject is the agentic force or 'thing' power (Bennett, 2010b) of the material and discursive elements of the assemblage.

We see this at work in the research artifact. Both human and nonhuman agents are part of this acting network, this assemblage, this apparatus: Amelia, the small conservative town in which she resides, a working-class education that further inscribes traditional gender behaviors, small-town schooling that attempts to keep people in their place, the practices of a former preacher contrasted to the practices of the current preacher, Amelia's internal milieu of her own emotional terrain, sounds of a garage door and heavy footsteps, and so on. To further extend Barad's statement, agency can be thought as attributable to a complex network of agents 'continually coming into being, fading away, moving around' (Pickering, 1993, p. 563), in a mutual and emergent production. It is this concept of agency as attributable to a complex network of agents that we work to think voice in a similar fashion (see Jackson, 2013 for a reading of data as/in/of the assemblage, or mangle). That is, we maintain that the voice that is claimed is *not attributable* to Amelia, but rather *bound to* the assemblage in which practices of etiquette; the presence or absence of spouses, pastors, children, old friends; status in the community; material surroundings; institutional discourses; objects that are both symbolic and agentially real—all are elements of the assemblage that are joining forces in this moment in an emergence of this posthuman voice. In the research artifact, there is no voice to be extracted from the assemblage that stands alone. Without the intersection and intra-action of forces in the agentic assemblage, there is no posthuman 'voice,' only words on a page. Therefore, voice in the agentic assemblage emerges as the 'sum of the vital force of each materiality' (Bennett, 2010b, p. 24).

Conclusion: Voice as a *doing*

Expression is not in a language-using mind, or in a speaking subject *vis a vis* its objects. Nor is it rooted in the individual body. It is not even in a particular institution, because it is precisely the institutional system that is in flux. Expression is abroad in the world—here the potential is for what may become. (Massumi, 2002, p. xxi)

In this article, we have been thinking voice in the assemblage. Doing so has allowed us to posit voice in educational research not as something that *is*, but rather as something that *becomes* in an emergent intra-action with other agents in the agentic assemblage. That is, we moved away from positioning voice as simply spoken words emanating from a conscious subject in the case of Amelia, to voice as constituted in the entanglement of *things* (footsteps, squeaky doors, verbal critiques, institutional discourses, feminine bodies, male privilege). We illustrated with an example from a conventional research artifact in the form of a transcript how voice was bound to an entanglement of forces, where human and nonhuman bodies and accounts (matter and meaning) reconfigured voice as no longer attached to a humanist subject. In doing so, we have constructed a methodological move that enables a more provocative outcome than does an attempt to determine what Amelia's voice might mean.

We end, then, not with a further delineation of what voice is, or might become, but a brief discussion of what might be made possible by thinking the methodological implications—of voice, of data, of analysis—in qualitative educational inquiry. Positioning voice, (and data, and analysis) in the agential assemblage presents three moves that we think warrant further attention in posthuman research practices in education.

First, positioning voice in the agentic assemblage takes us away from simple contextual analysis and forces us to pay attention to different spatial and temporal dimensions of voice. Doing so means that we recognize the agential cuts that are made, in the assemblage, and that forces an attentiveness on the part of researchers to everything, *including* what is said. We can no longer think of Amelia's voice as separate and individual but only within the entanglement it immediately becomes and continues to become as it joins other enactments, other assemblages. The artifact or *voice* is no longer a story of Amelia, or of her experience—but a mutual constitution produced by material and discursive forces that make the assemblage. Like Pickering's description of agents continually coming into being, and like Coole's description of agentic capacities that are contingently identified with individual agents, voice in the agentic assemblage is there right now in that moment, called up by the materiality of particular matter histories, discourses, signs, utterances, and so on. *It is not a matter of how a human voice articulates those things, but how the intra-action is an agential cut that assembles them and territorializes a space.*

Kirby (2011), in her reading of Barad, makes clear that in any entanglement, the entities do not exist separately or act independent of each other; 'entanglement suggests that the very ontology of the entities emerge *through* relationality: the entities do not preexist their involvement' (p. 76). Based on this assertion, we treat voice as one such entity. Attention to these onto-epistemological entanglements make matter matter, enable an analysis that decenters the intentional human subject, and distributes agency among all of the *things* in an assemblage that is continually making and unmaking itself. Again, we assert that nothing is mediated; everything is made, including voice.

Second, if voice is no longer something to be retrieved to provide an account of a participant's experience, then data analysis is no longer a practice of providing a representational account. This move of intra-acting with the territorializations of the agentic assemblage is a practice that not only pushes against (over) simplified treatments of voice-as-data but also the traditional, interpretive analytic strategies that tend to take for granted what voice 'is' and what voice 'does' in educational research. We think this makes possible an uncontainable voice in the assemblage that incites becomings and new ontological entanglements, new territories and de-territorializations.

Thinking voice, and analysis, thus provokes a different set of analytic questions when voice can only be thought *in* the agentic assemblage. Approaching analysis as a 'plugging in' (Deleuze & Guattari, 1987; Jackson & Mazzei, 2012), that opens up potentialities, we advocate analysis as a process of developing analytic questions that seek the provisional emergence—of voice, subjects, agents—in the assemblage.[1] For example, returning to the conversation with Amelia and informed by the theoretical concepts that we have presented: agency, the assemblage, intra-action, we might ask:

How does Amelia intra-act with the materiality of her world in ways that produce different becomings?
What are the points on the spectrum (of motherhood; small-town living; being a 'good' Christian, etc.) that co-exist and intra-act?

Finally, thinking a posthuman voice in educational inquiry also requires a rethinking of interviewing. The research artifact presented above does not represent Amelia or her own, individual 'lived experiences' but an assemblage of points on the spectrum (Amelia, other women like and unlike her, small towns, gender norms, disappointments, pleasures, place, and so on) that can produce a different set of questions and research practices that do not rely on a single *source* of knowledge. A posthuman voice in the agentic assemblage draws us to the present-ness and potentialities of that which did not unfold linearly via neat and tidy causality. That is, the elements in the assemblage (or entanglement) are not single sources of knowledge or agency—the footsteps did not cause Amelia to act anymore than Amelia rushed to get her voice/critique 'heard' before her husband arrived home. We need not separate the acts or agents to prove 'some sort of mysterious connection among them' (Kirby, 2011, p. 77). Research artifacts are each *one* moment in *one* assemblage—or *one* particular entanglement. The point, for interviewing practices, is to notice how these elements—including voice—are joined in a particular way, 'in the sheer wonder of the spacetime entanglement at work' (Kirby, 2011, p.77).

Such a scenario certainly requires a de-centering and de-privileging of the method of interviewing in posthuman educational research. Thinking the practice of interviewing in the assemblage necessitates that as researchers we produce practices that are themselves entangled in order to allow the mutual emergence and production of forces to join other enactments and assemblages—kitchens, footsteps, husbands, hometowns. It means that we try to think 'research as the machine that is a hub of connections and productions, with interviewing being just one of those connections' (Mazzei, 2013, p. 739).

In returning to the artifact from our conversation with Amelia, her words (her voice) do not exist apart from her or us, but in the assemblage, as a *voice without organs* (see Mazzei, 2013), as a knot of forces between the material and discursive. We follow Braidotti (2013), who writes, 'The collapse of the nature-culture divide requires that we need to devise a new vocabulary, with new figurations to refer to the elements of our posthuman embodied and embedded subjectivity' (p. 82). It means that as educational researchers, we are challenged not only to devise a new vocabulary, but also to see what different possibilities might be produced for doing educational inquiry in the agentic assemblage.

Note

1. In the book, *Thinking with Theory in Qualitative Research*, the authors engage Deleuze & Guattari's concept, 'plugging in,' as a *process* rather than a *concept*. One aspect of this process involves putting philosophical concepts to work via disrupting the theory/practice binary in order to see what analytic questions are made possible as they *think theory and data together*.

Disclosure statement

No potential conflict of interest was reported by the authors.

References

Barad, K. (2007). *Meeting the universe halfway*. Durham, NC: Duke University Press.

Bennett, J. (2010a). A vitalist stopover on the way to new materialism. In D. Coole & S. Frost (Eds.), *New materialisms* (pp. 47–69). Durham, NC: Duke University Press.

Bennett, J. (2010b). *Vibrant matter: A political economy of things*. Durham, NC: Duke University Press.

Bonta, M., & Protevi, J. (2004). *Deleuze and geophilosophy*. Edinburgh: Edinburgh University Press.

Braidotti, R. (2013). *The posthuman*. Malden, MA: Polilty.

Coole, D. (2005). Rethinking agency: A phenomenological approach to embodiment and agentic capacities. *Political Studies, 53*, 124–142.

Deleuze, G., & Guattari, F. (1987). *A thousand plateaus: Capitalism and schizophrenia*. Minneapolis: University of Minnesota Press.

Hekman, S. (2010). *The material of knowledge: Feminist disclosures*. Bloomington: Indiana University Press.

Jackson, A. Y. (2003). Rhizovocality. *International Journal of Qualitative Studies in Education, 16*, 693–710.

Jackson, A. Y. (2013). Posthumanist data analysis of mangling practices. *International Journal of Qualitative Studies in Education, 26*, 741–748.

Jackson, A. Y., & Mazzei, L. A. (Eds.). (2009). *Voice in qualitative inquiry: Challenging conventional, interpretive, and critical conceptions in qualitative research*. London: Routledge.

Jackson, A. Y., & Mazzei, L. A. (2012). *Thinking with theory in qualitative research: Viewing data across multiple perspectives.* London: Routledge.

Kirby, V. (2011). *Quantum anthropologies.* Durham, NC: Duke University Press.

Lenz Taguchi, H. (2012). A diffractive and Deleuzian approach to analysing interview data. *Feminist Theory, 13*, 268–281.

Livesey, G. (2010). Assemblage. In A. Parr (Ed.), *The Deleuze Dictionary* (revised ed.) (pp. 18–19). Edinburgh: Edinburgh University Press.

MacLure, M. (2009). Broken voices, dirty words: On the productive insufficiency of voice. In A. Y. Jackson & L. A. Mazzei (Eds.), *Voice in qualitative inquiry: Challenging conventional, interpretive, and critical conceptions in qualitative research* (pp. 97–113). London: Routledge.

MacLure, M. (2013). Researching without representation? Language and materiality in post-qualitative methodology. *International Journal of Qualitative Studies in Education, 26*, 658–667.

Massumi, B. (2002). Introduction: Like a thought. In B. Massumi (Ed.), *A shock to thought: Expression after Deleuze and Guattari* (pp. xiii–xxxix). New York, NY: Routledge.

Mazzei, L. A. (2013). A voice without organs: Interviewing in posthumanist research. *International Journal of Qualitative Studies in Education, 26*, 732–740.

Pickering, A. (1993). The mangle of practice: Agency and emergence in the sociology of science. *American Journal of Sociology, 99*, 559–589.

Pickering, A. (1999). The mangle of practice: Agency and emergence in the sociology of science. In M. Biagioli (Ed.), *The science studies reader* (pp. 372–393). New York, NY: Routledge.

Ringrose, J. (2011). Beyond discourse? Using Deleuze and Guattari's schizoanalysis to explore affective assemblages, heterosexually striated space, and lines of flight online and at school. *Educational Philosophy and Theory, 43*, 598–618.

Snaza, N., & Weaver, J. (Eds.). (2014). *Posthumanism and educational research.* Florence, KY: Routledge.

St. Pierre, E. A. (2004). Deleuzian concepts for education: The subject undone. *Educational Philosophy and Theory, 36*, 283–296.

Images of thinking in feminist materialisms: ontological divergences and the production of researcher subjectivities

Hillevi Lenz Taguchi

Qualitative feminist studies are much challenged by the contemporary critique of social constructionist postmodernism, as well as the renewed search for the body and materiality. The result is (at least) two diverging research accounts: a *re*newed feminist materialism, relying on some foundational ontologies and what has been called a *new* materialist feminist account that constitutes radical onto-logical rewritings. The aim of this paper is to investigate what kind of researcher subjectivities these different accounts produce for qualitative inquiry. This investigation will be unfolded using an example from a collaborative research process involving 10 PhD students. The example is woven into Deleuze and Guattari's discussions on the Image of Thought and the three images of thinking outlined in *A Thousand Plateaus*. The investigation shows that although the aim of our collaborative process was to resist the assumed Cogito/"I" of philosophy and qualitative inquiry, we still got caught up in taken-for-granted images of thinking and doing analysis. A deterritorializing of habits of thinking and practicing in order for new and other researcher subjectiv-ities to emerge required collaborative efforts that put to work a rhizomatic image of thinking and operated from within an ontology of difference.

Outlining the problem: the conflict in feminist materialisms

This paper focuses on the problem of whether feminist research has, as St. Pierre asks (2011), managed to get away from the assumed "I" of qualitative inquiry; that is, "that there exists a subject 'I' that precedes the verb 'think'" (p. 40). St. Pierre's question addresses two issues: the images of thinking we enact when doing research and what it is to be/become a researcher. The relationship between processes of knowledge production and processes of being/becoming has been discussed in some current accounts of feminist materialist theorizing as they have tried to, in different ways, address the contemporary critique of social constructionist postmodernism. Examples of such accounts are *posthumanist* and *anti-anthropocentric* research (Åsberg, Koobak, & Johnson, 2011; Pedersen, this issue), *material feminisms* (Alaimo & Hekman, 2008), and *new* or *re*newed material feminisms (Coole & Frost, 2010; Dolphijn & van der Tuin, 2012). The question of what is or what is not *new* in these currently emerging feminist materialist accounts has been intensively discussed. Dolphijn and van der Tuin (2012) write that a radical rereading that *ontologically recreates* founding ontologies should be considered *new* (pp. 120–122). Thus, what have been labeled *new* materialisms claim to establish a radical break with both universalism and dualism as they theorize the co-consitutiveness of cultural discourse and materiality (Dolphijn & van der Tuin, 2012).

Another kind of material feminist theorizing, however, has engaged in *reactivations* of ontologies and epistemologies that constitute the very foundations of qualitative interpretive inquiry – phenomenology, hermeneutics, psychoanalysis, and the "old" materialism of Marxism (e.g. Ahmed, 2006; Sullivan, 2012). Their advocates have therefore labeled them "*re*newed [feminist] materialisms" of "neglected and marginalized currents in modern thought" that "deserve a reactivating in new modes of research" (Coole & Frost, 2010, p. 4). In other words, the conflict in feminist materialisms, and whether they are considered *re*newed or *new*, concerns the question of ontology, and thus what kind of researching "I" (St. Pierre, 2011) and (researcher) subjectivities they produce.

The aim of this paper is to investigate more closely what kind of researching "I" or subjectivity gets produced by the two different feminist accounts of *re*newed materialisms and *new* materialisms. This investigation will be unfolded using an example from a collaborative research process that involved 10 PhD students during a period of seven months during 2005–2006 (Lenz Taguchi, in press). The example is woven into Deleuze's (1994) and Deleuze and Guattari's (1987, 1994) discussions on the Image of Thought. In the first chapter of *A Thousand Plateaus*, they describe three different images of thinking as three figurations of root-systems and connect them to the image of the book. The first image of thought is the Cartesian tree-like root-thinking that relies on a principal root. Such thinking produces what they call root-books, which are underpinned by a representational and binary logic. The second image of thought relies on a phenomenological ontology producing the figure of a multiple root-system *without* a principal root or center. Nevertheless, these multiple roots inevitably form a unitary and coherent so-called fascicular root-system and book (like the roots of scallion). The third image moves away from trees and unitary root-systems to rhizomatic root-systems without trunks or stems that do not form coherent units. They spread in all directions, moving inbetween, across, and through, creating a pluralism or multiplicity like that of weeds or grass: the rhizome book.

In this paper, I weave these three images of thinking into the process of shifting and transforming researcher subjectivities as they were produced during the collaborative coursework. I first introduce the coursework and then show how, despite our intentions, we got caught up in the very classical root-book-thinking rejected by *both re*newed and *new* feminist materialisms. It is, however, important in this context to show not only how easily this practice of thinking is activated but also how it implicitly resides within the interpretive style of thinking that dominated the next phase of our work, what Deleuze and Guattari call fascicular root-thinking. This is the image of thought of the subject-dependent phenomenological researching "I/eye" (Sullivan, 2012) present in *re*newed critical feminist materialisms. In order to illustrate the methodological process and consequences – if only in a cursory fashion – I will introduce some data. This data will also be taken up in the last section, where the *new* materialist account will be discussed in relation to our collaborative work, and Deleuze and Guattari's image of a rhizomatic image of thought. This practice of thinking produced a researching subjectivity that I have called a *collective-researcher-assemblage* of movement and transformation in its engagement with theory and data as mutually active agents (Lenz Taguchi, in press). The paper concludes with a brief summary.

The Cartesian self-reflexive "I" and "root-book" thinking

I read St. Pierre's (2011) refusal to accept an assumed "I" of qualitative inquiry in parallel to the outspoken aim I had formulated together with 10 PhD students who asked me to arrange a feminist course on deconstruction. As a group of nine women and one man from four different social science disciplines, we aimed to challenge the image of *Man* as the universal, self-evident ground of thinking and philosophizing who produces woman as his Other (Lloyd, 2002). We made it our task to try to develop other possible images of thinking, theorizing, and doing analysis by enacting what we understood as a collaborative endeavor of "put[ting] theory to work" (Spivak as cited in Lather, 2007, p. 157).

The coursework started with studying texts on deconstruction with the aim of deconstructing our own "take ups" of the texts. We aspired to make ourselves aware of our respective epistemological presuppositions as we battled with trying to make sense of texts by John Caputo, Jacques Derrida, Gayatri Spivak, and Martin Mac-Quillan. Although this kind of disclosure of our discursive tool-boxes helped us displace, and even unhinge, our taken-for-granted thinking, this process still relied on an assumed "I" as the taken-for-granted starting point of thinking. That is, we assumed a rational and self-reflexive mind trying to trace her/his thinking understood as different viewpoints or perspectives in order to understand or *interpret* what deconstruction is. A subject position from which to read data in this way is produced by an understanding of *difference* as marks of alterity or as a necessary othering of an unknowable Other. Such differences are, as Deleuze (1994) writes, a *negative* difference that necessarily divides something *from* something else for its identity to emerge: woman as different from man, etc. This way of understanding difference produces binary thinking and dichotomous realities. Deleuze and Guattari (1987) write, "this is the most classical and well reflected, oldest, and weariest kind of thought" (p. 5), it is "the law of the One that becomes two, then of the two that becomes four … Binary logic is the spiritual reality of the root-tree" (p. 5). Hence, in a habitual style of thinking, we would treat these texts as what Deleuze and Guattari (1987) have described as "root-books" (p. 5). This tree-like thinking means treating the texts (or data) as imitations or reflections of reality (Deleuze & Guattari, 1987, p. 5). The original idea or ideal (in this case deconstruction) is supposed to emanate from the root that produces its representation: "one becomes two" (p. 5). As the texts produce different understandings in the participants' readings of them, this merely unmasks how the participants are discursively inscribed in different ways, while the original meaning lies within the root-book itself.

Just as there must be a necessary separation between the reality of "the world" and "the book" imitating it, the researching "I" produces her/his representations of this reality at a distance, or at arms' length, from the texts (or data). This is the process of Cartesian *mindwork*: the pure self of "I think" as the beginning of thinking that Deleuze has critiqued throughout his writings. However, as will be discussed in the next section that illustrates a fascicular thinking, Deleuze (1994) shows how a representational thinking resides in fascicular thinking as well (p. 138). In fact, all major modern philosophies presuppose the human being, her thinking, or her experiencing or language making, as the only possible starting-point of knowledge production. "I think" and the mere "habit of saying I," says Deleuze (1994), become the most general ground and principle of representation, and the source that unites other and connecting faculties such as "I conceive, I judge, I imagine, I remember and I perceive" as branches of the Cogito and its being, thinking and experiencing (Deleuze, 1994, p. 138; St. Pierre, 2011).

Seriously questioning this representational image of thought constitutes a major ontological shift. It is in relation to this shift that the debate between feminist materialist accounts reveals how the *new* materialist accounts must be understood to ontologically diverge in essential ways from the *re*newed accounts. Regardless of these fundamental differences, what seems to have caused confusion in the debate (Ahmed, 2008; Sullivan, 2012) is that *both* accounts unanimously reject the Cartesian notion of knowledge production as an exclusively *human* affair and as a rational self-reflexive mindwork. They *both* ask the crucial question of whether it is at all possible to pull apart the knower from the known (St. Pierre, 2010), and both answer in unison "No." Where they diverge is in how it is possible to consider material agents and bodies as central in the production of knowing.

Materiality as *given* to the human subject: fascicular root-thinking as a corrective to social constructionism

The *re*newed feminist materialisms, relying on the subject-dependent ontologies of Edmund Husserl, Maurice Merleau-Ponty, and Martin Heidegger, have been presented in terms of a "practicing of critical materialism" in response to criticism of radical constructivist and deconstructionist approaches (Coole & Frost, 2010, p. 25). To think that gender is simply a social construction constitutes, for these *re*newed accounts, an impossible reduction of what is foremost an embodied lived experience. It is simply not enough to *think* in order to know that you exist as a gendered being, so this is not an exclusively human affair. Rather you need to experience something *outside* the mind to understand who you are; that is, experiencing your own body and its relation to the material world (Ahmed, 2006, 2010). In other words, you cannot pull apart the knower (subject) from the known (object). Or, to rephrase this from within a phenomenological epistemology: the knower (subject) is what is to be known, because the subject is also the object of study, the so-called body-subject. Gendered bodies are understood to materialize in an inseparable relation to material objects that subjects *orient* themselves towards, handle or "*do* things with," and thus become meaningful to them in particular ways (Ahmed, 2010, p. 249). Ahmed (2006, 2010) studies the conscious acts of human subjects orienting themselves differently in relation to the material world. She writes, "To be oriented in a certain way is how certain things come to be significant, come to be objects *for me*" (2010, p. 235).

Hence, there is no universal or principal ideal, or root, in the world outside the subject in a phenomenological ontology. "The principal root is aborted, or its tip has been destroyed" (p. 5), as Deleuze and Guattari (1987) explain. Instead, we have what they call a fascicular root-system that concerns the lifeworld of human subjects only. It consists of a multitude of "secondary roots," as in fibrous roots bundled tightly together, or multiple experiences of the already given material world forming a strong unit of a human lifeworld. The outermost aim of a phenomenological analysis is to bundle together and describe what are considered the general structures of human subjects' *firsthand perspectives*. So, despite the lack of a principal root, the fascicular root-system of multiple and seemingly chaotic roots pertain to the fascicle that affirms a superior unity or a hidden truth or meaning and, adds a higher spiritual – *transcendental* – dimension (Deleuze & Guattari, 1987, p. 5). Deleuze and Guattari (1987) write, "the root's unity subsists as past, as yet to come, as possible" (5). This constitutes a transcendental negative ontology, where difference is understood to derive always from a state of lack in relation to an unknown Other, or to what has been, or what might be possible, as a transcendental ideal. What this amounts to, in the words of Deleuze and Guattari (1987), is that:

> the fascicular system does not break with dualism, with the complementarity between the subject and an object, a natural reality and a spiritual reality: unity is consistently thwarted and obstructed in the object, while a new type of unity triumphs in the subject. (p. 6)

Unity is restored in the subject's interpretive control of a chaotic multiplicity of life-world experiences.

To summarize and relate the fascicular root-thinking to the *re*newed feminist materialist phenomenological account, they can clearly be understood to resurrect the formation of subjectivity by way of its conscious acts of making *meaning* of its bodily lived experience of the material world of things and power structures. But this is so only insofar as this materiality is *given* to this human subject for it to be perceived. It is in this way that the *re*newed critical materialist phenomenological research accounts have been understood as a corrective of social constructionist theorizing (Coole & Frost, 2010).

Doing fascicular root-thinking in processes of collaborative analysis

During the major part of the coursework, we engaged in performing collaborative analysis of excerpts of research data supplied by each of the participants (Lenz Taguchi, in press). We split into temporary groups of three to analyze our data in two or three steps. Typically, we would analyze our own data and the data of one other participant and send the analysis by email to the group participants. In the next step, we would perform an analysis of the other participants' already performed analysis and then critically deconstruct our own already performed analysis of our own data. Occasionally, we would undertake a third (and even fourth) round of *analyzing the analysis of the analysis.*

In order to discuss the emerging research subjectivities produced by this work, I will use an example. This data excerpt features an interview with a young Iranian woman (Wikström, 2007). The interviewer asked for a life-span narration, starting with questions about where the interviewee was born and major events leading up to the present time. "Fataneh" was born in Iran the same day the Iranian revolution began in April 1979. She describes what she remembers as a militant discipline in her primary school in Teheran, with corporal punishment and daily humiliating inspections of the girls' hair as the teacher unveiled them each morning. Fataneh came to Sweden when she was eight years old via India as a county of transit. She describes a series of transitions from refugee camps with mostly Iranian inhabitants, to living in a Swedish village with only three Iranian families and not being able to socialize with Swedes. Then she moved again to a larger city and began to socialize with Swedish-speaking immigrants from other countries as well as Swedes. In her later teens, she began to take an interest in Iranians again, only to find she had almost forgotten how to speak Persian. She then had to relearn Persian culture. Her interview ends with a description of her recent travels to Iran. At the time of the interview, she described Iran as a space where she can relax and be herself since no one knows what to expect from her.

In the first rounds of analysis made by Hanna Wikström and myself, it is obvious how we both got caught up in wanting to describe how Fataneh, as a body-subject, makes meaning of her lifeworld in the various places described in the interview. We both seemed to activate what Nikki Sullivan (2012) tellingly called a *somatechnics* analysis, where "'matter' is inextricable from the I/eye that perceives it: perception makes 'matter' matter … [making] 'it' intelligible" (p. 300). This is a process of making meaning of how something is made intelligible *for* a specific thinking "I/eye," where the researching subject is also such an "I/eye." Correspondingly, in our analysis, Fataneh's hair and girl-body is made intelligible and meaningful to her, as well as to us as researchers, as one who resists oppressive teachers, bullying Swedish kids, and demanding parents. This is a resistance that also seeks revenge in victorious fist-fights or by transgressing sexual or gendered norms at home or when traveling back to Iran as a young woman. Hence, *a lifeworld of resistance practices* of different kinds constitutes the bundles of meaning that this fascicular root-thinking produces.

What kind of researcher subjectivity is constituted by such fascicular root-thinking? In enacting this thinking, we emerged as intentional subjects, stretching ourselves towards the material world (and data) given *to* and *for* us as researching "I/eyes" to be perceived and experienced. The intentional and conscious "I/eye" tries to make meaning of the lifeworld of Fataneh by analyzing the "perceptual thereness" of Fataneh's hair, or of any other matter, in the data (Ahmed, 2006, p. 25). The meaning of matter emanates from and is determined by the consciously thinking and meaning-making researcher subject – making hair color meaningful in specific ways, i.e. as a resistance lifeworld. This means that the human meaning-making subject inevitably pre-exists its relations to the world as a taken for granted image of thought. To perform conscious acts of meaning-making, this researching "I/eye" needs to create a distance from the data (St. Pierre, 2011). Moreover, she needs to rid herself of any cultural and discursive inscriptions of the matter perceived to be able to perceive matters in the world as they are *for* the subject *before* discursive norms and inscriptions that might be oppressive of women or other subjects of race, ethnicity, sexuality, etc. As both Ahmed (2010) and Sullivan (2012) note, this kind of analysis makes possible new and other meanings *of* matter (as well as gender, sexuality, etc.) *for* human subjects. On the other hand, this renders matter itself passive in the relation and the human subject as the only agent of knowledge-production, intention, and transformation. To conclude this section, the problem with the *re*newed critical feminist accounts produced by a fascicular root-thinking is that although the knower cannot be separated from the known, and although matter is indeed crucial in the process of human subjects producing knowledge, the fundamental condition for this thinking still takes the human subject as a starting point, and thus produces a negative and dialectical ontology.

New material feminisms: from given to mutually constitutive intra-active relations

Dolphijn and van der Tuin (2012) have conceptualized *new materialism* as a *transversal* cultural theory that simultaneously cuts through realist positivism and social constructionist postmodernism to create something new. Hence, new materialism does not simply add on materiality as something else to be taken into account or propose a critical counter theory, each of which would simply maintain a transcendental dualism. Moreover, matter is not simply *given* to human body-subjects to be perceived, but human agents and matter are *mutually constitutive* of each other in a process of "making themselves intelligible to each other" in their inevitably ongoing intra-active relations (Barad, 2007, p. 185). The production of "knowing" is thus taking place on a "two way track" between matter and discourse (Dolphijn & van der Tuin, 2012, p. 110). This means a shift to rethinking matter in a *radical sense of materialism* instead of starting from human meaning-making. A radical rethinking of matter means that not only perceiving human body-subjects can act intentionally, orient themselves, and have agency to know themselves. In new materialist ontology, intention is something distributed and emerging in complex networks of human and nonhuman material agents that include historically specific sets of material conditions that are effects of *materialdiscursive* and *natureculture* intra-actions (Barad, 2007).

Deleuze's project of pushing dualisms and difference to the limit can be understood as a basic underpinning of new materialisms thinking (Braidotti, 2012; Dolphijn & van der Tuin, 2012). In this philosophy of difference, difference is understood as a *practice* rather than defining identity in relation to another. Hence, it is the process and effects of *differing* and differentiation – that is, *difference in itself* as an ongoing flow of affirmative relations – that is constitutive of existence (Deleuze, 1994). This radical way of understanding difference (as an ongoing practice) diverts from transcendental ontologies that understand difference as marks of alterity in terms of identity or as a necessary othering of an unknowable Other – that is, as a *negative* difference. Braidotti (as cited in Dolphijn & van der Tuin, 2012) writes that this translates difference into binary and hierarchical relations of "worth-less-than" (p. 99). Divergent to this negative difference that underpins a root-tree image of thought, difference, in the rhizomatic image of thought, is something performative that "'refer[s] to other differences which never identify it but rather differentiate it'" (Deleuze, as cited in Dolphijn & van der Tuin, 2012, p. 130). It produces, alters, transforms, creates, and invents as an ongoing metamorphosis (Braidotti, as cited in Dolphijn & van der Tuin, 2012, p. 107).

A rhizomatic image of thought and a cartographic methodology

A rhizomatic practice of thinking did not emerge in our collaborative work until we had to give in to the overwhelming diversity of different readings produced from the data excerpts. Analyses seemed to grow wildly like weeds or grass from our collaborative engagements with each other's data. When we met to discuss this multiplicity of analyses, starting literally anywhere – *in the middle* – helped us break out of assumed research practices of root-thinking and fascicular root-thinking as described earlier. The analyses performed on already-written analysis as a second, third (and occasionally fourth) step, produced an expansive and almost uncontrollable multiplicity of new readings that thwarted ordering and ruined binary logic, opening up creative and inventive offshoot readings. Some of us had provided physical space in our analytical charts in the computer software, where what Deleuze and Guattari (1987, p. 9) call "lines of flight" readings might be invoked.

The multiplicity of analyses of Fataneh's story can be understood as a complex rhizome that contains not only what Deleuze and Guattari (1987) call segmentary lines that organize, stratify, and signify the rhizome but also lines of deterritorialization and "lines of flight" (p. 9) according to which the rhizome can transform and expand. Deleuze and Guattari (1987) write, "The rhizome operates by variation, expansion, conquest, capture, offshoots" (p. 21). Moreover, all of these readings, as different segmentary lines or lines of flight of the rhizome, can be laid out as a "map," but not an ordinary map that accurately represents a space of geography. Deleuze and Guattari (1987) think of the map as a composition of different lines that is "detachable, connectable, reversible, modifiable, and has multiple entryways and exits and its own lines of flight. /.../ the rhizome [as such a 'map'] is an acentred, non-hierarchical, nonsignifying system" (p. 21). Hence, the "map" does not concern itself with interpretation, meaning, and defining a body's limitations or form but with the investigation of forces and intensities in the events as the different lines connect, intersect, or traverse each other. This kind of rhizomatic and transversal analysis can show how different realities of Fataneh are materially actualized and realized as concrete practices, but it might also be productive of new and other possible realities of Fataneh. Deleuze and Guattari (1987) call this a methodology of cartography (p. 12).

Let us enter the map of multiple analyses of Fataneh's story at various points to try to identify and follow the different lines that connect or traverse each other, looking for ruptures and differences that get made. One analysis performed on an initial fascicular reading radically deterritorialized the taken-for-granted segmentary (story)line of such a reading. Here, Fataneh understands herself in a linear fashion: first as a refugee and then as an immigrant girl, a relatively assimilated Swedish teenager, before "becoming Persian" again. Instead, we read the lines of how Fataneh's body responds to the different forces in the material and discursive (semiotic) flows and environments that she encounters and inhabits. In other words, we install ourselves in the embodied affective events, as Deleuze and Guattari (1994) suggest (p. 111) in order to sense how the material and discursive flows connect, reinforce, and become co-productive. For example, Fataneh's dark hair powerfully connects to and interacts with the discriminating semiotic force (discourses) and bullying practices of the Swedish kids in what can be understood as a material discursive engagement. These intensive relational entanglements co-produce new effects and events such as fistfights in the schoolyard. The victorious outcomes of these fights involve the material flow of Fataneh's hair, clothes, and embodied ways of being in new sets of relational flows of matter and semiotic discourse, now making the other kids watch out for Fataneh and keep their mouths shut.

In these relations, hair and bodies as materialities cannot be understood as passive substances that can only be given agency by ways of intentional human subjects. Rather, discourse and matter as flows and intensities are mutually implicated and co-constitutive in these relations. Matter is understood to transform and change language and discourse in these events just as much as discourse is constitutive of material realities. In a rhizomatic image of thought, all kinds of matter, including human discourse (or what Deleuze and Guattari call collective enunciations), are involved in processes of making themselves intelligible to each other in events of knowledge-production (Barad, 2007, p. 185). One example of this is the collective enunciations produced by frequent media images and discourses in which immigrant women are depicted as victims of their "homeland" cultures. They produce strong segmentary lines that interact with matter such as hair and skin color.

When following the lines of the different analyses of Fataneh's story and letting them traverse each other, it was possible to extend and expand some of our analyses into new imagined (virtual) possible realities (Lenz Taguchi, 2012). Fataneh's subjectivity can be understood to multiply rather than always being reduced to a negative difference *from* the Other and thus understanding herself *either* as (mostly) Iranian *or* (mostly) Swedish. When multiplying, she becomes more of everything and different in herself – *a subjectivity in transposition* (Braidotti, 2006, p. 5). It becomes possible to be 100% Iranian and 100% Swedish as a complex multiplicity of intersecting cultural, gendered, and other differences. Braidotti (2006) thinks of subjectivity in transposition as involved in affirmative transversal leaps from one code or field into another, corresponding to Barbara McClintock's "jumping genes" and the epigenetic interactivity and flexibility of the genome. Subjectivity, says Braidotti (2012), is determined by its capacity to be both *grounded* in what is *already given*, and to simultaneously *flow* and change in relation to what is *given* in new events of encounters with other bodies, matter, or concepts/discourse (p. 22). A nomadic subjectivity in transposition constitutes the possibility of weaving together different strands and indicates (as in music) "variations and shifts of scale in discontinuous but harmonious patterns" (Braidotti, 2006, p. 5). In this way, we can think of Fataneh's subjectivity in musical terms of "playing the positivity of differences" (p. 5).

A collective-body-assemblage researcher subjectivity

In a rhizomatic image of thinking, Deleuze and Guattari (1987) describe the "book as an assemblage" or a "rhizome book" (p. 23). This image of the book goes against the idea of the book "as an image of the world. A rhizome-book, [and] not a dichotomous, pivotal, or fascicular book" (p. 23). The rhizome book has no clear division between "a field of reality (the world) and a field of representation (the book) and a field of subjectivity (the author)" (p. 23). Rather, a book as an assemblage is, as I have tried to show, establishing connections between these different fields where different flows (a semiotic, a material, and a social flow) act and are acted upon, intersecting, overlapping, and traversing each other. This means that rather than tracing what emerges in the practice of analysis to a root of origin or essence or trying to order the chaos of differences, stacking them into bundles, themes, or categories in our analysis as an invisible hand of a researching "I" (St. Pierre, 2011), we start in the middle to look for what emerges in the connections among these different fields and flows.

   In order to get to this analysis of connections on the "surface" of an extending cartography map, we need to distort assumed practices of thinking, analyzing, and interpreting and produce a researcher ontology of *multiplicity*. "The multiple *must be made*," (p. 6) write Deleuze and Guattari (1987). The multiplicity of different kinds of readings of data that our collaborative work produced helped us create such a multiplicity of fields and flows. In the middle of such a multiplicity, it became possible to *acentre* and *asubjectify* ourselves in a way that produced a researcher reality that I have called a collective-body-assemblage, and/or a collective-researcher-assemblage (Lenz Taguchi, in press). In line with Deleuze and Guattari's (1987) thinking, we operated in a practice of subtraction (subtracting also ourselves) in order for a multiplicity to be produced. They write: "Subtract the unique from the multiplicity to be constituted; write at $n - 1$ dimensions. A system of this kind could be called a rhizome" (p. 6). "/.../ Flat multiplicities of n dimensions are asignifying and asubjective" (p. 9). Thus, our individual subjectivities were severely obscured by the multiple foldings and unfoldings of analyses, produced as effects of effects of effects in the process. The further away we got from tracing roots and bundling up lifeworld experiences into neat categories, the closer we got to reading data *trans*corporeally (Alaimo, 2010) as a fluidity between and through the collective-body-assemblage. Here, matter, such as Fataneh's hair, was understood as a forceful material agent that connected to other flows of collective enunciations (discourse on what it is to be Swedish) and children's violent talk and discriminating practices in the flow of the production of knowing. It is in this way that rhizomatic thought might be productive of what St. Pierre (2011) has called post-qualitative and post-interpretive analysis. This kind of analysis can produce a different kind of knowing produced in a co-constitutive relation between matter and discourse where it is impossible to pull apart the knower from the known.

Toward the end of the seven months, we began to slowly recognize the emancipatory effects of being involved in this rather messy collaborative endeavor. Being subtracted as the assumed researching "I," we were simply "tools for thinking" in events that exceeded us as individual researchers because it is *"thought itself* that requires the thinker" (p. 69, emphasis added), as Deleuze and Guattari (1994) write. We came to understand this decentered researcher subjectivity, of being *used by thought*, in terms of a deep loading interconnectedness and companionship with our fellow researchers, the data, and the material discursive places and spaces where this research was enacted.

Summary

This paper has tried to investigate the ontological divergences and the production of researcher subjectivities produced by two feminist materialist accounts in qualitative research that both address the contemporary critique of social constructionist postmodernism: *new* materialisms and *re*newed materialism. In line with St. Pierre (2010), it is important that we ask ourselves whether it is possible (even as a deconstructive gesture), to remain within the enclosures of interpretivist or intersubjective phenomenological ontologies while at the same time trying to trouble them. As this paper shows, when relying on any kind of subject-dependent ontology, whether it concerns the thinking "I" of the self-reflexive Cartesian subject, or a phenomenological intersubjective firsthand perspective, this cannot be understood in any other way than always presuming "a subject before the verb /.../ a doer before the deed / .../ an a priori subject that exists ahead of [and apart from] language and cultural practice" (St. Pierre, 2010, p. 3).

The investigation performed in this paper, analyzing an example of researchers actively trying to resist taken-for-granted researcher practices and subjectivities, shows that even as poststructuralist-informed feminist researchers, we were still drawn into habitual practices of producing root-book-thinking and having problems getting past an irresistible fascicular root-thinking. The territory of qualitative inquiry is so heavily sedimented that it requires very hard collaborative work to deterritorialize its habitual ways of thinking and practicing in order for new and different researcher practices and subjectivities to emerge. However, as this paper has illustrated, a rhizomatic image of thinking, operating from within a Deleuzian ontology of difference, can cut qualitative inquiry loose from old tools to invent new ones. This is not something that can be done only *once*, but it has to be done over and over again, in an ongoing flow of differentiation. Our researcher practices can never be fixed, but must be invented again and again.

Acknowledgements

I want to thank Patti Lather for her constructive comments to help me improve this paper.

References

Ahmed, S. (2006). *Queer phenomenology: Orientations, objects, others*. Durham, NC: Duke University Press.

Ahmed, S. (2008). Open forum imaginary prohibitions: Some preliminary remarks on the founding gestures of the "new materialism". *European Journal of Women's Studies, 15*, 23–39.

Ahmed, S. (2010). Orientations matter. In D. Coole & S. Frost (Eds.), *New materialisms. Ontology, agency, and politics* (pp. 234–257). Durham, NC: Duke University Press.

Alaimo, S., & Hekman, S. (Eds.). (2008). *Material feminisms*. Bloomington, IN: Indiana University Press.

Alaimo, S. (2010). *Bodily natures. Science, environment, and the material self*. Bloomington, IN: Indiana University Press.

Åsberg, C., Koobak, R., & Johnson, E. (2011). Beyond the humanist imagination. *NORA – Nordic Journal of Feminist and Gender Research, 19*, 218–230.

Barad, K. (2007). *Meeting the universe halfway: Quantum physics and the entanglement of matter and meaning*. Durham, NC: Duke University Press.

Braidotti, R. (2006). *Transpositions. On nomadic ethics*. Cambridge, MA: Polity Press.

Braidotti, R. (2012). Interview with Rosi Braidotti. In R. Dolphijn & I. van der Tuin (Eds.), *New materialism: Interviews & cartographies* (pp. 19–37). Ann Arbor, MI: Open Humanities Press.

Coole, D., & Frost, S. (2010). Introducing the new materialisms. In D. Coole & S. Frost (Eds.), *New materialisms. Ontology, agency, and politics* (pp. 1–46). Durham, NC: Duke University Press.

Deleuze, G. (1994). *Difference and repetition*. (P. Patton, Trans.). New York, NY: Columbia University Press.

Deleuze, G., & Guattari, F. (1987). *A thousand plateaus. Capitalism and schizophrenia*. (B. Massumi, Trans.). Minneapolis, MN: University of Minnesota Press.

Deleuze, G., & Guattari, F. (1994). *What is philosophy?* (G. Burchell & H. Tomlinson, Trans.). London: Verso.

Dolphijn, R., & van der Tuin, I. (2012). *New materialism: Interviews & cartographies*. Ann Arbor, MI: Open Humanities Press.

Lather, P. (2007). *Getting lost. Feminist efforts toward a double(d) science*. New York, NY: State University of New York Press.

Lenz Taguchi, H. (2012). A diffractive and Deleuzian approach to analyzing interview-data. *Journal of Feminist Theory, 13*, 265–281.

Lenz Taguchi, H. (in press). Becoming "molecular girl": Transforming subjectivities in collaborative doctoral research studies as micro-politics in the academy. *International Journal of Qualitative Studies in Education*.

Lloyd, G. (2002). Maleness, metaphor, and the "crisis" of reason". In L. M. Antony & C. E. Witt (Eds.), *A mind of one's own: Feminist essays on reason and objectivity* (2nd ed., pp. 73–89). Boulder, CO: Westview Press.

St. Pierre, E. (2010, April 30–May 4). *Resisting the subject of qualitative inquiry*. Paper presented at the annual meeting of the American Educational Research Association, Denver, CO.

St. Pierre, E. (2011). Refusing human being in hmanist qualitative inquiry. In N. K. Denzin & M. D. Giardina (Eds.), *Qualitative inquiry and global crisis* (pp. 40–55). Walnut Creek, CA: Left Coast Press.

Sullivan, N. (2012). The somatechnics of perception and the matter of the non/human: A critical response to the new materialism. *European Journal of Women's Studies, 19*, 299–313.

Wikström, H. (2007). *(Im)possible positions. Families from Iran & postcolonial reflections* (PhD thesis in social work). Gothenburg University, Gothenburg, Sweden.

Learning to be affected: Matters of pedagogy in the artists' soup kitchen

Stephanie Springgay and Zofia Zaliwska

ABSTRACT
Expanding on the robust contributions by feminist new materialist scholars this essay focuses on two concepts—affect and rhythm—in order to elaborate on matters of pedagogy and a politics of attunement. If one of the key challenges that arises from feminist new materialism is that the human can no longer be taken for granted, then this prompts us to open ourselves to other ways of thinking, knowing, and doing. Being attuned to the agency of all matter offers a way of looking at how pedagogy is constituted as material, affective, and in rhythm, and this attention to the mechanisms of pedagogy can in turn affect a politics of attunement. In order to problematize an affective pedagogy we turn to a socially enagaged performance called The *Artists' Soup Kitchen*.

Introduction

Across the social sciences and humanities, feminist new materialism is increasingly being used as a methodology that seeks to emphasize the materiality of matter in research. For feminist new materialism, the human no longer assumes priority as the knowing subject or the organizer of inquiry. Focus shifts towards *what* participates in knowledge production, not just who, emphasizing that the what is never fully containable or knowable beforehand. Drawing from discursive and materialist turns in cultural theory (Butler, 1993; Haraway, 1988; Harding, 1986), feminist new materialism 'comes back to persistent troublings' (Hughes & Lury, 2013, p. 787) concerning feminist theory, and intra-acts with the recurring debates around representational thinking, causation, an understanding of time as non-linear, and theory as inventive (Coleman, 2014). In other words, feminist new materialism is not a paradigm shift, but rather, an exploration and *rethinking* of what is 'new' in feminist new materialism. As a methodology that grapples with and is constituted by the phenomenon it seeks to understand, it conceives of theories as performative (Barad, 2007) and thinking as immanent (Van der Tuin & Dolphihn, 2010). A feminist new materialist methodology thus aims to make room for generative matter that forces us to 'engage affirmatively with the present, accounting for some of its features in a manner that is empirically grounded without being reductive and remains critical while avoiding negativity' (Braidotti, 2013, p. 5). This radical relationality calls for a new politics of attunement and responsibility, one that contributes to 'the differential mattering of the world' where 'we are responsible for the cuts that we help enact not because we do the choosing, but because we are an agential part of the material becoming of the universe' (Barad in Coleman, 2014, p. 43). This inventive politics, we argue, is being increasingly taken up in the field of education, where feminist new materialists are reconsidering what these new engagements with matter do to educational practices and what pedagogical processes are opened up as a result.

For example, the 2013 special issue of *Gender and Education* on new material feminisms highlights the ways in which educational scholars are drawing on this new shift towards the material in order to think about education 'in terms of change, flows, mobilities, multiplicities, assemblages, materialities and processes', (Taylor & Ivinson, 2013, p. 665) while simultaneously theorizing the newness of this radical break with dualism. This requires a particular ethics from the researcher, one that takes seriously their messy involvement in knowledge production. This radical ontology, or what Barad (2007) calls ethico-on-to-epistemology, is at the heart of the special issue, forcing educational scholars to pay attention to what matters (and consequently what does not matter) and to grapple with the uncertainty of their own position. Mazzei (2013) reflects on her own use of theory through Barad's methodology of diffraction, helping her to explore her embodied relationship with the data she is attempting to understand. In challenging conventional modes of analysis, Mazzei is able to theorize the ways in which the agential matter of data may rework the researcher's positionality. Hughes and Lury (2013) rework the feminist concept of situatedness in order to advance potential tools of analysis for understanding the entangled processes of co-invention. In re-thinking situatedness as more than strictly a position or an identity, Hughes and Lury (2013) rework the concept to understand it more ecologically, paying attention to the patterns of movement 'that constitute the moving surface or ground of figures of knowledge' (p. 792). Using the feminist materialist concepts of cuts, knots, contrasts, fractals and figures, the authors offer ways to map patterns of movement 'such that the multiple relations between figure and ground, object and subject become visible as matters of concern' (p. 795). What is captured in this particular special issue, and continues to proliferate in educational journals, is a feminist new materialist attention to analysis, highlighting this traditional category as matter of concern (Niccolini & Pindyck, 2015; Rotas & Springgay, 2013; Springgay & Zaliwska, 2015; St. Pierre, 2013).

Feminist new materialism is concerned with ongoing affective and transcorporeal relations of becoming, emphasizing experimentation, process and novelty. For many new materialist scholars, the return to matter requires an attention to process and the unpredictability of research. As Tiainen, Kontturi, and Hongisto (2015) contend, new materialist researchers should 'let the concepts she or he works with re-singularise in connection with the vibrant, never fully containable processes that are being explored' (p. 6). They suggest that it is 'the co-affective relations of material, conceptual, histor-ical and social elements that reconfigure spheres of knowledge by way of singularisation' (p. 6). For example, MacLure (2013) conceptualizes the unpredictable and creative process of research through the intensity of wonder. As a movement of desire and intensity, wonder can be located and produced in the entangled relationship of data-and-researcher. Suspended in a threshold between knowing and unknowing, wonder has the potential to relieve data from conventional inquiry so that it can grasp us in unanticipated ways. Wonder, according to MacLure, is not necessarily a positive affect. As a force that disrupts epistemic certainty, wonder 'shades into curiosity, horror, fascination, disgust, and monstros-ity' (p. 229). The event of wonder is unannounced and cannot be found, but rather, is something that requires attunement and an ability to respond so that we can experiment with its invitation.

Expanding on the robust contributions by feminist new materialist scholars this article focuses on two concepts—*affect and rhythm*—in order to elaborate on matters of pedagogy and a politics of attunement. If one of the key challenges that arises from feminist new materialism is that the human can no longer be taken for granted, then this prompts us to open ourselves to other ways of thinking, knowing and doing. Being attuned to the agency of all matter offers a way of looking at how pedagogy is constituted as material, affective, and in rhythm, and this attention to the mechanisms of pedagogy can in turn affect a politics of attunement that captures 'the intensity of the in-bracing to remain cor-related, to coordinate, to move inventively together in concerted action—crucially, without erasing the attuned differences' (Massumi, 2015, p. 117). Unlike more conventional politics of pedagogy, the aim of this article is to flesh out a politics of attunement that forces us to consider pedagogy as a 'live mapping of the process under transition' (Massumi, 2015, p. 118) and invites us to learn to be affected.

In order to problematize an affective pedagogy we turn to a socially enagaged performance called *The Artists' Soup Kitchen*. We understand this event as a practice of research-creation, a propositional and experimental mode of activity; a process of 'speculative eventing' (Manning, 2013). As opposed to representing the particular concepts we take up in this article, the soup kitchen, we contend instantiates them. This is not to suggest that art is Deleuzian or new materialist. Rather, the theorists we use provide concepts that are useful in understanding a particular dimensionality of art and pedagogy. Here we draw on the work of performance philosopher Laura Cull (2012) who argues that the performance practices she writes about do not illustrate the

> concept of immanence in a representational fashion, so much as they try to perform immanence; it is less a matter of trying to show what immanence looks like and more a matter of figuring out how to be inside it and then seeing what comes out of that experience to immanence itself. (p. 13)

One of the challenges with thinking theory alongside the object of study is that we have a tendency to apply theory, as if one proceeds the other. Thinking immanently is what Erin Manning (2013) calls a question of composition. In thinking experience experimentally we want to consider the affective dimensions of the *Artists' Soup Kitchen*. This requires a shift from asking questions about how bodies experienced the event, or how to interpret the art, to thinking about the doing of the performances; what kinds of territories, milieus, refrains and deterritorializations are produced and productive in the event? Understanding the work as an affective event, rather than a pre-formed object opens up the potential for a process of collective individuation. This potential resonates with a politics of attunement that thinks pedagogy differently, as 'an event snapping us to attention together, and correlating our diversity to the affective charge this brings, energizing the whole situation' (Massumi, 2015, p. 115).

McCormack (2013) notes that 'affects of site-specific encounters have the potential to return again and again, simultaneously interrupting and supplementing thought at odd moments, taking place, repeatedly, through sometimes novel configurations of bodies, concepts, and objects' (p. 7). It is this rhythm, or repeatability of difference, that Deleuze and Guattari (1987) map out in their plateau on the refrain. Traversing through their writing, and contemporary thinkers who similarly write about affect and the refrain, our goal is to address how the soup kitchen as a queer feminist art practice offers new ways of conceptualizing pedagogy, art, and politics, or to put in another way, helps us to reimagine the politicality of art and pedagogy. We imagine what it would mean to gain attunement within the affective terrains of feminist new materialist practice, or what Elizabeth Grosz (2008) would call blocs of sensation—art's politicality. Art, she notes, is political not because of its interpretive frameworks, but

> in the sense that it elaborates the possibilities of new, more different sensations than those we know. Art is there the becomings of the earth couple with the becomings of life to produce intensities and sensations that in themselves summon up a new kind of life. (p. 79)

These site-specific encounters, we hope to show, summon matters of pedagogy that depend on a politics of attunement.

The article begins with a brief contextualization of cooking and art in order to situate the *Artists' Soup Kitchen* within a broader art historical field. From there, we move into a discussion around affect theory and the apparent challenges in defining affect as an intensity. In this section, we turn to various performances from the soup kitchen to illustrate the capacity for a body to be affected and to affect, charting a politics of attunement. The following section explores the materiality of eating through Deleuze and Guattari's concept of rhythm and the refrain in order to map out how intensities come together and habits come to matter. Finally, we move towards conceptualizing what art's politicality could do to approaching pedagogy as an event of becoming affected that requires a particular expression of attunement. Here, we flesh out a politics of pedagogy as an event that pays attention to the material forces and entanglements in bodies and matter.

Food as art

The concept of a kitchen—of preparing, cooking and serving food—as art is not new. Kitchen type projects include: *Conflict kitchen*, Rirkrit Tirivanija's *Untitled (Free)*, Michael Rachowitz's *Enemy Kitchen* and *The American Reputation Aid Society* (ARAS) Aid Wagon and mobile kitchen. These examples use food to disturb the ocularcentrism inherent in visual art, as a way of gathering people together, as an invitation to dialogue, as a form of trade or exchange and as a political gesture. The *Artists' Soup Kitchen,* which prepared lunchtime meals over six Mondays in the winter of 2011, is embedded within this robust history of social practice and performance art [www.artistsoupkitchen.com]. The project, curated by Jess Dobkin and Stephanie Springgay, in the former Raging Spoon café in Toronto's Queen West neighborhood, served more than 100 community members each week including local artists, academics, students, queer activists and people who resided in the Queen West area who simply arrived off the street. With the help of more than 25 volunteers and café staff, food was prepared and planned in conjunction with the featured weekly artist's performative project.

Some examples of the various live performances included: Helen Reed and Hannah Jickling's *Mystic Pizza*. Guests were invited to choose one of four specialty pizzas, prepared with ingredients that corresponded to an aspect of life as an artist. After their meal, guests could have their crusts and crumbs 'read' by a divination specialist. Helen and Hannah hand-printed paper placemats that introduced and guided guests through 'crust divination' techniques. Annie Cheung's *I Want More*, a scaled-small installation and collective performance action, served quarter-sized portions with scaled down dishes and utensils. Guests were required to ask for second or third servings of food using a wooden cut-out hand, which they had to raise in order to signal a server who would then come around with a megaphone. The diner had to request 'more food' through the megaphone, which signalled another server to come and provide additional helpings of food and drink. This sequence of actions encouraged lunching participants to consider the labor and risk involved when demanding satisfaction during unsatisfactory circumstances. The final week brought Swintak's[1] broth to the Soup Kitchen. Swintak boiled herself into a broth for two days in a large metal vat over a fire with a nice selection of winter vegetables, reducing the body broth to about 48 litres, the approximate amount of her body water. Inspired by a passage from Leonora's Carrington's surrealist work, 'The Hearing Trumpet,' where an old woman finds herself helplessly in a soup, Swintak instead created a situation where she was simultaneously both the chef and the food being served. Guests had the option of eating either 'Swintak Broth' or a vegetarian version that was offered alongside a range of toppings reminiscent of body parts, such as toenails or loose skin. The banquet included a two channel-video documenting the making of her broth.

Food related performances have often been theorized for their sensory contributions to an otherwise overly visual field, examined in relation to the kinds of 'lived experiences' generated, or framed through relational aesthetics and the value of conviviality (Banes & Lepecki, 2007; Bourriaud, 2002; Fischer, 1999). Often classified as socially engaged art, food performances are rooted in multi-disciplinary inquiry, gathering insight from a combination of disciplines including ethnography, anthropology, communication and pedagogy. Turning to educational practices as a framework for understanding socially engaged art, Helguera (2011) outlines the ways in which educational practices such as engagement with audiences, inquiry-based methods, collaborative dialogues and hands-on activities are being taken up by artists who are compelled to break away from and to challenge the discipline(ing) of art, and to instead inhabit more ambiguous positions. Furthermore, he discusses the ways in which socially engaged art practices are pushing the field of education to reconsider or perhaps to remember the sociality and politicality of pedagogy. In what follows, we hope to build on this turn towards the pedagogical, taking the focus away from the conflation of art and pedagogy towards a feminist new materialist understanding of the matters at stake within the disciplinary fusion.

Learning to be affected

In the opening passages of the *Affect Theory Reader*, the challenges and tensions of defining affect become apparent. While Seigworth and Gregg (2010) contend that 'affect arises in the midst of inbetween-ness; in the capacities to act and be acted upon' (p. 1) they unfold 'an inventory' of various theoretical frameworks by which affect has come to be known. One of many understandings of affect is by Deleuze and Guattari who posit a distinction between affect and emotion. Affect for Deleuze and Guattari is not personal and thus is not the same as feeling. Affect is the becoming sensation, a force or intensity manifested at the surface of the body. Feeling or emotion occurs once that intensity becomes personal and is perceived as a particular quality—such as happy, sad or fear. Massumi (2002) contends that 'an emotion is a subjective content, the sociolinguistic fixing of the quality of an experience which is from that point onward defined as personal. Emotion is qualified intensity' (p. 28). For example, an affective understanding of Cheung's *I Want More* performance would differ from a phenomenological understanding. Phenomenologically we might understand her project eliciting feelings of guilt, anxiety and discomfort when a guest had to ask for more food publically using the megaphone. These feelings are personal; they are attached to a subject, and they already pre-exist the event itself. The affective moment of sensation occurs outside of this personal or cognitive mapping. Massumi notes that 'emotion is the way the depth of that ongoing experience registers personally at a given moment' (as cited in Zournazi, 2002, p. 213). Thus, Cheung's performance understood affectively isn't about how it makes us feel (emotionally), or the kinds of experiences it elicits, but the capacity it enlivens in the body to be affected and to affect. The art exists in a moment of resonate intensity. In this way, Cheung's performance affects the body not from the outside as what we know to be guilt or shame, but enables heterogeneous intensities to 'come together, move each other, and transform and translate *under or beyond* meaning, semantics, fixed systems, cognitions' (Bertelsen & Murphie, 2010, p. 147; italics in original). Thinking about affect as sensation is important because it considers 'feelings' from an anti-essentialist, anti-hierarchical place that associates sensory knowledge with racial others, women, children, animals and the feral. Feminist scholar Elspeth Probyn (1995) draws on Deleuze's work to think about the body not as lack or latent, but as a surface; a surface of intensities. If, according to Deleuze affects are not 'things' but created through encounters, which force us to thought, then in performance there is a difference between the audience feeling emotions that are already recognizable for example guilt, and an unfamiliar affect that unsettles and forces us to resist identification (Cull, 2014).

Colebrook (2002) notes that 'once something appears to us we have already organized it into a certain perspective' (p. 18). On the contrary, encounters between bodies—sounds, food, artist's bodies, chairs, cups, projections, candles, guests, cooks etc.—activate affective intensities of singular relations. For example, art can present the affect of fear without feeling scared ourselves. Colebrook (2002) provides the example of a poem in which the rhythms and pauses, the halting and hesitation creates an affect of fear; 'a fear that is not located in a character nor directed to an object' (p. 22). It is not that affectively we cannot sense fear, but that fear is not known or pre-supposed beforehand. Affect is 'the virtual co-presence of potentials' (Massumi cited in Zournazi, 2002, p. 213). While philosophy creates concepts, art, Deleuze and Guattari contend, also thinks through the creation of affects and percepts. Art's thinking is not in the creation of meaning but in the particular intensity of sensation that it brings about.

Returning to the soup kitchen, the affect of the performances underscores our capacity for action, our body's immersion in the world; a worlding (Manning, 2013). Affect approaches everyday life—like a kitchen—through force. For example, take Swintak's broth. Presented in canning jars and offered in shot glasses to guests, the brown, murky liquid assaulted participant's palate as 'not being food.' However, affectively the feeling of disgust is not attached to the broth, 'to a form already taken' (Manning, 2013, p. 21), but rather in the eating of the broth, the refrains or affective modulations that reorganize territories, allows us to break with old habits and perhaps form new ones. If we think of affect as intensity and the capacity for movement and change, then there is an affect associated with everything a body does, from sitting in a chair, to moving your lips as you chew food. 'Affect', writes Massumi 'is simply a body movement looked at from the point of view of its potential—its capacity to come to be, or better, to come to do' (cited in Zournazi 2002, p. 215).

This 'coming to do', is of utmost importance to Deleuze and Guattari, who draw on the work of Spinoza. As Grosz (1994) contends,

> the body is regarded as neither a locus for a consciousness nor an organically determined entity; it is understood more in terms of what it can do, the things it can perform, the linkages it establishes, the transformations and becomings it undergoes, and the machinic connections it forms with other bodies, what it can link with, how it can proliferate its capacities. (p. 165)

Her emphasis on *doing* is reverberated in Deleuze and Guattari's (1987) writing when they state that we can't know anything about the body

until we know what a body can do, in other words, what its affects are, how they can or cannot enter into composition with other affects, with the affects of another body, either to destroy that body or to be destroyed by it,
either to exchange actions and passions with it or to join with it in composing a more powerful body (Deleuze &
Guattari, 1987, p. 257)

In the *Soup Kitchen,* the work of the artists was not to represent an experience of emotion through food
but 'to devise a procedure to extract the affects of bodies, to somehow reconstruct in performance the
power of another body to pierce us like an arrow, to force us to think, and enable us to act in new ways'
(Cull 2014, p. 193). Learning to be affected disables stasis, compartmentalisms and habit gives way to
the excess of an ongoing process. The various foods on offer in the soup kitchen, the performances,
props, volunteers and the café space provide conditions, platforms for potential actions. For example, a
chair creates anticipation of a habitual action, sitting, and in this way works to order the space. Likewise,
a sandwich can condition a habitual action. Conditions can enable as much as they can restrain, and
in enabling they propose new actions. Eating as art, devouring a slice of pizza and having your crusts
read, green eggs and ham, a meal of only red food, tiny sandwiches, opens bodies to a wider field of
sensitivities which might then produce a suspension in-process, a cut, or a dephasing out of habitual relations, evoking a sensation of being, as Manning (2013) contends 'always more than' a subject.
Braidotti (2000) uses terms like figuration or fabulation to describe this politics of non-representation,
the anomalous and the monstrous. Feminist theories, particularly those that focus on affect, or think
about the body outside of essentialist and biological determinates, are crucial in thinking about power
relations and the repositioning of the subject.

Entering into the café space, diners were met at the door by a volunteer greeter, often in a costume
in concert with the performance of the week. For example, for Cheung's performance volunteers wore
tall chefs hats and aprons. Once in the café space, participants were given a wooden hand, lead to the
seating area and provided instructions on how to ask for food using the megaphone. On the Mystic
Pizza, week diners entered a candle lit space, where everyone spoke in hushed tones, diviners lined
the outer walls talking quietly to those they were reading, and the entire space felt as if it was cloaked
in heavy velvet. For Naty Tremblay's performance, narrating stories of land, settlerism, transbeing and
Franco-Canadian language, the café was strewn with hay and farming equipment. Naty periodically
jumped onto the tables and 'planted' seeds. This jolt from our typical eating habits shifts us out of
habitual inattention and forces a new concentration on what is going on in the moment rather than
preformed assumptions of relation. This sensation of disorientation might be experienced in the everyday when there is an unexpected loss or distortion of sense perception. According to Grosz, 'habit is
change contracted, compressed, contained' (Grosz, 2013, p. 221). Considering that eating has become
part of our everyday habits of carrying on in a world that has no time to wait, how we eat—its affect—is
rarely addressed. However, as a habit where change is contracted, eating can 'outstrip the change it is to
address' (p. 221). In other words, the everyday act of eating has the potential to reveal, to decompress,
its material forces. Broth made with an artist's body, barely bite sized servings that force the consumer
to demand more, or a divined crust, have the potential to actualize the material forces of eating. If we
are to understand eating as an orderly process where matter settles into objects, processes and fields,
then the disruption of these processes can reveal a virtual mode of addressing a future change. The
habit of eating can 'provide the ability to change one's tendencies, to reorient one's actions to address
the new, and to be able to experience the unexpected' (Grosz 2013, p. 221). Affect propels. It activates
thresholds that disperse and differentiate into something new. This involves what Deleuze and Guattari
call refrains.

Eating as refrain: the becoming expressive of art

The expressive is primary in relation to the possessive; expressive qualities, or matters of expression, are necessarily
appropriative and constitute a having more profound than being. Not in the sense that these qualities belong to a
subject, but in the sense that they delineate a territory that will belong to the subject that carries or produces them.
These qualities are like signatures, but the signature, the proper name, is not the constituted mark of a subject, but
the constituting mark of a domain, an abode. (Deleuze & Guattari, 1987, p. 316)

'One ventures from home on the thread of a tune, along sonorous, gestural, motor lines' (Deleuze & Guattari, 1987, p. 311). Bodies spilling into the space, warm candles flickering and shadows dancing on the walls. Smells curling and mingling with bodies, mouths eating, the sounds of performances and the steady swell of murmuring voices, milieus of indeterminable relational fields. Milieus are not spatial; they are not yet territories, but affective vibratory blocks of space-time. A territory becomes into being through the force of a rhythm, which is the transcoded passage between milieus. Rhythm, according to Deleuze and Guattari (1987), however, is not denoted by a regular measure, but rather is 'always in a process of transcoding' (p. 326). Rhythm as such is difference or relation 'the in-between whereby milieus communicate with one another' (Bogue, 1991, p. 88). Territories are created when assemblages of different and multiple milieus come together. As Grosz (2008) states

> it is only when a rhythm and a milieu cohere, form internal relations with each other, induce each other to come together, the rhythm functioning now as that particular temporal form of a region, that a territory can emerge, that the raw materials of art can erupt and the processes of deterritorialization, which are the conditions of art, can begin. (pp. 47–48)

Refrains emerge as the differential patterning through the relations between milieu, rhythm and territory. Deleuze and Guattari (1987) use the notion of the refrain to describe any type of pattern or code that creates a territory. The refrain territorializes in three ways: first the refrain creates stability in a field of chaos; second it marks a stable habitat around that point of stability; and third the refrain opens out into cosmic uncertainty, or as Deleuze and Guattari (1987) write 'the bird [that] sings to mark its territory … a little tune, a melodic formula that seeks recognition' (p. 312). The refrain of eating functions to territorialize chaos into rhythmic, coded patterns. Refrains are how assemblages of heterogeneous elements come together as matters of expression. Deleuze and Guattari (1987) write 'what holds an assemblage together is not the play of framing forms or linear causalities but, actually or potentially, its most deterritorialised component, a cutting edge of deterritorialisation. An example is the refrain' (p. 336). The refrain becomes an assemblage of 'different loops, knots, speeds, movements, gestures and sonorities' (Deleuze & Guattari, 1987, p. 312) connecting different milieus and rhythms. As a kind of repeating process of differentiation, eating as art 'is how rhythm stakes out a territory from chaos that resonates with and intensifies the body' (Bertelsen & Murphie, 2010, p. 145). These territories open up onto new spaces that the refrain itself has created with just enough stability to resist chaos, without succumbing to rigidity. Thus, a refrain clearly involves an element of recurrence. But recurrence is neither mimesis nor simulacra. It is not a repetition of the same, or a copy, but a production that is singular—'a repetition with a difference'. Rather, its significance is what it *does*; its expressive qualities. Even art, according to Deleuze and Guattari (1994) is territorializing. Art creates affects and percepts and thus involves the selection of a milieu (color, form and rhythm), which is then made expressive.

The refrain of mindless eating, then, includes rhythm, patterns, 'that shape the vibrations of milieus into the harmonics of territories, the organization of a wall or barrier' (Grosz, 2008, p. 54). Eating as art is the reverse movement, the freeing of such patterns to become that which is not-yet-conceivable on the plane of composition. It is art that uproots the refrain from its territory. The plane of composition through which articulation emerges is populated by the thought of the work, its inner rhythm (Manning, 2009). Deleuze and Guattari call this inner rhythm a 'block of sensation; we paint, sculpt, compose, and write with sensations' (1994, p. 166). Blocks of sensation are forces that compose the work's durational attitude. 'By means of the material, the aim of art is […] to extract a block of sensations, a pure being of sensation' (1994, p. 167).

Art is an escape from the refrain even as it engenders the refrain simultaneously. Eating as art, thus 'breaks and dislocates; it breaks down the refrain, it dislocates it from its home and from the safety zone it marks around itself' (Grosz, 2008, p. 58). Art intensifies, it enables chaos to appear as sensation. Deleuze and Guattari write: 'The work of art is a being of sensation and nothing else' (1994, p. 164). This is not the phenomenology of perception that Dewey speaks of, a sensation located in the perceiving subject, but a movement-sensation of the event of art itself. As Grosz notes, 'sensation lives, not in the body of perceivers, subjects, but in the body of the artwork' (2008, p.73). Sensation is not a color or a taste of food. Rather through the artwork are coloring, flavoring and sounding forces. Deleuze and

Guattari write, art 'confides to the ear of the future the persistent sensations that embody the event' (1994, p. 174).

Movement, in this instance, is not understood as a displacement, but as sensation where rhythm is the emergent quality of felt intensity, affect, a moving-toward of duration itself (Manning, 2009). For Massumi (2002) affect is how intensities come together. Affect is the pre-personal transition from one state to another. Affectivity, then, does not belong to the order of the individual or of the human as such, but emerges precisely as the change or variation that occurs when bodies—both human and non-human—enter into new relations. Writing about Bacon, Deleuze states 'there are no feelings … there are nothing but affects; that is sensations and instincts' (Deleuze cited in Massumi, 2002, p. 39). In other words, we don't have to feel a particular emotion about the soup kitchen, but that refrains as affective modulation 'bring us forces or take them away, acting via reorganization of sensations and instincts' (Bertelsen & Murphie, 2010, p. 149). Refrains are expressive; they are ethico-aesthetic, in and of affect. In contrast to relational aesthetics that focuses on convivial moments of affiliation, the refrain's power resides in the continual variations in the culminating points that can either lead us 'back to the opinion from which we wanted to escape' or precipitate us 'into the chaos that we wanted to confront' (Deleuze & Guattari, 1994, p. 199). As a queer feminist art practice, the soup kitchen asks that increased affectual capacity be experimented with; new assemblages emerging between the milieus of food, performances, bodies; a new collectivity that expands their potential and expression. But more than this, eating as art engages with not only what is perceptible, but also what is felt by all the components of the event, those feelings not immediately perceptible to us but nevertheless part of the becoming of the event (Manning, 2013). As a queer feminist art practice, its politics does not arrive as the representation of an 'issue', but rather emerges in the dynamic exchange of force that unfolds the larger shared potentiality of the event. It is political in that it 'connects up different aspects of life' (O'Sullivan, 2006, p. 74), multiplying refrains through which differential patterns emerge. This, according to Deleuze, (1994) is art's ethics in that it is a practice of expression and composition, rather than representation.

Matters of pedagogy: towards a politics of attunement

Learning to be affected, we contend, is an anticipatory experience, where we learn to maintain ourselves in the differential entanglements between past and future, hope and despair (Zaliwska, 2013) and non-relational relations (Massumi, 2011). Learning *to be in* this way—to remain in movement—is simultaneously an invitation to becoming something else—something unexpected. Learning to be affected, to reside and co-invent on the refrain, necessitates a particular politicality, a differentiated ethics that demands a particular attunement to the matters at play. Writing about art's rhythmic, irreducibility, Grosz (2008) reminds us that the ethico-political in learning to be affected is that 'we cannot live these forces, although they act through and on us; what we can do is extract something of these forces, nothing that resembles them, for they cannot present themselves, but something that partakes of them' (p. 86). A feminist new materialist understanding of affect as a pre-personal movement of relation complicates the traditional standards of learning as a process of transmitting knowledge. Learning to be affected cannot be predicted nor can it be qualified in the traditional empirical sense. This is why we turn to the inventive language of Deleuze and Guattari, Massumi and Manning and feminist scholars of matter, to think about pedagogy in terms of response-ability to matters of expression, to the 'melodic formula that seeks recognition' (Deleuze & Guattari, 1987, p. 312). A different understanding and approach to attunement is at the heart of accepting the invitation from the vibrant matters, one that we can no longer risk ignoring. We turn to Massumi's (2011) notions of activist philosophy to help articulate an experience of movement where action-thinking-feeling create platforms from which we can (re)act. Specifically, we turn to his concept of *middling* to tease out what this 'somewhere in the middle' could do for a feminist new materialist understanding of attunement. According to Massumi (2011), middling is an affective entanglement that signals an event coming into its newness. This is an event that is simultaneously felt and perceived: 'they are dual immediacies of process' (p. 3). In other words, middling is both a moment of feeling, something coming into being and reflection. Middling would not hold together without the dynamic unity of feeling and reflection. This dynamic unity is constantly on the move, 'gathering the prior phase's momentum into its own unfolding' (p. 3). Middling spawns, it creates an event that comes back through itself, creatively leaving behind a place of rest in order to move onto the next.

This looping movement helps us to understand attunement as being tied to the temporality of the event. This form of attention does not happen before or after the event, but constitutes the dimensionality of the event. According to Massumi (2015), attunement in relation to middling is pragmatically predisposed. In other words, our everyday mode of attention, of looping through the world, is performed intuitively and perceived directly without having to think about it. We take this future anterior movement for granted—we have not yet actualized the full potential of our attunement, the very thing that motivates our ways of being in the world. The potential to radicalize or politicize our attunement resonates in a collective field of relations where there are correlated but differential middlings. In other words, an awareness of our middling—a politicized attunement—crystallizes when different attunements occur across individual differences. A radical politicization of attunement is not simply an awareness or consciousness, but rather, a technique of immanence that 'wells up from within that more-than of ourselves' (Massumi, 2015, p. 124). A radical attunement is always partial, there's no position of mastery as there is no way to comprehend a field that you are being changed by. It is thus experimental and ethical, and requires a deliberate re-chunking of our habitual ways of being in a field of relations.

Learning to be affected and a politicized attunement are co-dependent. This is something that the soup kitchen is provoking in terms of its proposition of eating as art, not only as an expression that interrupts forces of habit, but also as a platform for creating a new concept of matter that involves the untangible and the incorporeal, 'a spark of virtuality that enables life to emerge' (Grosz, 2011, p. 17). In other words, in revealing the taken-for granted labour of eating, eating as habit opened up the 'the charge of being-otherwise' (p. 19), an extra-materiality that offers potential for realignment and reorganization. This extra-materiality of eating, the more than compressed material forces, 'entails not only a politics of the force of encounters that yields events but also an ethics of bearing this burden of indeterminacy, its pointing to singularities whose alignment could be otherwise' (p. 21). To bear the recognition of the hidden forces of our everyday habits requires us to become affected. To become affected, we argue, is a pedagogical moment where pedagogy is not about a particular form, but comes into being through compositions of expression.

The soup kitchen 'carries subjectivities elsewhere, to new territories and a dismantling of the old, ever toward the infinite possibilities and power contained within our bodies, our friends (and our foes), and their ecological contexts' (Guattari quoted in Bertelsen & Murphie, 2010, p. 153). If 'affective intensity is literally the life of territorial processes' (Bertelsen & Murphie, 2010, p. 152) then the becoming-art of eating carries with it the potential for things to turn out differently—affect's virtuality of the future potential.

Affect, writes, Shukin (2000) is one of Deleuze's most valuable contributions to feminist figurations. Similarly, Åsberg, Thiele, and Van der Tuin (2015) argue that feminist new materialism must be invested in 'becoming-with-context, situated knowledges and speculative alter-worlding' (p. 164) This, we contend, necessitates a thinking about pedagogy as attunement and responsibiltiy. This responsibility, however, is never determined prior to the event of pedagogy. As Manning writes:

> Working collectively from this vantage point asks us not to put ourselves in a pre-planned position of benevolence or generosity or accommodation as though there were an outside of the event. Rather, it pushes us to develop ways of conceiving of event-generosity—where it is the event that creates conditions for its own potential openings. (Manning in Massumi, 2015, p. 137)

Eating as art, as a pedagogy and politics of attunement, enters into compositions in unprecented ways, not through some external reference but through affective and rhythmic actions and modulations that unfold in novelty. Art, in creating aesthetic figurations, in challenging the coherence of commonsense experience, compose sensations, which defy the necessity of a coherent self, where flesh is never separate from the world.

Note

1. Artist uses only last name.

Disclosure statement

No potential conflict of interest was reported by the authors.

Funding

This work was supported by the Social Sciences and Humanities Research Council of Canada.

References

Åsberg, C., Thiele, K., & Van der Tuin, I. (2015). Speculative before the turn: Reintroducing feminist materialist performativity. *Cultural Studies Review, 21*, 145–172.
Banes, S., & Lepecki, A. (2007). *The senses in performance*. New York, NY: Routledge.
Barad, K. (2007). *Meeting the universe halfway*. Durham, NC: Duke University Press.
Bertelsen, L., & Murphie, A. (2010). An ethics of everyday infinities and powers: Félix Guattari on affect and refrain. In M. Gregg & G. J. Seigworth (Eds.), *The affect theory reader* (pp. 138–161). Durham, NC: Duke University Press.
Bogue, R. (1991). Rhizomusicosmology. *SubStance, 20*, 85–101.
Bourriaud, N. (2002). *Relational aesthetics*. Paris: Les Presses du Reel.
Braidotti, R. (2000). Teratologies. In I. Buchanan & C. Colebrook (Eds.), *Deleuze and feminist theory* (pp. 156–172). Edinburgh: Edinburgh University Press.
Braidotti, R. (2013). *The Posthuman*. Cambridge: Polity Press.
Butler, J. (1993). *Bodies that matter: On the discursive limits of 'sex'*. New York, NY: Routledge.
Colebrook, C. (2002). *Gilles Deleuze*. New York, NY: Routledge.
Coleman, R. (2014). Inventive feminist theory: Representation, materiality and intensive time. *Women: A Cultural Review, 25*, 27–45.
Cull, L. (2012). *Theatres of immanence: Deleuze and the ethics of performance*. London: Palgrave.
Cull, L. (2014). Performance philosophy: Staging a new field. *New Arts – Journal of the National Academy of Art, 34*, 15–38.
Deleuze, G. (1994). *Difference and repetition*. New York, NY: Columbia University Press.
Deleuze, G., & Guattari, F. (1987). *A thousand plateaus: Capitalism and Schizophrenia*. Minneapolis, MN: University of Minnesota Press.
Deleuze, G., & Guattari, F. (1994). *What is philosophy?*. New York, NY: Columbia University Press.
Fischer, B. (1999). *Foodculture: Tasting identities and geographies in art*. Toronto: YYZ Books.
Grosz, E. (1994). *Volatile bodies*. Bloomington: Indiana University Press.
Grosz, E. (2008). *Chaos, territory, art: Deleuze and the framing of the earth*. New York, NY: Columbia University Press.
Grosz, E. (2011). Matter, life, and other variations. *Philosophy Today, 55* (Suppl.), 17–27.
Grosz, E. (2013). Habit today: Ravaisson, Bergson, Deleuze and us. *Body and Society, 19*: 217–239.
Haraway, D. (1988). Situated knowledges: The science question in feminism and the privilege of partial perspective. *Feminist Studies, 14*, 575–599.
Harding, S. (1986). *The science question in feminism*. Milton Keynes: Open University Press.

Helguera, P. (2011). *Education for socially engaged art: A materials and techniques handbook*. New York, NY: Jorge Pinto Books.

Hughes, C., & Lury, C. (2013). Re-turning feminist methodologies: From a social to an ecological epistemology. *Gender and Education, 25*, 786–799.

MacLure, M. 2013. The wonder of data. *Cultural Studies ↔ Critical Methodologies 13*, 228–232.

Manning, E. (2009). *Relationscapes*. Cambridge, MA: MIT Press.

Manning, E. (2013). *Always more than one*. Durham, NC: Duke University Press.

Massumi, B. (2002). *Parables for the virtual*. Durham, NC: Duke University Press.

Massumi, B. (2011). *Semblance and event*. Cambridge, MA: MIT Press.

Massumi, B. (2015). *Politics of affect*. Cambridge: Polity Press.

Mazzei, L. (2013). Materialist mappings of knowing in being: Researchers constituted in the production of knowledge. *Gender and Education, 25*, 776–785.

McCormack, D. (2013). *Refrains for moving bodies*. Durham, NC: Duke University Press.

Niccolini, D., & Pindyck, M. (2015). Classroom acts: New materialisms and haptic encounters in an urban classroom. *Reconceptualizing Educational Research Methodologies, 6*(2), 1–23.

O'Sullivan, S. (2006). *Art encounters Deleuze and Guattari*. New York, NY: Palgrave.

Probyn, E. (1995). The outside of queer cultural studies. *University of Toronto Quarterly, 64*, 536–546.

Rotas, N., & Springgay, S. (2013). 'You Go To My Head': Art, pedagogy and a politics to come. *Pedagogies, 8*, 278–290.

Seigworth, G., & Gregg, M. (2010). *The affect theory reader*. Durham, NC: Duke University Press.

Shukin, N. (2000). Deleuze and feminisms: Involuntary regulators and affective inhibitors. In I. Buchanan & C. Colebrook (Eds.), *Deleuze and feminist theory* (pp. 144–155). Edinburgh: Edinburgh University Press.

Springgay, S., & Zaliwska, Z. (2015). Diagrams and cuts: A materialist approach to research-creation. *Cultural Studies ↔ Critical Methodologies, 15*, 136-144.

St. Pierre, E. A. (2013). The appearance of data. *Cultural Studies ↔ Critical Methodologies, 13*, 223–227.

Taylor, C., & Ivinson, G. (2013). Material feminisms: New directions for education. *Gender and Education, 25*, 665–670.

Tiainen, M., Kontturi, K., & Hongisto, I. (2015). Framing, following, middling: Towards methodologies of relational materialities. *Cultural Studies Review, 21*, 14–46.

Van der Tuin, I., & Dolphihn, R. (2010). The transversality of new materialism. *Women: A Cultural Review, 21*, 153–171.

Zaliwska, Z. (2013). *The pedagogy of existential questioning* (Masters Thesis). University of Toronto, Toronto.

Zournazi, M. (2002). *Hope: New philosophies for change*. Annandale: Pluto Press Australia.

Objects, bodies and space: gender and embodied practices of mattering in the classroom

Carol A. Taylor

This article focuses on objects, bodies and space to explore how the mundane materialities of classrooms do crucial but often unnoticed performative work in enacting gendered power. Drawing on ethnographic data from a UK sixth form college study, the article analyses a series of 'material moments' to elaborate a material feminist analysis of embodied practices of mattering. I argue that 'practices, doings and actions' (Barad, K. 2007. *Meeting the Universe Halfway: Quantum Physics and the Entanglement of Matter and Meaning*. London: Duke University Press), while often hidden or taken for granted, are a constitutive material force in producing what and who matters within classrooms. By highlighting objects, bodies and space as entangled material agencies, the article raises new questions about gendered pedagogic practices. It proposes the necessity to rethink classroom space as an emergent intersection of multiple, mobile materialities, and argues that doing so is a crucial task for a material feminist praxis.

1. Introduction

This article focuses on objects, bodies and space as vital materialities which possess active, dynamic agency. Through an analysis of the complex choreographies within which object and bodily materialisations are enacted, power relations are mobilised and educational space is continually re-constructed, the article sheds light on how material cultures of everyday classroom life are both active and constitutive in processes that recreate gender inequalities. Drawing on an ethnographic case study of a UK A Level Sociology classroom, the article elaborates a material feminist analysis which empirically takes forward Barad's (2007, 170) argument that 'bodies do not simply take their place in the world ... rather "environments" and "bodies" are intra-actively constituted'. In doing so, it shows that space is not simply a physical container; objects and things are not inert, fixed or passive matter awaiting 'use' by human intervention; nor is the body a mere corporeal vehicle to be moved by the mind. The article draws new attention to how objects, bodies and spaces do crucial but often unnoticed performative work as vital materialities within the classroom. To explore how objects and bodies work to produce the classroom as a gendered space of differential matterings, I focus on a number of 'material moments' – including the manner in which a chair is occupied, the irregular use of a pen and the wearing of a particular t-shirt – to illuminate how that which is resolutely mundane within everyday pedagogic practice nevertheless possesses a surprising material force. My central argument is that bringing to the fore how material things act on and with us reveals educational practices to be a constellation of human–nonhuman agencies, forces and events.

The arguments I put forward are informed by post-human material feminist theorisations of matter (Barad 2007), understandings of objects from material culture (Bissell 2009; Miller 2010) and analyses of space which originate in human geography (Hubbard, Kitchin, and Valentine 2004; Massey 2005). Drawing together these interdisciplinary threads provides an analytical purchase on the detailed specificity and density of the material moments and enables us to grasp the force of the material in its speed and evanescence. This close empirical focus on embodied practices of mattering discloses how 'bodies are understood and lived spatially as much as are topographical sites in the landscape' (Shields 1997, 186) and I put Barad's (2007) concepts of 'intra-action', 'cut', 'phenomena' and 'apparatus' to work in developing a material feminist analysis of the body in the 'fullness of its materiality'. The article thus contributes a distinctive feminist intervention in the emerging field of 'Barad studies'. Furthermore, in its deployment of a 'diffractive' approach the article works as a methodologically strategic act of experimentation which unsettles some of the usual conventions of article writing, and I do this to demonstrate how a post-human research practice brings to the surface our ethical entanglement as researchers in enacting practices of knowledge production.

The article begins with a discussion of the main theoretical confluences which inform the ensuing empirical analysis. After an account of the data, and a discussion of the importance of utilising a diffractive methodology within material feminist analyses, the article turns to a detailed empirical exploration of a number of material moments to show how objects–bodies–spaces 'work' within the spatial assemblage of the classroom. A performative account of instantiating a diffractive methodology as an act of experimentation, and the differences this makes to the production of knowledge, is woven through the empirical analysis. The article concludes by highlighting the importance of things and bodies as vital players through which gender gets done, power is worked and inequalities re-embedded within the space of the classroom.

2.   Theoretical contexts: space, objects, bodies and materiality

This section provides an account of the theories which inform the subsequent empirical analysis. Both here and later, my aim is to bring material culture studies (Miller 2010) and material feminism (Barad 2007; Bennett 2010; Coole and Frost 2010) into relation with spatial understandings (Massey 2005) to indicate, theoretically and empirically, what educational analyses have to gain from viewing classrooms as an entangled 'mosaic' of 'vital matter' (Bennett 2010, 22). This interdisciplinary theoretical enterprise is, I suggest, generative for understanding the agentic force of material objects, analysing the minutiae of bodily practices, and highlighting what can be gained from this novel way of apprehending objects–bodies–space as intra-actively entailed material agencies within the assemblage of the classroom.

Borrowing from human geography, I have found Massey's (2005, 9) notion of space as a 'practiced place' which is always open, contemporaneously plural, emergent and 'under construction' useful. Her theorisation of space as 'the sphere of relations, negotiations, practices of engagement, power in all its forms' (Massey 2005, 99) helps raise some new questions about the micro-practices of matter, bodies and space and reveal what an intensely political, contested and unequal space the gendered classroom can be. The recent 'spatial turn' has brought renewed attention to educational space, as demonstrated by recent edited collections by Boys (2010) and Brooks, Fuller, and Waters (2012) and studies by Allen (2012), Hirst and Cooper (2008), Jones (2013b) and Mahony, Hextall, and Richardson (2011). It is perhaps worth remembering that a rich seam of analyses which touches on space already exists, albeit emanating from other research traditions, including classroom ethnographies (for example, Delamont and Galton 1986), and studies from within critical pedagogy of schools, politics and place (Di Leo and Jacobs 2004). Foucault's (1979, 1984) discursive genealogies also offer radical re-evaluations of modern institutional space and have informed studies on educational architecture (Burke and Grosvenor 2008), teachers' discursive practices within classroom and staffroom space (McGregor 2001), as well as feminist studies of space (Dunne 2007; Quinn 2003; Tamboukou 1999). However, the 'spatial turn' has usefully refocused attention on micro-level spatial practices, and brought theories of space into productive relation with studies of pedagogy and materialities (Fenwick and Landri 2012; Ivinson 2012; Mulcahy 2012; Palmer 2011; Zembylas 2007). Studies such as these lend support to my argument for understanding space as a material 'multiplicity' (Massey 2005, 9).

Analyses which focus on the contemporaneous plurality of spatial practices resonate with recent shifts towards recognising the force of 'thing-power' (Bennett 2010). Giving due regard to the material force of objects, and seeing objects not as commodities and artefacts but as things with their own sense of agency is, I suggest, a valuable move towards a post-human understanding that 'objects make us, as part of the very same process by which we make them' (Miller 2010, 60). While it is not my intention to argue that the agency of objects is 'like' human agency in degree or kind, thing-power discloses agency as 'congregational' or 'confederate' (Bennett 2010, 20) rather than a matter of individual human will, and this opens up new ways of seeing and thinking about how classroom space is made, transformed and continually re-made through the concerted co-constitutive acts of objects–bodies–spaces. Likewise, I argue that the body is a vital material agency in the classroom. Taking forward Shields's (1997, 186) view that 'bodies are understood and lived spatially as much as are topographical sites in the landscape', I develop a material feminist account which includes in its frame Foucault's (1979, 1984, 1988) considerations of bodily discipline and Butler's (1990, 1993) notions of gender performativity, as reformulated by Barad (2007) to include a post-human recognition that all bodies, things and matter – not just human bodies – are active material-discursive agents. Embodied practices, doings and actions are central to the account I develop because, as Stengers (2007) reminds us, practices are always collective.

As indicated earlier, the article also works as an act of methodological experimentation to indicate the potential of material feminism to unsettle conventional ways of thinking about and reporting research. In its use of a diffractive methodology to show that knowledge is an emergent and embodied 'practice of knowing in being' (Jackson and Mazzei 2012, 116), the article brings to the fore our ontological, epistemological and ethical responsibilities as producers of knowledge, which is what I turn to now.

3.   Diffracting the methodology: reflecting on data

To highlight what new openings material feminism offers as a way of producing knowledge, I begin by presenting a familiar account of my data as a qualitative research case study. I follow this by highlighting some of the key differences that doing a material feminist diffractive analysis might make.

There are currently more than 150,000 students studying at sixth form colleges (Igoe and Kewin 2013). As post-compulsory educational institutions, sixth forms are often but not always places of greater relative freedom than schools but, like many other classrooms, they are redolent with material-discursive practices of gendered power. The empirical data I draw on were part of a wider ethnographic case study of the strategies sixth form students deploy in forming their identities in relation to A Level curriculum subjects, knowledge hierarchies, pedagogic practices and spatial formations, both inside and outside their college location. The data were collected during 2005–2006 in two sixth form colleges in South-East England. Both colleges had a predominantly white student and teacher population and, in both colleges, young women outnumbered male students by 2:1 in the seven curriculum subjects sampled. In its entirety, the data set includes classroom observations, interviews with students, teachers and Principal Examiners, my research diary and field notes. The data extracts included here originate in six two-hour observations in an A Level Sociology class at Seaside College, and a teacher interview, chosen because of the acute concerns they raise about the 'micro-physics' of gendered power in classroom space. The account just given lays out clearly the scope of the study, its sample, and the rationale for choice of data extracts to be used in the ensuing meaning-making procedures. So, what new ways of looking at research practice does a diffractive approach make possible?

Research protocols often remain caught within assumptions of a transparent relay between data and meaning in which data is envisaged as inert, passive 'stuff' we (humans) go out and 'collect', return with and then pore over to analyse, code and thematise. In treating data as 'evidence' in this way, data is rendered, contained, controlled, indeed it is condemned to the death-like status of object (Koro-Ljungberg and MacLure 2013). In contrast, a vital materialism prompts us to think of data as lively matter – as a material actant – and research practices as 'encounters between ontologically diverse actants, some human, some not, though all thoroughly material' (Bennett 2010, xiii–xiv). I bring out the import of these material entwinings in my reflections on observation notes in the following section. A second novel implication of the use of a diffractive methodology turns on the difference it makes to acknowledge our capacity to be affected by data. Such concerns are usually excised from written research accounts but many of us as researchers feel haunted by 'our' data long after collecting 'it', and I take up this idea later to show how and why these affective engagements matter. And thinking data's liveliness leads to a third point, the often insistent invitation data makes to us to follow it on nomadic theoretical journeyings, on to-and-fro zig-zags and 'backwards' readings as we work 'on' it to make sense of it. Following the data-theory in this way interferes radically both with the presumed linearity of 'rational' sense-making procedures, and even the iterative accounts of post-structuralism which still usually 'end' in forms of transparent representability. Instead, a diffractive methodology helps highlight 'knowledge-ing' as a messy multiplicity, a point I pick up again later. Fourth, and added to this, a diffractive methodology is most persistent in calling us to account in new ways for the choices we make by including *these* data and *these* incidents and not others. I follow this line of thinking through in relation to Barad's (2007) concept of the 'agential cut', an analytic practice which both separates out 'something' – an object, practice, person – for analysis from the ongoing flow of spacetimemattering, but which, at the same time as separating and excluding, entangles us ontologically with/in and as the phenomena produced by the cut we make. I show the ethical import of cuts which hold us to account in my later analysis of Malky, 'Sheila', and 'Brains', cuts which make it apparent that in an entangled materialist ontology 'knowing does not come from standing at a distance and representing but rather from a direct material engagement with the world' (Barad 2007, 49).

A diffractive methodology, then, encourages new ways of thinking about and relating to data and meaning-making. It offers a critical practice of interference which pays attention to what we don't normally see, to what is excluded; as such, it urges 'a commitment to understanding which differences matter, how they matter, and for whom' (Barad 2007, 90). In addition, it offers to be a creative methodology which opens ways of undoing traditional, humanist epistemic codes so we may do, present and write research differently. In the next section, I put a diffractive methodology to work, and thread the somewhat abstract methodological points made just now into the ensuing empirical analysis where I focus on those 'small but consequential differences' (Barad 2007, 29) from which knowledge about objects, bodies and spaces is produced in the gendered practices of everyday classrooms.

4. His magisterial chair

That teachers control the 'action zone' at the front of the (their) classroom is a commonplace, of a piece with Bourdieu, Passeron, and Saint Martin's (1965, 10) observation, made some time ago, that 'space is a source of pedagogical distance'. However, their subsequent comment – that pedagogic authority is conferred by the 'magisterial chair which consecrates him' – has largely gone unnoticed, although Jones's (2013b) article is a notable exception. Asking the question 'what does a chair do?' prompts a reconceptualisation of things, bodies and pedagogic space as an assemblage of intra-active, ongoing and productive happenings entailing multiple agencies.

> Malky had his desk and chair at the front and his resources laid out around him on adjoining tables and didn't move out of his zone. Straight in front of his desk, the students' desks were in a complete square and it was not possible to get inside it, so physical movement towards and proximity to students was out of the question. (Observation No. 1 Notes)

> He had his 'instruments' laid out like a pilot's flight deck around him. He glided in his chair between his things, pushing himself off with his heels from a still point with speed and grace, like a practiced dancer. His body language is totally relaxed and expansive. (Observation No. 2 Notes)

> I'm getting more of a feel for Malky and how he conducts his lessons … He is leaning back in his chair and controlling the space at a distance. He decides who should talk and when they should talk. He's like a radiating star … everything comes from him and goes back to him. When the students discuss things in pairs this is set off by Malky and he controls how long they talk to each other. Other than that the whole focus of the class is on Malky. (Observation No. 3 Notes)

I said in the previous section that data was 'lively matter' and that agential cuts work both to separate and entangle. In integrating these observation notes at this point I enact an agential cut which focuses attention on the chair-body assemblage. This cut counts as a meaning-making practice in precisely these ways: it separates the chair-body assemblage from the ongoing 'context'; it foregrounds the material agency of my observation notes in producing this particular textual incarnation; and it entangles me, and you as reader, materially, cognitively and sensorially with the data and, through the data, with the participants and the classroom they emerged from. Thus, the data have done and continue to do their agentic work *with* me on this page: they assist me to make the cut. Why is this significant? In both separating out (chair-body) and suturing together (me, objects, participants, you), the cut's significance is that it constitutes onto-logically entangled phenomena, it installs a relational materiality at the heart of this account and, Barad would argue, at the heart of all worldly events. I pick up some implications of this further on. Now, I return to the data to trace what emerges from making the cut regarding Malky's chair-body assemblage.

Malky's chair was no mere piece of furniture. As an object with thing-power, it took its place as a material-discursive agency within a classroom space saturated with gendered meanings. It was a seat positioned for a material performative of gen-dered bodily power, as well as a physical location from which the teacher could direct his gaze at his students and ensure all were looking at him at all times. As the data extract indicates, the mobility of Malky's chair-body assemblage worked to mate-rialise what Mulvey (1975) calls the male gaze, a visual technology of power which gave Malky visual freedom to roam over the static bodies of the students fixed as they were behind immobile desks in unmoving chairs. In Malky's classroom, the small-scale panoptics enacted through the arrangement of tables and chairs served as a material reminder of Foucault's (1979, 25) point that 'it is always the body that is at issue – the body and its forces, their utility and their docility, their distribution and their submission'.

The materiality of the chair – an elegant, black and chrome, decidedly 'office' chair, on casters and with a tilting facility, the only one of its kind in classrooms throughout the college, all the others being fixed and upright, moulded red or orange plastic – con-ditioned the possibilities of mobility and stasis. Unless exiting the chair for the occasional virtuoso performance like the ones I discuss below, Malky remained seated in his chair throughout the class. The chair and his body formed a human–nonhu-man assemblage which freed him up to glide, slide, spin, twirl, tilt, lean, roll and spring. The vitalism of the chair-body assemblage created momentary eruptions in the lessons (my observation notes record) which disrupted traditional notions of how teachers sit, stand and physically behave as, for example, when chair-and-Malky whizzed to the computer to display a powerpoint in which 'Max [Weber] goes walkabout', or when Malky leaned back in the chair to the tipping point in an embodied display of adult hegemonic masculine nonchalance (young men and boys, unlike girls, routinely tip backwards in chairs to embody resistance and/or aggression in pedagogic authority contexts). The variability, flexibility and mobility instantaneously enacted by the tea-cher's chair-body assemblage contrasted markedly with the obdurate materialities of the students' chairs and desks, the walls with their posters of the 'founding fathers' of Sociology, windows and a classroom door which Malky closed with a flourish at the start of each lesson. These harder, more solid materialities and their immobile moor-ings (Urry 2003) enacted physical barriers which constrained who was free to move (the teacher) and, crucially, who couldn't (the students). Ivinson (2012, 490) notes that such regulative disciplining of educational bodies into stasis has its roots in a mon-astic legacy which sought to separate the contemplative and the intellectual life from 'the dirt and labour of mundane life', a point I return to below.

It was not simply that Malky occupied the 'chair', his manner of occupation was important. Notes from the second observation record that:

> The power clearly resides with him. He is totally relaxed and expansive in his body language, leaning back in his chair and controlling the space at a distance.

I wrote that 'he never leaned forward' and there are repeated comments on his 'even, quiet and controlled' tone of voice. I record that he often 'adopted the open bodily stance of a genial, chat show host', and that this relaxed, embodied stance remained in vibrant tension with the eruptive dynamism of chair-body movement and the occasional, exuberant out-of-chair performance (see below). Ironic humour was central to Malky's embodied and vocal practices. He interlaced extended stories, jokes and anecdotes with information about key sociological figures, their research and the pre-eminence of Sociology as a mode of knowledge production. My fieldwork diary records that, from his chair, he choreographed his lessons as a 'stand-up comedy routine', that his lessons were a 'wise-cracking performance' and that his 'repartee' was delivered in a 'sardonic tone reminiscent of Jack Dee'. I aimed to capture the 'logic of sense' of one lesson as follows:

> Malky covered topics as various as a J. K. Galbraith, a Lyndon Johnson 'piss story', a man who hallucinated on the 'jazz woodbines', moonies, smoking, pub quizzes, student dreams, chair design, renaissance female artists, the ugliness of Southampton, the church's abolition of limbo, postmodern relativism, contemporary musicals, ice cream and sex, and 15% mortgage rates under the Tories. All of this with a deadpan delivery in an atmosphere in which you could hear a pin drop as he was talking, followed by out-bursts of extended laughter from students at each punch line. (Research Diary)

Then, as researcher, I was 'taken up' by all of this and I relished the potentially rich, if difficult, data this would give me. *Now* (revisiting the data via a diffractive method-ology) I see not only how Malky's embodied practices work by his agential cuts in the spacetimematter of the classroom which enact a spatially authoritative, urbanely flexible and powerfully dominant masculine performative, but also, what my data does as an 'ontologically diverse actant' to use Bennett's phrase cited earlier: it hails me, it hauls me in and perplexes me with its material embrace.

Barad (2007, 159) argues that 'bodies in the making are never separate from their apparatuses of bodily production' and, as I have noted above, chair, objects and bodies are entangled intra-active forces in the spatial assemblage of the classroom. The concept of intra-activity is particularly useful in making sense of Malky's embodied doings because it encourages us to contend directly with material practices which bring into being subjects and objects. As Barad (2007) notes, agencies do not precede their interaction but emerge through an intra-active process. Thus, Malky's individualistic and idiosyncratic flair, the material force of the chair-body assemblage and the spatiali-sation of his capacity to entertain and hold students' attention emerge as intra-active con-stituting forces in the ongoing flow of spacetimemattering. These intra-active materialisations enact tropes of masculine confidence, power and authority vis-à-vis stu-dents, they produce boundaries between his chair-body physical ease and their immobile attention, his voice and their silence, his wit and their receptivity to his humour, his knowledge and their lack. This is why Malky's (and by extension all teachers') intra-active cuts count: they enact 'differentness' (Barad 2007, 137), maintain hierarchies and instantiate gendered power. Of course, boundary-making practices are endemic in teaching contexts. However, seeing Malky's embodied practices as intra-active cuts which enact micro-level gendered differentiations encourage us to rethink teacher–student–space–object relations as an intra-active co-constitutive accomplishment which show materially that some bodies (and some chairs!) matter more than others. Focusing on Malky's chair brings to the surface the usually unnoticed dynamic force of things and their capacity for confederate intra-action with human agencies. It encourages us to notice how much the thing-power of the chair contributes to Malky's gendered practices and how the chair-body assemblage together choreographs a material practice of mattering in this classroom space. Having asked 'what does a chair do?' in the classroom in the following section I ask 'what do things do?'

5. 'Come here Sheila'

My observation notes above remark on how Malky's panoply of materialities – objects, coursework, resources, desk furniture, along with chair and desk arrangements – separated him spatially from the students. More than that, what was interesting was how Malky pressed various material 'instruments' into action in an embodied orchestration of gendered pedagogic action. Three instances of mattering within the human–nonhuman assemblage of the classroom are worthy of note.

'Sheila' occupied a position on the right hand side of Malky's desk, spending most of the time unnoticed and unobserved until summoned into action by Malky with the commanding phrase 'come here Sheila'. In this, 'Sheila' was just like the many other things which inhabit our spaces but which we often don't 'see' because the 'work' they do accords with our sense of what is natural, commonplace and culturally familiar. Their very invisibility determines expectations and produces the required effects of normality. My observation notes record two 'come here Sheila' moments when 'Sheila', the flipchart stand with paper displaying a pre-drawn sociological model or theory, was hauled or dragged over by Malky to front centre stage. Malky performed his man-handling of 'Sheila' with physically expansive aplomb in an exhibitive spatial display which each time generated laughter from the students. Re-positioned, revealed and brought to sight, 'Sheila' exhibited all the virtues of a compliant Stepford wife and dutiful hand-maiden to the man, shocked into silence by her unexpected and unwanted visibility.

Mundane as this example is, it is no little matter that the flipchart was given the name 'Sheila' because, while the anthropomorphisation of matter has a long and complex cultural history, in this instance, it tells us a lot about the gendered dynamics of this classroom in which control of space is key, and the appropriation, use and movement of things is so very clearly and visibly (albeit humorously) put into the service of a masculine performative of ownership. And more than that, we can see that it installs the notion of binarised space within the classroom, in which the sexual specificity of gendered identities are predicated on an essentialist normative male/female binary, which ontologically articulates male to action, thought and Logos and female to stasis, matter and mute passivity (Grosz 1994). Likewise, it is a matter of note that the flipchart was given the name 'Sheila' which is derogatory slang for woman in Australia. Seen diffractively through the lens of post-human materialist feminism, Malky's repeated embodied practice of possessing, containing and mobilising 'Sheila' is perhaps an indication of hegemonic masculine anxiety in the face of thing-power, or perhaps a gendered need to establish and display authority in the potentially unruly space of the classroom (even if it did carry shades of a knowingly exaggerated post-modern performance of authority). Nevertheless it shows how things make people and how people make things (Miller 2010) as well as how things work within a spatial assemblage of lively material events.

A second material moment concerns past students' coursework which sat in three large piles on the left hand side of the desk and from which Malky regularly extracted work graded A (the highest grade) to read out or refer to. While human endeavour was no doubt required to activate the coursework, we could also say that the coursework 'issued a call' (the phrase is Bennett's 2010, 4) which summoned human agency into response. Many teachers use past students' coursework as exemplars to motivate and challenge current students, and such uses are undoubtedly effective pedagogic practice (Gibbs, 2010, notes that high expectations work well in engaging students). But perhaps we also need to keep in mind coursework as matter which inhabits class-rooms, desks, drawers, cabinets and cupboards, which regulations demand we keep, which we posit future pedagogic use for and thus don't/can't throw away. Seen in this way, coursework as matter acts in confederation with space, objects and bodies as an apparatus, that is as a 'practice of mattering through which intelligibility and materiality are constituted' (Barad 2007, 170). In the instance under discussion, course-work serves to materialise and insistently memorialise the credentialism, high grades culture and intensification of national A Level meritocratic educational regimes here and now in the proximate space of the classroom. And there is, too, a very particular gendered inflection to the summons issued by coursework, one which plays into young women's anxieties to produce themselves as 'good girls' and 'good students' by materialising themselves as coherent subjects within dominant neoliberal discourses of 'successful girl' (Ringrose 2007; Taylor 2011).

Pens mattered in Malky's classroom. My observation notes contain a surprising number of references to students' pens which leads me to suggest that it is worth taking notice of pens as material agencies within 'object assemblages which make things happen' (Bissell 2009, 112). The following exchange with a male student occurred during the first observation:

Malky: If you don't stop whistling down that pen top I'll have to punch you.
Student: Sorry.

And this one in the second observation, said to female student holding a pen with a fluffy top to it:

Malky: Spongy, is that a sociologist's pen?
Student: No (laughter).

Pens as singular items of matter may be considered inconsequential, peripheral to pro-cesses of cognition and intellection, a mere adjunct to and device for recording the dis-cussions arising in collaborative pair or group learning contexts, or nowadays as increasingly redundant in the face of iPads, tablets and other mobile learning devices. This, though, would be to mistake the identity investments students make in and publicly attach to such mundane material articles as pens, pencil cases and bags, albeit that these patterns of consumption, display and use are highly gendered. Both examples I discuss highlight what can be at stake in having and holding a pen. The second example designates a fluffy-top pen as obviously inappropriate to the matter of being a serious, cerebral (and, by implication, male) sociologist, and uses a comedic put-down to make a powerful point about the gendered hierarchies of aca-demic knowledge, a point I return to later.

However, the whistling noise made in an un-thought way by pen-mouth-hand assemblage in the first example was clearly sufficient to provoke Malky into offering an extreme and violent retribution as payback for the momentary auditory annoyance it caused (I hadn't even registered it as a noise). In this example, both cuts – that made by the pen/noise and that made by Malky's comment – produce rapid, successive interventions which constitute the dynamic of mattering very differently for the individuals involved. The student, on the one hand, felt compelled to provide an immediate apology; publicly positioned as 'wrong' and verbally chastened/threatened he enacts an embodied, instantaneous and felt recognition that his momentary capture of auditory space is something not to be tolerated: this is, after all, Malky's classroom. On the other hand, threatening as this comment is especially in written form above, *in situ* Malky's tone and verbal delivery, given from a relaxed reclining sideways position in his chair, was mild, courteous and calm, and elicited class laughter. His cut was not embodied materially or spatially as a particularly threatening cut, nevertheless it intra-actively instantiated a threat. In drawing attention to the materiality of this instance of incipient gendered violence called into action by a pen, a material feminist account helps complicate some of the universalistic theorisations of gendered violence which would position Malky's response as hegemonic masculinity, the student's apology as dominated, and the class response as complicit (Connell 1995). No doubt that is also the case but I want to emphasise how this mundane example of the pen's materialisation in a human–nonhuman apparatus of mattering brings to the fore the conduct of human relations between people in a classroom, in all their visceral, emotional and ethical import.

The agential cuts I enact in this section have produced empirical instances which illuminate what things do, how things work within gendered relations of power, and how things materialise actions and relations in human–nonhuman apparatuses which complicate notions of human agency and human relationality. I have suggested that mundane things choreograph an 'invisible pedagogy' (Bernstein 2004) of relations which matter; and I have shown how things as mobile elements enfold matter and meaning at a micro-level in a complex spatial web within classrooms. Furthermore, in 'diffracting the methodology' above, I noted the invitations data offers for theoretical journeyings and that these nomadic zig-zags disclose knowledge-ing as a messy multiplicity. As illustration of this, the three instances discussed in this section emerged and concretised through 'backwards', 'circular' and 'forward' readings in which I sited the lively data (for example, 'Sheila') alongside Butler alongside Foucault alongside Deleuze and Guattari alongside Barad, reading each theoretical account diffractively through the others. This is not a particularly idiosyncratic or unusual approach to meaning-making (is it?). However, with its lines of flight, heterogeneous bricolage and fortuitous findings, it follows a logic of sense and intuition rather than a logic of rationality and deduction. I use this to illustrate that, in its undoing of linearity, and in highlighting 'knowledge-ing' as a messy multiplicity, always mediated through the material body of the researcher, a diffractive methodology is valuable in enabling us to notice, pinpoint and perhaps value more openly than we usually might, how that which is utterly provisional (knowledge) is smoothed, soothed and straight-jacketed into a 'finished' academic article which, whether in its solid paper materiality or virtual online im/materiality, offers (as I do above with 'Sheila' and the pen-mouth-hand assemblage) a 'final' account.

Returning from this diffractive interference, and having raised some important concerns about objects in this section, the discussion next turns to clothes.

6. 'If these were brains, I'd be a genius'

The data in this section have been the most troubling/troublesome. MacLure (2013) talks about the wonder of data, of data which 'glow', and it is certainly the case that the data I dice with here feel like shining points or 'hotspots'. I referred earlier ('diffracting the methodology') to data's affective power, its capacity to haunt us through ongoing entanglements. The agential cuts I have made which have produced these data and these phenomena testify to the power of Malky's glamour (in the archaic sense of casting a spell), which caught me out (as novice researcher) and caught up the students (another funny day in class) in its allure.

Clothes as markers of class, status and identity, and the communicative function of clothes, have been discussed within Cultural Studies, Material Culture studies and Anthropology for some time, and there is a growing body of feminist scholarship on how clothes produce gendered and aged subjectivities (Jones 2013a; Pilcher 2013; Renold 2005). In studies of education, however, clothes have mostly received attention in relation to how pupils express individuality, conformity and resistance to the homogenisation effected by school uniforms (Park 2013). In Sixth Form College settings clothing is crucial, as sixth forms are usually much less regulated spaces than schools for the expression of young people's individuality, sexuality and peer group or sub-cultural affiliations. Many of the participants in my study said they partly chose Sixth Form College over school sixth form because it enabled them to leave school uniform behind. In this section, I pursue a material feminist analysis of clothes. By focusing on clothes as 'vital players' (Bennett 2010, 4) in classroom space, I bring new attention to the powerful but usually unremarked material-discursive work they do in installing gendered practices through their entanglement with bodies and space.

Butler (1997, 5) has spoken of the 'inaugurative' power of naming both as a means for a person to be recognised as a viable subject in discourse and as a process which produces a 'fundamental dependency on the address of the Other'. 'Brains' functioned as one such name. 'Brains' was the nickname Malky used to a young woman who had once worn a t-shirt with the logo 'if these were brains I'd be a genius'. Other students also had nicknames and, while students did not use these names, neither did they contest their usage in class (although in interviews two students expressed their disapproval of the naming of other students). Malky used the names in class in a humorous, bantering tone accompanied by praise and positive feedback. While recognising the social and performative power of names, the name 'Brains' is of particular interest when considering clothes from a material feminist angle. That such naming is a form of gendered 'power over' (Kreisberg 1992) is obvious but how does this 'power over' do its work materially? Much like Sera and her suit (Jackson and Mazzei 2012), the t-shirt and the student interact in a mutual production of agency, the t-shirt has thing-power, it has a life of its own and we can see how the t-shirt–body–classroom apparatus works in an intra-active dynamism. We can, however, take things further.

I suggest that the repeated naming of 'Brains' functions as a micro-practice of the power of the male gaze. 'Brains' calls attention to one part of this particular student's body (her breasts), while at the same time the name – '*Brains*' – materially *dis*-embodies the body. The power of this name designates the body as partial, reduced to placid, receptive matter and, as in pornography, insistently summoned up in fragmented form, in a spatial field of dispersed panoptics, which regulates this individual student body and, undoubtedly, serves the larger purpose of regulating all student bodies in that proximate space. But the material feminist reading I have just offered is, when thinking diffractively, complicated by other material feminist possibilities. The student chose to wear this t-shirt with its material alliance of breast-brains-genius, and this prompts me to suggest that what this t-shirt seeks to do is entangle feminist with post-feminist discourses in a materiality which knowingly sexualises the feminist body as a paradoxical means to demonstrate sexual and intellectual autonomy under/from the male gaze. In that case, like Aschenbrand (cited in Genz 2006, 345) who says 'I am on a mission to change things – one pair of tits at a time', this particular t-shirt–body–name–space assemblage becomes an unruly, energetic and threatening irruption in the classroom space, and one which materialises broader concerns about sexualisation and 'pornification' of young people's cultures (Renold and Ringrose 2011; Ringrose and Renold 2012). In drawing attention to how clothes matter material feminism, like feminism more generally, is a valuable resource which opens an emergent field of analytical possibilities, some of which may be in tension. A material feminist reading of the 'if these were brains' t-shirt example undoubtedly undoes the dualistic presumption of the Enlightenment ego that clothing is exterior to us, mere cover, or surface, there to hide or represent the 'real me' within. It shows how clothes as materialities become with us as we become with them in an open, contingent unfolding of mattering.

I include now, as my data compel me to, a discussion of Malky's clothing. Malky, on every occasion I observed his lessons, was smartly dressed in a dark grey or navy tailored suit, with white shirt, tie and leather shoes. His suited neatness and close-cropped hair expressed 'classic' understated masculine elegance, and these material elements worked in confederation to ensure his body remained at all times the 'clean body' of the 'privileged subject' (Ahmed 2000, 93). That Malky's suit worked in a choreography of materialities in much the same way as his desk – as border and boundary to separate him from the students – became apparent with his comment in interview: 'if I see one more belly top I'll puke' (short, tight t-shirts, which made girls' midriffs visible, were in fashion at that time), a comment which, as glowing data hotspot, invites me to conjecture that his physical loathing of young women's display of flesh is tied to the materialisation of their abjection (as in the name 'Brains') and to the spatial arrangements of his room. Pursuing this line leads me to propose Malky's clothes as a material 'intensification of [his] being' (Simmel, cited in Carter 2012, 352).

So much for t-shirts and suits. What about jumpers? On more than one occasion Malky criticised, and encouraged students to laugh at, the male Physics teacher's jumpers (Observations 2 and 3), commenting 'oh you are a bitch you' in response to one male student's laughter (which provoked yet more class hilarity). And in one lesson I observed, Malky had the students crying with laughter as he gave a virtuoso embodied performance of 'Physics student', in which he slouched around caveman-style at the front of the class, dribbling, with his knuckles touching the floor, speaking incomprehensible words. This performance was followed by a verbal diatribe about Physics students which exhibited perfect comic timing:

> Geeks, with spots, who wear clothes bought by their Mum, they don't see daylight, they only talk to other geeks on the web, they wear trainers with no logos on them, also bought by their Mum. (Observation 3)

In this momentary transformation of classroom space into an arena of entertainment, however uncomfortable I felt, how could I remain 'outside' the laughter? As novice researcher, what would you have done? The materially embodied spatialisation of

Malky's production and reproduction of 'Physics' as an undesirable, even despicable, 'other' to Sociology had, by this point in the educational lifecycle of this teacher and his students, becomes routinised, acceptable and fun. 'Sociology', sociological knowledge, Sociology students and teachers were, incontrovertibly, superior physically, socially and intellectually, to everything and everyone pertaining to 'Physics'. The very materiality of Malky's stylishly suited body in this Bakhtinian, carnivalesque performative was sufficiently incongruous to make the point. Malky's material enactment of comedic routines pathologised 'Physics' through powerful categories of normalisation and exclusion. In this way he spatially reconstructed *his* classroom as serious, theoretical and analytical, and materially installed himself in that space as 'authentic knower and keeper of knowledge' which, as Francis (2008, 113) notes, is a 'profoundly masculine' enactment. Based on the data discussed here I propose that one good answer to the question 'what do clothes do?' is that clothing produces 'pleasure, exuberance and vertigo' (Caillois 2003, 49). In this instance, clothing's 'vertigo' works materially as a regulative ontological and epistemological disciplining which, as I noted early, separates the cleanness of an authentic intellectual life from the grubby social ineptitude of its despised 'others'. The practices enacted by Malky's clothed body show that 'nothing is more material, physical, corporal than the exercise of power' (Foucault 1980, 57).

And so, another cut has been made; and this cut puts the data which has troubled me so long on the page from where it continues to glower at me, even scold me. I noted earlier the profound responsibility that comes with making cuts in a material feminist diffractive approach. This is because 'the primary ontological unit is not independent objects with inherent boundaries and properties but rather phenomena', whereby 'phenomena are the ontological inseparability/entanglement of intra-acting agencies' (Barad 2007, 139). These intra-active entanglements make ethical relationality a touchstone, a key to the process of 'worlding' which involves us all, humans and non-human agencies together. The 'Physics' instance indicates the material force of classroom space to homogenise consent, provoke collective endeavour and marginalise dissent. In bringing to the fore that our ethical responsibilities arise from our entangled ontologies a diffractive methodology can prompt new ethical attention to our 'direct material engagement with the world' (Barad 2007, 49). This, undoubtedly, has profound implications for how we conduct research *in situ*.

7. Materialising a diffractive analysis

My aim has been to write this article as an accessible and practical illustration of what it means to undertake and write about how a diffractive methodology, inside a feminist materialist approach to how gender matters, can work, and what it can do. Choosing to weave diffractive interferences into the empirical account the article no doubt offers an irruptive reading experience, as does the direct address to 'you' the reader, in your entangled materiality, as I invite a comment, reflection or even judgement.

This act of experimentation in writing diffractively has been my attempt to instantiate both the critical and the creative potential of this approach. Thinking about data as matter returns me to Koro-Ljungberg's (2012) question *'what do data want?'* Perhaps, I suggest, what data want is a risky encounter. Recognising data's troublesome agency, its affective scope to unsettle our grooved, established research practices, may help us 'think with the uncertainties of knowing' (Lather 2007, 156) and open research to new ways of seeing and more plural, innovative practices.

8. Towards a conclusion

This article has contributed to moving forward educational analyses of objects, bodies and space through its use of a material feminist analysis of embodied practices of mattering in the classroom. In disclosing empirically the material multiplicity of classroom space, the article has indicated how space works as, at one and the same moment, entertainment space, performative space, epistemological space, ontological space and pedagogic space. Through a focus on objects and matter within the classroom, new attention has been drawn to space as a distributed confederacy of agentic materialities, within which differential gendered subjectivities are produced and enacted co-constitutively in vital human–nonhuman assemblages. By asking the questions 'what does a chair do?', 'what does a body do?', 'what do things do?' and 'what do clothes do?' I have illustrated matter's thing-power and the importance of attending to that which is so often unnoticed, unremarked, or passed over as mundane in the materiality of the classroom.

My argument has been that the confederacy of materialities means we can no longer think of agency as an individual, willed and bounded human property; agency is, instead, distributed, confederate, brought into being though the co-constitutive enactments of human–nonhuman apparatuses. This has profound ontological and ethical implications for classroom practices. In relation to gender, I have shown how the spatial multiplicity of the classroom in question was 'cut' by powerful gendered performatives of masculinity and how, in the space of entertainment, it was the player who occupied 'the chair' who was able to have the most fun.

The article has also made an original methodological contribution by instantiating one way of doing a diffractive analysis. This has enabled me to illustrate how a diffractive methodology enables a livelier, emergent and more open interaction between data and researcher and thus how it may suggest 'critical practice[s] for making a difference in the world' (Barad 2007, 90). In foregrounding Malky's glamour and my cuts I noted my material entanglement as researcher with data which was and still is troubling. This led me to propose the advantages to be gained in deploying a material feminist approach both as an ethical research practice and as a final nail in the coffin of objectivist, rationalist Enlightenment presumptions. In putting to work various concepts as tools for thinking from Barad – intra-action, entanglement, phenomena, apparatus, cut – I argued the necessity of plunging into particularity, of getting down and dirty in the empirical details. In this way, we can create a space for material feminism to work its way into our lives and embodied educational practice as we seek not just to fight the familiar but to change it through our feminist praxis.

References

Ahmed, S. 2000. *Strange Encounters: Embodied Others in Post-coloniality*. London: Routledge.

Allen, L. 2012. "Behind the Bike Sheds: Sexual Geographies of Schooling." *British Journal of Sociology of Education* 34 (1): 56–75.

Barad, K. 2007. *Meeting the Universe Halfway: Quantum Physics and the Entanglement of Matter and Meaning*. London: Duke University Press.

Bennett, J. 2010. *Vibrant Matter: A Political Ecology of Things*. London: Duke University Press.

Bernstein, B. 2004. *Pedagogy, Symbolic Control and Identity: Theory, Research, Critique*. Revised ed. Oxford: Rowman.

Bissell, D. 2009. "Inconsequential Materialities: The Movements of Lost Effects." *Space and Culture* 12 (1): 95–115.

Bourdieu, P., J. C. Passeron, and M. de Saint Martin. 1965. *Academic Discourse*. Oxford: Polity Press.

Boys, J. 2010. *Towards Creative Learning Spaces: Re-thinking the Architecture of Post-compulsory Education*. London: Routledge.

Brooks, R., A. Fuller, and J. Waters, eds. 2012. *Changing Spaces of Education: New Perspectives on the Nature of Learning*. London: Routledge.

Burke, C., and I. Grosvenor. 2008. *School: Iconic Architecture*. London: Reaktion.

Butler, J. 1990. *Gender Trouble: Feminism and the Subversion of Identity*. New York: Routledge.

Butler, J. 1993. *Bodies that Matter: On the Discursive Limits of 'Sex'*. New York: Routledge.

Butler, J. 1997. *Excitable Speech: A Politics of the Performative*. New York: Routledge.

Caillois, R. 2003. *The Edge of Surrealism, A Roger Caillois Reader*. Durham, NC: Duke University Press.

Carter, M. 2012. "Stuff and Nonsense: The Limits of the Linguistic Model of Clothing." *Fashion Theory* 16 (3): 343–354.

Connell, R. 1995. *Masculinities*. California: University of California Press.

Coole, D., and S. Frost. 2010. *New Materialisms: Ontology, Agency, Politics*. Durham, NC: Duke University Press.

Delamont, S., and M. Galton. 1986. *Inside the Secondary Classroom*. London: Routledge and Kegan Paul.

Di Leo, J., and W. Jacobs. 2004. *If Classrooms Matter: Progressive Visions of Educational Environments*. New York: Routledge.

Dunne, M. 2007. "Gender, Sexuality and Schooling: Everyday Life in Junior Secondary Schools in Botswana and Ghana." *International Journal of Educational Development* 27 (5): 499–511.

Fenwick, T., and P. Landri. 2012. "Introduction: Materialities, Textures and Pedagogies: Socio-Material Assemblages in Education." *Pedagogy, Culture & Society* 20 (1): 1–7.

Foucault, F. 1979. *Discipline and Punish: The Birth of the Prison*. London: Peregrine Books.

Foucault, M. 1980. *Power/Knowledge: Selected Interviews and Other Writings 1972–1977*. New York: Harvester Wheatsheaf.

Foucault, M. 1984. "Space, Knowledge, and Power." In *The Foucault Reader*, edited by P. Rabinow, 239–256. London: Penguin.

Foucault, M. 1988. *The History of Sexuality*. Vol. 3. *The Care of the Self*. Harmondworth: Viking.

Francis, B. 2008. "Teaching Manfully? Exploring Gendered Subjectivities and Power via Analysis of Men Teachers' Gender Performance." *Gender and Education* 20 (2): 109–122.

Genz, S. 2006. "Third Way/ve: The Politics of Postfeminism." *Feminist Theory* 7 (3): 333–353.

Gibbs, G. 2010. *Dimensions of Quality*. York: Higher Education Academy.

Grosz, E. 1994. *Volatile Bodies: Toward a Corporeal Feminism*. Bloomington, IN: Indiana University Press.

Hirst, E., and M. Cooper. 2008. "Keeping Them in Line: Choreographing Classroom Spaces." *Teachers and Teaching: Theory and Practice* 14 (5–6): 431–445.

Hubbard, P., R. Kitchin, and G. Valentine. 2004. *Key Thinkers on Space and Place*. London: Sage.

Igoe, D., and J. Kewin. 2013. Creating a Level Playing Field in Sixth Form Education, White Paper, Sixth Form Colleges Association.

Ivinson, G. 2012. "The Body and Pedagogy: Beyond Absent, Moving Bodies in Pedagogic Practice." *British Journal of Sociology of Education* 33 (4): 489–506.

Jackson, A. J., and A. Mazzei. 2012. *Thinking with Theory in Qualitative Research*. Oxon: Routledge.

Jones, L. 2013a. "Becoming Child: Becoming Dress." *Global Studies of Childhood* 3 (3): 289–296.

Jones, L. 2013b. "Children's Encounters with Things: Schooling the Body." *Qualitative Inquiry*. doi:10.1177/1077800413494348

Koro-Ljungberg, M. 2012. "What do data want?" Conference presentation, American Educational Research Association Annual Meeting, Vancouver, Canada.

Koro-Ljungberg, M., and M. MacLure. 2013. "Provocations, Re-Un-Visions, Death, and Other Possibilities of 'Data'." *Cultural Studies=Critical Methodologies*. doi:10.1177/1532708613487861

Kreisberg, S. 1992. *Transforming Power: Domination, Empowerment and Education*. Albany, NY: SUNY Press.

Lather, P. 2007. *Getting Lost: Feminist Efforts Toward a Double(d) Science*. Albany, NY: SUNY Press.

MacLure, M. 2013. "Classification or Wonder? Coding as an Analytic Practice in Qualitative Research." In *Deleuze and Research Methodologies*, edited by B. Coleman and J. Ringrose, 164–183. Edinburgh: Edinburgh University Press.

Mahony, P., I. Hextall, and M. Richardson. 2011. "'Building Schools for the Future': Reflections on a New Social Architecture." *Journal of Education Policy* 26 (3): 341–360.

Massey, D. 2005. *For Space*. London: Sage.

McGregor, J. 2001. "Making Spaces: Teacher Workplace Topologies." Paper presented at the British Educational Research Association Annual Conference, Leeds University, September 13–15.

Miller, D. 2010. *Stuff*. Cambridge: Polity Press.

Mulcahy. D. 2012. "Affective Assemblages: Body Matters in the Pedagogic Practices of Contemporary School Classrooms." *Pedagogy, Culture & Society* 20 (1): 9–27.

Mulvey, L. 1975. "Visual Pleasure and Narrative Cinema." In *Feminist Film Theory: A Reader*, edited by S. Thornham, 58–69. Edinburgh: Edinburgh University Press.

Palmer, A. 2011. "Performative Strategies and Diffractive Thinking as Methodological Tools for Rethinking Mathematical Subjectivity." *Reconceptualizing Educational Research Methodology* 1 (1): 3–18.

Park, J. 2013. "Do School Uniforms Lead to Uniform Minds? School Uniforms and Appearance Restrictions in Korean Middle Schools and High Schools." *Fashion Theory* 17 (2): 159–178.

Pilcher, J. 2013. "'Small But Very Determined' A Novel Theorisation of Children's Consumption of Clothing." *Cultural Sociology* 7 (1): 86–100.

Quinn, J. 2003. "The Dynamics of Protected Space: Spatial Concepts and Women Students." *British Journal of Sociology of Education* 24 (4): 449–461.

Renold, E. 2005. *Girls, Boys and Junior Sexualities: Exploring Children's Gender and Sexual Relations in the Primary School*. London: RoutledgeFalmer.

Renold, E., and Ringrose, J. 2011. "Schizoid Subjectivities: Re-Theorising Teen-Girls' Sexual Cultures in an Era of Sexualisation." *Journal of Sociology* 47 (4): 389–409.

Ringrose, J. 2007. "Successful Girls? Complicating Post-Feminist, Neoliberal Discourses of Educational Achievement and Gender Equality." *Gender and Education* 19 (4): 471–489.

Ringrose, J., and E. Renold. 2012. "Slut Shaming, Girl Power and 'Sexualisation': Thinking Through the Politics of the International Slutwalks with Teen Girls." *Gender and Education* 24 (3): 333–343.

Shields, R. 1997. "Spatial Stress and Resistance: Social Meanings of Spatialization." In *Space and Social Theory: Interpreting Modernity and Postmodernity*, edited by G. Benko and U. Strohmayer, 186–202. Oxford: Blackwell.

Stengers, I. 2007. "Diderot's Egg: Divorcing Materialism from Eliminativism." *Radical Philosophy* 144 (July/August): 7–15.

Tamboukou, M. 1999. "Spacing Herself: Women in Education." *Gender and Education* 11 (2): 125–139.

Taylor, C. 2011. "'Hope in Failure': A Level Students, Discursive Agency, Post-Feminism and Feminism." *Gender and Education* 23 (7): 825–841.

Urry, J. 2003. *Global Complexity*. Cambridge: Polity.

Zembylas, M. 2007. "Risks and Pleasures: A Deleuzo–Guattarian Pedagogy of Desire in Education." *British Educational Research Journal* 33 (3): 331–349.

Gettin' a little crafty: Teachers Pay Teachers©, Pinterest© and neo-liberalism in new materialist feminist research

Elizabeth A. Pittard

ABSTRACT

In this paper, I share data from a year-long study investigating the manifestations of neo-liberalism in the working lives of five women elementary school teachers in the United States. I discuss how gendered discourses of neo-liberalism construct what is understood as possible in the material-discursive production of the women's subjectivities concerning a surprising market created by teachers for teachers that is largely promoted through the social media site, Pinterest©: Teachers Pay Teachers©. Utilising new materialist feminist theory [Braidotti, R. 2000. "Teratologies." In *Deleuze and Feminist Theory*, edited by I. Buchanan, and C. Colebrook, 156–172. Edinburgh: Edinburgh University Press; Dolphijn, R., and I. van der Tuin. 2012. *New Materialism: Interviews & Cartographies*. Ann Arbor, MI: Open Humanities Press], I analyse how the teachers intra-act [Barad, K. 2007. *Meeting the Universe Half Way: Quantum Physics and the Entanglement of Matter and Meaning*. Durham, NC: Duke University Press] with curricular material actants [Bennett, J. 2010. *Vibrant Matter: A Political Ecology of Things*. Durham, NC: Duke University Press] that have the capacity to alter the course of events in women's work and lives. I argue that these material actants further entangle the material-discursive, virtual-real production of subjectivity and influence women teachers in variegated but particularly gendered ways that ultimately reinforce emerging theories around the gendered nature of neo-liberal subjectivity [Gill, R. 2008. "Culture and Subjectivity in Neoliberal and Postfeminist Times." *Subjectivity* 25 (1): 432–445. doi:10.1057/sub.2008.28; Walkerdine, V. 2003. "Reclassifying Upward Mobility: Femininity and the Neo-liberal Subject." *Gender and Education* 15: 237–248. doi:10.1080/09540250303864].

Joplin and I sat in her fifth-grade classroom at Creekveiw Elementary School.[1] The students had left for the day, and she was giving me a tour of her classroom via her pointed finger while we remained seated at children's desks in the middle of the room. While this was only our second meeting for the purposes of this study, I'd been in this space many times before, as Joplin and I were colleagues during my five years teaching fifth grade at Creekview and remained friends after I no longer taught elementary school.

However, with each bulletin board she described, each buzzword she used and each resource she explained, I became increasingly aware that I no longer recognised this once-familiar space. It was not so much the aesthetics of her classroom that had changed, but it was instead the curricular materials and educational resources she described that were completely unfamiliar to me. She continued showing me around her classroom using new words such as *strategy groups* and *task cards*. This language confused me.

Thinking it must be the result of some new textbook or computer-based resource due to the recent implementation of the Common Core State Standards (CCSS),[2] I asked her to tell me more about the curriculum they were using. She immediately replied, 'The [Common Core] standards are the curriculum ... The only curriculum we've got is the standards.' She elaborated in telling me how the school district provided pacing guides detailing when each standard for each subject was to be taught but how the curricular materials she and her colleagues used to plan and implement instruction was increasingly *not* provided by the district. In other words, even though the standards driving the mandated content had changed over the past school year, the district had not purchased new textbook series to address the new standards. Teachers were instructed to retrofit the textbook series and curricular resources that were aligned with the former state standards to the new standards when possible and to supplement with other resources where it was necessary so that they could address content that was not required under the former set of standards.

Adequately creating materials for the content that was previously taught in other grade levels proved to be extremely time-consuming, and Joplin told me that she refused to work the extra and unpaid hours, as it required to produce materials for four reading groups on a daily basis in addition to the other four subject areas she was responsible for teaching. As a result, she had begun using more of her own money than she had in previous years to buy curricular materials to teach the required standards/curriculum. In describing the process of gathering materials to teach the new CCSS she said, 'So then I got a little crafty, and I was like screw it, I'm just going to start buying things on Teachers Pay Teachers' – which was a marketplace I had never heard of before. As Joplin got up to retrieve and subsequently discuss an at least three-inch thick binder full of Teachers Pay Teachers© (TpT©) lesson plans (each of which contain *task cards* that focus on a particular skill that is to be used in a *strategy group*), I realised that the work of teaching at Creekview had changed significantly since my departure just two short years before. As I continued discussions about their working lives with more teachers, I soon found out that the work of teaching had changed in other places too and that Joplin was not the only one getting 'a little crafty' in obtaining curricular materials.

Context of the study

Over the past several decades, neo-liberalism has significantly shifted sociopolitical landscapes on a global scale (Harvey 2005; Ong 2006; Klein 2007; Steger and Roy 2010; Peck 2013). The impacts of neo-liberalism specific to educational institutions, policies and discourses have been widely theorised in contexts outside of the United States (e.g. Davies 2005; Davies and Bansel 2007; Duncan 2007; Watkins 2007; Connell 2008; Ball 2012) as well as within the United States particularly around education policy (e.g. Bartlett et al.

2002; Taubman 2009; Baltodano 2012; Costigan 2013; Gabriel and Lester 2013). Relatedly, there is an emerging body of scholarship theorising the gendered nature of neo-liberalism and neo-liberal subjectivities (e.g. Walkerdine 2003; Walkerdine and Ringrose 2006; Gill 2008), and it is important for feminist educational researchers to further investigate how this gendered nature of neo-liberalism manifests itself within the subjectivities available to women broadly conceived as well as the overwhelmingly feminised teaching force in potentially problematic ways. Indeed, Gill (2008) speaking to the gendered subject of neo-liberalism posits, 'Further exploration of this intimate relationship is urgently needed to illuminate … contemporary neoliberal social relations' (443).

This neo-liberal subjectification in addition to the pervasive and persistent 'bad teacher' narratives within media and popular discourses (Kumashiro 2012; Goldstein 2014) as well as the myth that 'since women can now do anything, only the least able become teachers' (Maher and Tretreault 2000, 199), it appears as though women teachers in neo-liberal times are up against seemingly impossible odds. Taking a nuanced look at the working lives of women teachers within localised contexts can tell us a great deal about how gender and neo-liberalism are operating within not only these localised contexts but also potentially more broadly as well.

The well-established bodies of scholarship around the history and impacts of the feminisation of the work of teaching (Grumet 1988; Nias 1989; Biken 1995; Munro 1998; Bartky 1990), the impacts of capitalism on teaching (Giroux and McLaren 1988; Apple 2001; Saltmarsh 2007; Sleeter 2008; Casey 2013), and the relationship that exists between the two (Apple [1986] 1988; Weiler, 1988; Luke 1992; Coffey and Delamont 2000; Miller 2005) significantly informs the research on neo-liberalism, gender and teaching presented in this study. However, it is important to acknowledge that while neo-liberalism is an extension and intensification of capitalism in the arenas of policy formation, ideological discipline and modes of internalised governing (Connell 2008; Foucault [2004] 2008; Brown 2015), neo-liberalism and capitalism are by no means interchangeable entities. As such, the analysis presented here is situated against the backdrop of this scholarly work around capitalism, gender and teaching as well as the literature concerning neo-liberalism and teaching and seeks to extend these analyses considering the ways in which discourses of neo-liberalism are particularly gendered and functioning in the working lives of teachers.

There are very few studies investigating the manifestations of neo-liberalism in the daily lives of teachers in the United States (see Duncan 2007; Watkins 2007; Ball and Olmedo 2013 for examples of this type of analysis). I contend there is a need to investigate the entanglement of gendered and neo-liberal discourses from the ground-up perspective of women teachers, as material and discursive entities produce the conditions for what becomes possible in how people might live (Foucault [1984] 1997; St. Pierre 2004; May 2005). Through this investigation, we can also look for ways of resisting damaging subjectification that is often implicit in the gendering effects of neo-liberal discourses.

In this paper, I share data from a year-long study investigating the sociopolitical, embodied, discursive and material manifestations of neo-liberalism in the working lives of five women elementary school teachers in the Southeastern United States. One aim of this study was to theorise how gendered and neo-liberal discourses contribute to what counts as *good enough* in teaching while simultaneously producing and upholding the pervasive yet impossible subject position of the *good enough (woman) teacher*. The concept of the good enough teacher serves as an analytical tool for deconstructing and problematising the impossible situations in which teachers find themselves in current sociopolitical contexts and is further discussed throughout this paper.

Early in the course of the study, conversations with participants revealed a surprising market created by teachers for teachers that is largely promoted through Pinterest©:[3] TpT©. I discuss data from interviews and websites concerning TpT© and Pinterest© to provide an example of one way neo-liberalism manifests itself in the gendered work of teaching as well as its role in persistently making over what counts as good teaching.

I use new materialist feminist theory (Braidotti 2000; Dolphijn and van der Tuin 2012) to analyse how women elementary school teachers *intra-act* (Barad 2007) with curricular *material actants* (Bennett 2010) produced for and consumed via TpT© and argue that these material actants have the capacity to alter the course of events in teachers' lives. Further, these material actants, which are most often obtained in the technological spaces of Pinterest© links to TpT©, further entangle the material-discursive and virtual-real production of subjectivity and influences women elementary school teachers in variegated but particularly gendered ways that ultimately serve to reinforce feminist understandings of neo-liberal subjectivity (Walkerdine 2003; Gill 2008). In later sections of the paper, I describe new material feminism and the unique analytical perspective it offers around the mutual constitution of material and discursive entities (Barad 2007). But I first outline the methods of data generation and provide a briefly introduce the participants in this study.

Methods of data generation and participant overview

As discussed above, this paper analyses data from a broader study around the gendered nature of neo-liberalism and its manifestations in the work of teaching. Once I obtained approval from the institutional review boards at both my university and the local school district, I began the process of soliciting participants via email communication with three local school administrators with whom I was personally acquainted asking them to distribute my initial invitation to participate in the study to teachers who worked in their schools. As a result of the initial email solicitation, all three administrators agreed to distribute the letter of invitation, and five teachers from two schools, Creekview and Townsend Elementary Schools, ultimately agreed to participate. Figure 1 provides general information about each teacher.

Because Creekview was one of the schools in which I worked during my career as a teacher, three participants were former colleagues of mine. These interpersonal relationships are important to note because they impacted my position as a researcher as well

Participants	Years of Experience	Current School	Years at Current School	Highest Degree
Gretta	15	Creekview Elementary	15	Educational Specialist
Joplin	8	Creekview Elementary	8	Masters
Natasha	17	Townsend Elementary	4	Masters
Rose	6	Creekview Elementary	6	Doctorate
Taylor	5	Townsend Elementary	3	Masters

Figure 1. General information about study participants.

as the conversations that were possible with each participant in unique ways. Specifically, I was a participant in Rose's doctoral study, so she readily volunteered to participate. Another participant, Joplin, and I stayed in touch after I left teaching to pursue graduate work full time and often had discussions about her work and life, so our conversations for this study were familiar and comfortable from the start. Finally, I knew Gretta from our experience as colleagues from my earliest days teaching. Joplin, Rose, Gretta and I had a foundation upon which to begin our discussions and each of the women were eager to share their opinions about the state of education in both local and national contexts.

I did not personally know Natasha and Taylor who worked at Townsend Elementary prior to beginning the study. Much of our time together in the beginning of the study was spent getting to know each other and building trusting relationships. Both Natasha and Taylor seemed to become comfortable in our conversations after the first few meetings, and they each noted how they looked forward to what they called our bi-weekly 'therapy' sessions.

While each of the women in the study at one point or another discussed engagement with Pinterest© and TpT©, Joplin, Rose and Taylor are centred in this analysis, as they were most actively engaged in the buying and selling on TpT©. I can conjecture several reasons for their engagement including but not limited to years of experience and age. Gretta and Natasha had been teaching many years longer than the other participants, and they had saved curricular materials from over the years that they could use as supplemental resources. They were also hesitant to consider purchasing curricular materials with their own money. It is also possible that Joplin, Rose and Taylor being in their 30s are demographically situated in an age range more likely to engage the social media space of Pinterest©, which is the primary advertising platform for TpT© sellers.

Pinterest© and TpT©

Pinterest© is a popular social networking site outnumbered only by Facebook© and Twitter© in its number of users (Phillips, Miller, and McQuarrie 2013) (Figure 2).

Based on techniques of collecting *ideas* or *things* made possible by constructing bulletin boards, collages or scrapbooks, Pinterest offers a virtual space to construct similar collections but in the context of the practically infinite space of the Internet. The overwhelmingly feminised user base uses the application to 'pin' images on different 'boards' about topics in which they are interested. The user-created boards on Pinterest© house images about topics ranging anywhere from decorating ideas to recipes to inspirational quotes – and pretty much anything else imaginable.

For example, a user who is a teacher might go to Pinterest© for ideas about lesson planning, bulletin boards and classroom décor in addition to other 'Pinteresting' topics relevant to them such as parenting advice, party planning or gardening. A teacher looking for specific lesson ideas could enter a search for it using keywords such as '5th grade math fractions ideas.' Like Google©, Pinterest© will suggest other typical words or categories that complement, extend or narrow the search. Once users decide on a search, they scroll through pictures in the results and decide which ones to pin on the board titled to describe the topic at hand on their personal Pinterest© page. The boards on a

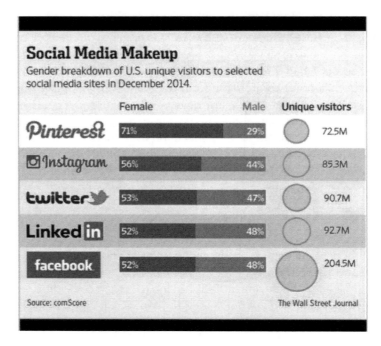

Figure 2. Data on unique visitors by gender for popular social media sites.

user's page-make-up projects, products or ideas that users think is appealing in some way. Users can also follow other people's boards and 'like' their pins similar to how one might 'like' a post on Facebook© or 'favorite' something on Twitter© (Figure 3).

Soon after beginning this study, I decided to try using Pinterest© myself. At the time, I was teaching math to a group of four home school students ranging from fifth to ninth grade one day per week. I thought trying Pinterest© might provide me with new instructional ideas from the perspective of a practicing teacher as well as prove beneficial in my upcoming conversations with women elementary school teachers regarding the possible influence of Pinterest© in their teaching lives. In learning to use Pinterest© from the perspective of a teacher, I began to recognise three prominent types of pins regarding teaching: curricular materials such as lesson plans and anchor charts, classroom décor such as themed classroom bulletin boards and matching door decorations, and inspirational or funny quotes about teaching (Figure 4).

Through searching for curricular materials to support my instruction with my homeschool students, I noticed that many resources that seemed like they may be helpful almost always linked to TpT© website, and I was reminded of the conversation I had with Joplin described above and other conversations that I had with other women teachers in my study. In finding out more about this website that seemed to keep coming up, I learned that TpT© is an online, user-generated marketplace where merchants who are almost always teachers upload and sell lesson plans for other teachers to purchase.

Users can choose to filter content by categories such as grade level, subject area and price. Each seller is scored by consumer rankings from one to four stars, and shoppers

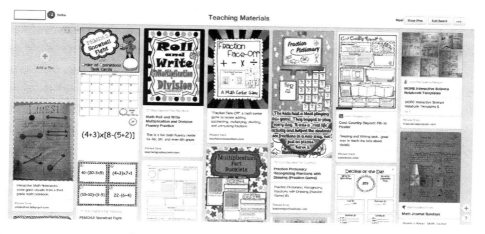

Figure 3. Personal Pinterest© page that was used when looking for materials to support instruction.

can create wish lists much like any other retail site. TpT© 'makes "resource sharing" into a full- featured shopping experience, where teachers can simultaneously be an entrepreneur and a customer' (www.edsurge.com, 2014). Additionally, it is widely recognised

Figure 4. Two screenshots from the TpT© website.

among TpT© sellers that the primary and 'required' (www.tptschool.com, 2014) marketing tool for TpT© merchants is Pinterest©. According to blogger, author and teacher Chris Kesler who after selling on TpT© for a little over a year was making '4-figure monthly pay-checks' (www.tptschool.com, 2014), Pinterest© is essential in driving

> the majority of traffic to TpT. You can't upload a product and expect it to take off if you're relying on the TpT search function to get it noticed. Pinterest is my only method of marketing, so I'm really deadly serious about it. (www.tptschool.com, 2014)

In other words, it is common knowledge among TpT© merchants that Pinterest© is essential to a successful business.

Success on Pinterest© can mean six figure salaries for teachers previously making a mere fraction of that annually. For example, Deanna Jump, a private school kindergarten and first-grade teacher (who continues teaching in Georgia, USA) has made over a million dollars selling lesson plans on TpT©, and the newly appointed CEO of TpT© (formerly the CEO of Etsy.com©) does not think the revenue will slow down any time soon (http://mashable.com/2012/05/17/teachers-pay-teachers/). He describes the TpT© market as 'massive and growing' as the site possesses over 22 million pieces of educational material that have generated over $86 million dollars in revenue since the site's launch in 2006 (http://mashable.com/2012/05/17/teachers-pay-teachers/).

The implications for such phenomenon seemed potentially wide reaching and game changing concerning the work of teaching. While millions of people participate in social media on a daily basis, there is almost no literature discussing social media and teaching. I was interested in finding out if and how the social media site Pinterest© was influencing the working lives of the women teachers in my study. Based on my own experiences and with the ultimate aim of informing broader questions of how neo-liberalism influences the subjectivity of women elementary school teachers, I anticipated that TpT© might come up in discussions with participants about Pinterest©. However, I was surprised when four out of five of the women in the study mentioned Pinterest© or TpT© before I asked specifically about either one.

For example, TpT© came up three times in my first interview with Rose, another fifth-grade teacher at Creekview with whom I had also worked previously. As a part of the first discussion with each participant, I asked about general background information such as how and when each of them decided to become teachers, their experiences as a teacher such as describing a typical day at work, and their lives outside of work such as social supports and roles outside of teaching.[4] When I asked Rose to tell me about her responsibilities outside of work, she mentioned schoolwork for her doctoral degree, household chores, weekend festivals where she promoted and sold a children's book that she authored, and complicated family relationships with her parents, sister and niece. In addition to each of these responsibilities, she concluded by adding, 'I opened my teachers pay teachers store – which is really exciting because even though I'm only making, like, 30 cents, 50 cents at a time, I'm still just – the fact that someone else wants my stuff – I like that.'

Rose mentioned TpT© a second time when I asked her to walk me through a typical day in her life in noting that on any given day she might make a new lesson for her TpT© store. She brought up TpT© a third time when I asked about when she feels most accomplished. Rose began by explaining that she has 'different definitions of accomplishment for everything' that she does. After explaining what makes her feel accomplished as a partner, an author, a doctoral student and as a teacher and colleague, her voice got louder and more lively as she concluded by describing accomplishment as a TpT© seller:

> Seeing the email from teachers pay teachers saying, 'Congratulations! You've made a sale on Teachers Pay Teachers!' I'm like, *Yes!* That feels like a *huge* accomplishment, you know? I don't know why. That's so weird, because it's like, 30 cents. [laughing] Seriously. But its just that whole: I've made something, do you want it? *Yes! I want that.*

After explaining that earning 30-cents selling one TpT© lesson felt like more of an accomplishment than selling 9 of her books totalling approximately $130 in earnings at a recent weekend festival, Rose comments on how she is not quite sure why she felt this way. Then, in theorising why the feeling she gets when selling lesson plans as a teacher might be different than the feeling she gets when selling books as an author, Rose continued,

> It's very foreign to me from a teacher's point of view. Cause, I get it as an author, but that's a different – That's a different me. You know? And so … from a teacher's perspective, I'm making these things and other teachers want it – for their classroom. I'm like, *Okay!* Like, that feels really good.

For Rose, selling lesson plans is seemingly more valuable than selling copies of her book because even though it might provide less money per transaction, there is something about successfully selling the TpT© lessons that makes her feel more accomplished. It was as though, for Rose, authors were *supposed* to make money selling their books, but teachers, on the other hand, were not supposed to make money selling lesson plans. However, if they did, as she had selling lesson plans on TpT©, that was in many ways going above and beyond the expectations she had for herself as a teacher. Promoting educational materials on Pinterest© to subsequently sell on TpT© was rewarding for Rose in a significantly different way than other types of teaching-related work accomplishments. The personal satisfaction Rose experienced becomes more intelligible when presented within the context of neo-liberal subjectivity.

Neo-liberal subjectivity

Following feminist educational scholars Walkerdine (2003) and Davies (2005), I use the term *neoliberal subjectivity* to refer to what Foucault ([2004] 2008) described as a fundamental shift from earlier classical liberal understandings of the *homo economicus* in that with neo-liberalism, labourers are no longer considered separated from labour power but are considered 'active economic subject[s]' (Foucault [2004] 2008, 223). With this shift, the 'wage is an income, not the price at which he sells his labor power' (223). With this economic analysis of labour, the neo-liberal subject embodies 'capitalization of existence itself' (Davies and Bansel 2007, 252), and 'the new worker is totally responsible for their own destiny and so techniques and technologies of regulation focus on the self-management of citizens to produce themselves as having the skills and qualities necessary to succeed in the new economy' (Walkerdine 2003, 240).

In other words, neo-liberal subjectivity is legitimised through the production of an individual who is capable of responsibly choosing the most efficient means to market oneself in ways that will be most economically profitable. On the one hand, with liberal ideology, workers were produced in the image of the factory so that they were efficient in their work while they were in the enclosed spaces of the factory. On the other hand, with neo-liberal ideology, an income includes a wage but also extends beyond the money a person makes to include the subject positions that become available through their work – subject positions that, in the case of teachers creating curriculum for individual monetary profit, were formerly only available to textbook publishers or other educational companies who sell curricular materials. Additionally, neo-liberal work is no longer enclosed in spaces like the factory because neo-liberal societies are not closed off by space and time. Workers can always check their email, work from home and produce income outside of any fulltime job.

With this understanding of neo-liberal subjectivity, Pinterest© is an interesting and important site of study concerning teaching, as images in the form of *pins* overwhelmingly link users to websites where they can purchase the items being pinned. With the understanding that the neo-liberal subject is considered most successful when they properly 'sell' themselves, it becomes possible to recognise different explanations for Rose's feelings of accomplishment than otherwise could have been imagined.

Rose was no longer just another teacher who sells her labour power in exchange for the wage provided through the work of teaching. She instead was distinguished from other teachers with the same educational qualifications and pay grade because she had successfully sold lessons that were unequivocally hers to other teachers who, by way of their purchasing power, had proven that they wanted what she had to offer.

As I became more familiar with TpT© via Pinterest©, I realised that Rose and other teachers like her were at the forefront of creating and maintaining what counts as *good enough*[5] in elementary school teaching. I was learning to recognise what 'Pinterest worthy' classroom materials looked like, and if teachers could not re-create these ideas because of lack of ability or time, they could still gain access to *good enough* – if they were willing and able to pay for it. In the next section, I discuss new material feminist theory and why it is useful in analysing the material and embodied production of what counts as good teaching within neo-liberalism and neo-liberal subjectivity.

New material feminist theory

New material feminist theory is a recent hybridisation of post-structural and feminist theory that allows researchers to remain committed to feminist understandings of embodied materiality while simultaneously drawing from post-structural understandings of discourse, power and space. Specific to the data presented here, new material feminist theory offers interesting ways to think about how virtual spaces like Pinterest© and TpT©, as well as materials such as lesson plans and student activities, have the capacity to alter what teachers understand as possible in the production of their subjectivity. The user-generated search results found on Pinterest© that link to a teacher's TpT© store produce conceptual and literal re-configurations of teachers' understandings of what counts as *good enough* within the context of teaching. This version of neo-liberal subjectivity is constantly in motion through material and discursive collisions and negations – or what has been called *intra-action* (Barad 2007; Taguchi 2012) in new materialist feminist research.

Barad (2007) defines the concept of *intra-action* as 'the mutual constitution of entangled agencies' (33), so in the example presented above, technology (that is most often, by the way, accessed via smartphones and tablets which are increasingly considered necessary appendages to the body) provides access to a kind of monetary and professional satisfaction previously unavailable. In other words, through intra-action with products she sells on TpT©, discourses of neo-liberalism, and her virtual production of subjectivity, it became possible for Rose to experience a new kind of accomplishment.

Taguchi (2012) extends the concept of intra-action in positing that intra-active entities are 'understood *not* to have clear or distinct boundaries from one another' (271, emphasis in the original). In new materialist feminist research there are no subject/object, no mind/body, no material/discursive binaries, as none of these entities have predetermined agency outside of intra-action. Drawing again from Rose's feelings of accomplishment produced when she was notified that another teacher purchased her lessons on TpT©, it was the combination of the lesson plan, the TpT© website, the Pinterest© application where she advertises her lessons, the email notification from the TpT© website and the monetary reward intra-acting in that moment to produce the feeling of accomplishment she described – an event that none of the events or materials could produce without their intra-action with the others.

With the continuously moving target of what counts as *good enough* in teaching and the shiftiness inherent in neo-liberal subjectivity, it is increasingly difficult to pin down exactly how various material-discursive entities operate in the lives of women elementary school teachers. In other words, the target of *good enough* follows the pattern of the neo-liberal, capitalist education market's perpetual changing requirements because this change fuels the need for an endless supply of products to buy and sell. With new materialist feminist theory, subjectivity is understood as always *becoming* (Deleuze and Guattari [1980] 1987) through *intra-actions* (Barad 2007) with technological, material, discursive, virtual and spatial apparatuses in unpredictable ways, prompting new material feminist Braidotti (2000) to call for 'new frames of analysis' (163) that might be capable of analysing this more rhizomatic understanding of subjectivity. This call is particularly timely for me as a researcher who is interested in studying the material effects of discourse in women's lives to investigate the macro- and micro-levels of critique that might create the conditions necessary for women teachers to imagine and thus create more equitable and ethical ways of being and knowing both within and against neo-liberal modes of governance.

Finally, as I discuss below, pin boards on Pinterest© along with lessons and activities sold on TpT© contribute to the production of the subjectivity through what new material feminists have called *material actants* (Bennett 2010). These non-human material actants can produce a shift that changes what becomes possible. In this onto-epistemological reconfiguring, a person's knowing-through-being is altered through an ongoing process of *becoming* (Deleuze and Guattari [1980] 1987). In other words, the entanglement of the ethics of knowing and being is continuous in how we live together in the world. As Goodings and Tucker (2014) have pointed out, 'Socially mediated bodies emphasise the ways that technologies … have the capacity to shape people, places and things through the joint enactment of humans and technologies' (40).

Put another way, subjectivity and agency in new material feminist theory are understood as part of the ongoing process of *becoming* (Deleuze and Guattari [1980] 1987; Ivinson and Renold 2013). While a subject cannot rationally *will* her own becoming (as she exists only with other material and discursive entities), subjects *can* experience a shift in what Foucault ([1976] 1990, 93) has called their *grid of intelligibility* – what they understand to be thinkable and thus possible. These moments of imagining the previously unimaginable lead to the ability to think and thus live differently. In what follows, I describe how the materials on TpT© change what counts as *good enough* in teaching in neo-liberal times.

In the next section, I return to Joplin's explanation of her intra-actions with TpT© which produced very different effects than those described by Rose. Then I turn to another participant, Taylor, who also had intra-actions with TpT© materials in her experiences teaching fifth grade at Townsend Elementary, another school in the same district as Creekview.

Teachers talk about materials

Like my first interview with Rose, TpT© came up in my first discussion with Joplin as well, but Joplin mentioned Rose in response to my asking what she does when she has time for herself. She began by explaining that she usually does not take work home on the weekends and continued:

> This is what I'm doing now. Instead of trying to create things – Cause I have found that is not my strong suit: creating meaningful activities. I have started to buy tons of crap off of Teachers Pay Teachers and today I spent $20 ... Now, Rose goes home and creates things to put on Teachers Pay Teachers ... But if I can use somebody else's stuff that is good, I will do that now. I am not ... I'm [laughing] – I pay for stuff.

Because Joplin does not feel like she is good at 'creating meaningful activities,' she turns to purchasing them instead. Additionally, she brings up the fact that her colleague, Rose (who is discussed above) has her own TpT© store implying that she is good at creating meaningful activities. Further, she makes it clear that she does not spend her time on the weekend creating activities.

Joplin mentioned both Rose and TpT© again in our second meeting for this study. As described in the opening section of this paper, she first discussed using TpT© as her way of getting 'crafty' in coming up with lesson planning since it has in her opinion become increasingly difficult to find curricular materials to support her instruction since the implementation of the new CCSS curriculum. Later in that same discussion, I pointed out that when she, Rose and I worked together that we almost never bought curricular materials with our personal money. We sometimes bought supplies required for lessons such as food items or brought things from home like extra construction paper, but I could not recall a single time that any of us bought formal curricular materials such as worksheets or practice activities either in a store or online. I was curious about this shift to purchasing lesson plans. She responded:

> I needed stuff like this [pointing down to the thick binder filled with lessons and *task cards* that go with each lesson], and then I just kind of felt like Rose makes these great freaking lessons [when she's] in charge of writing and stuff, and I was in charge of the reading, and I just didn't feel like they were up to par, so I just got on Teachers Pay Teachers and I'm like, look at all this stuff. I'm just going to buy it.

The fifth-grade teachers at Creekview divided the lesson planning among each member of the team with one or two people working to plan each subject area. Each Tuesday, all grade-level teams across the school met to discuss pedagogical strategies that might be needed to enhance or extend the lessons each teacher had already planned for the upcoming week, and lesson plans were due to administration by 4 p.m. each Friday for the following week. In her statement above, Joplin feels like her lessons for reading are not 'up to par' with Rose's lessons in writing. Wanting to be an equal contributor to the team lesson planning, she began buying lessons on TpT©.

Trying to find out more, I asked her if anything had changed as far as the curricular materials the district provided and if she thinks that any of these changes had anything to do with her shift to buying lesson plans. She responded,

> I mean, even I thought this would be good' as she points to a workbook-style resource that the district did, in fact, purchase for the 5th grade students in lieu of another previously provided resource that teachers did not find useful at all. She continues explaining that she thought that as a result of the new resource she wouldn't 'have to buy anything.

However, the workbook turned out to be not as useful as the team thought it would be in addressing the required standards. Joplin compared it to a Basal reader and explained, 'I guess I just don't like Basals.' Then, turning to the binder of TpT© resources she continues, 'And who is going to make task cards on a certain – I mean, I could do this. I'm not going to do it. Rose would do it. Because she's creative like that. I would not do it.'

Of course, teachers have always bought supplies such as books, markers, glue and paper with their own money. The difference in the current technological and neo-liberal context is that the curricular materials are not the only things for sale. The teaching materials being created, bought and sold via Pinterest© and TpT© are bound up in the discursive production and maintenance of what counts as *good enough* in teaching which is ultimately bound up in the very subjectivities of women teachers buying, selling, pinning and creating lesson plans on TpT©. Again, teachers have always created lesson plans that they possibly shared with colleagues or their entire district of teachers or maybe even the state department of education.

However, with the understandings of success outlined in neo-liberal subjectivity, teachers' intra-actions with curricular materials via Pinterest© and TpT© provide a wider audience of customers within this specialised market. In other words, those who have the necessary extra resources can buy access to what counts as the *good enough* teacher within neo-liberal educational discourses. Further, it is not just the materials that are being bought, but an image of who gets to count as good enough in addressing mandated standards.

Joplin introduced me to the idea that good teaching is something that can be bought. She positions herself as being able, but unwilling to put the extra time into creating lessons that she thinks will be perceived as up to par or *good enough* within the context of the Common Core Standards, her students and fellow teachers. Joplin approached the pressure to produce curricular materials as a task that she could forgo by purchasing meaningful activities instead of creating them.

Another participant, Taylor, also bought lessons from TpT©. She made it clear from the very first interview that her 11-month-old child was her top priority and that she definitley relies more on her teammates more than before for lesson planning ideas. At the time of our third meeting, it was nearing the end of the school year and Taylor talked a lot about being reflective around that time of year and how she was thinking about how to do things better next year. She comments that on the one hand, 'good instruction takes planning' but on the other how she was 'tired of finding things' – meaning curriculum materials. She continues, 'Granted, you're never going to find a textbook or anything that has everything, or has it all the way you want it to, but it sure would be a starting point.'

When I asked her if she used TpT© in planning her instruction, she responded, 'Oh, god yes. Bless the people who have the time to put things on that website. It's a beautiful thing.' She continues, 'I have definitely found task cards from Pinterest – Like somebody pinned it on their board and then the link takes you to Teachers Pay Teachers … ' As she trails off she gets up and points me to at least six piles of laminated envelopes stacked behind her desk in crates. The sheer number of these envelopes shocked and per-plexed me[6] (Figure 5).

Taylor explained that each of these envelopes contained lessons she has bought on TpT© to use,

> because we have limited resources – because we, in the year 2014, still have to find all of our goddamn resources … Mary [her teammate] and I have bought a lot [of lessons off of Teachers Pay Teachers©] … I don't have to make it, but I still have to assemble it.

She continues discussing how her teammate, Mary, makes lessons to sell on TpT©. I ask how her teammate finds the time to make all the lessons, pin them on her Pinterest© page and then sell them in TpT© store. Taylor responds, 'Well, its like if she's making them, you might as well make money for it.'

Figure 5. Photograph of some of Taylor's TpT© lessons.

In this way, Pinterest© turns out to be understood as empowering for many teachers who share ideas that people like and make money for these ideas in return. Their ideas are *valued* in ways they might not be in the school or classroom (or other places in their lives). It could be argued, on the one hand, that this is one way teachers are resisting neo-liberal policy initiatives that strip funding for public services like education to in turn, pad the pockets of corporations providing consultation services, curricular materials and testing products. Following this rationale, teachers selling lesson plans could be understood as simply finding a way to take their own cut of the public money that is being funnelled into the private sector. Many teachers could see this as an opportunity to finally be compensated for the hours of formerly unpaid labour time spent developing lessons and activities after school. It also provides a way for teachers who do not feel as creatively inclined to have access to new ways of conceiving how to teach a particular lesson on a particular topic.

However, on the other hand, as Connell (2008) points out, 'Neoliberalism seeks to make existing markets wider, and to create new markets where they did not exist before' (175). Further, 'Markets are often presumed to be gender-neutral, and the neoliberal agenda should in that case have the effect of eliminating gender inequalities, over time' (Connell 2008, 177). With this, teachers have in fact created a market where it did not previously exist, and even though TpT© has recently added a purchase ordering option so that schools can buy lessons with tax dollars, the overwhelming majority of customers on TpT© are teachers spending their own money to purchase curricular materials for their classrooms. In this context, the emergence of TpT©, as a source of producing both income and curricular resources, has fulfilled twin needs.

Further, the teachers who *do* somehow find the time and energy to work this second job communicate a sense of accomplishment in the moments when as Rose put it, 'someone wants my stuff.' TpT© signals a dimension of entrepreneurial opportunity related to the profession of teaching that is entirely new, as the act of producing curriculum has not previously been conceived in terms of either its monetary value or in terms of the personal satisfaction of creating a product that someone else is willing to spend money to get. Teachers are all of a sudden thrust into a profitable domain previously limited to the sphere of textbook producers and curriculum writers. This supports Connell's understanding of neo-liberalism extending the market into previously unexplored domains.

However, this issue is further complicated for both the buyer and the seller. According to another participant, Greta, schools are beginning to tell teachers that the lessons they produce are not their own because they fall under intellectual property rights of the district. Additionally, teachers buying materials from TpT© have to agree that they will not share the lessons they have bought with anyone else, so while some women teachers who are Pinterest© users produce themselves online via the Pinterest© boards they construct based on the pins of others, others are pinning items they personally create and then intend to sell in the market of TpT©.

Implications

The technological space of Pinterest© and the site of each TpT© store intra-acts with the curriculum materials being put up for sale and the very subjectivity of the teacher who makes these materials available. With this gendered production of subjectivity within the context of neo-liberal education, she is not only constructing the teaching materials, but these material actants work, at the same time, on the material and discursive production of her subjectivity. This perpetual making-over of what counts as good teaching influences how other women and teachers produce and makeover themselves. In other words, for many women on Pinterest© selling items in TpT©, these material actants represent part of 'who they are' or who they want to be in the case of teachers who purchase rather than sell curricular materials. And within the context of neo-liberalism, these gendered and neo-liberal subjectivities are constructed as freely chosen and even sometimes empowering. Whether the teacher is buyer or seller, each teacher participating in Pinterest© boards about teaching and TpT© is continuously reproducing or making over what counts as good enough in teaching through representations of who they want to be and how these *things* could help them makeover their lives as teachers – even if that means making enough money to leave the teaching profession all together.

Feminist educational scholars Walkerdine and Ringrose (2006) have theorised how women are overwhelmingly the subjects called on to re-make themselves and how the idea of the makeover is different within neo-liberal discourses. They posit, 'The makeover is hardly new, but we would argue that these incitements have intensified and work in important ways to normalize the neo-liberal ethos of continuously maximizing, bettering and reinventing the self' (36). While women have practically always been the ones who are called upon to monitor themselves in addition to the material objects in their immediate surroundings, what is different with neo-liberalism is that women are not only being acted upon and disciplined by these external material actants but they are also taking part in this disciplining through the active production of themselves as the idealised feminine subject who is understood to be 'empowered' by the ways she 'chooses' to present herself in both real embodied ways and in virtual ways in online spaces. In neo-liberal discourses, empowerment and choice are held up as endless opportunities. However, feminists have pointed out how this discourse around empowerment and choice only works to further narrow the choices available to women (Walkerdine and Ringrose 2006; Gill 2008).

While the work of curricular production via Pinterest© and TpT© provides feelings of empowerment for some teachers, it serves to marginalise others who either do not feel like their curricular materials are *good enough* to post on TpT© or simply do not have or prefer to give the time it takes to essentially work this second job. Further, it also marginalises teachers who do not have the means to purchase these additional curricular materials. There are potentially damaging consequences for teachers when what counts as *good enough* can be bought because the women who cannot afford to purchase these materials or have time to produce 'Pinterest worthy' lessons may ultimately not have access to what counts as *good enough* in teaching.

Additionally, TpT© provides an example of teacher subjectivity is constructed and perpetually made-over through intra-action of these material and discursive productions. The highly visual space of Pinterest© and TpT© is online for anyone to view, thus the good enough teacher subject position that is both produced and maintained through these resources could potentially drown out other ways teachers are able to feel successful in their jobs.

Finally, this paper highlights just how swiftly *good enough* targets change or get made-over within the context of neo-liberalism. The vast differences in curricular materials from 2011 to 2014 at Creekview Elementary demonstrates how the moving targets of good enough are increasingly modelled after moving targets in the market, for both women and teachers. These perpetual changes that require women to consistently revise and reimagine how to be successful in their work and lives has very real implications for women teachers. Participants engaged in conversations about products many of them look at all the time without thinking about the ways they impact their lives because it is easy to get swept up in discourses of *good enough* and other enticing aspects of neo-liberalism's elusive grasp. I have noticed a similar trend with my teacher education students, and I am personally committed to assisting preservice teachers in questioning what counts as *good enough* in teaching and who gets to decide.

Understanding what becomes (im)possible in the lives of women using the conceptual tool of intra-action helps new materialist feminist researchers see the convergence of forces at work on and through the production of women's bodies and subjectivities against the particular backdrop of the gendered nature of neo-liberalism. Researchers interested in opening up more ethically oriented possibilities for how women teachers might live in neo-liberal society, must therefore persistently question and critique how neo-liberalism gets normalised in the work of teaching. Through this persistent critique, we can push back against neo-liberalism and offer more possibilities for what counts as *good enough* for women teachers.

Notes

1. All participants and school names are pseudonyms.
2. While not technically a requirement, many states applying for and receiving Race to the Top grants included the implementation of CCSS in their applications. Ultimately, forty-two of the 50 states in the United States have adopted the CCSS (www.corestandards.org).
3. Pinterest© is a social media website and smartphone application that allows users to browse content using a search function. All content are images that often link to an external website. Users then 'pin' images to their boards which they can sort by areas of interest. Figure 2 is a screenshot of a board on Pinterest.
4. Though I knew both Rose and Joplin prior to the study, I asked each participant the same questions in the first interview. These questions can be found in Appendix.
5. I have elsewhere (Author) theorized the *good enough teacher* subject position within the context of the neo-liberalisation of education. The *good enough teacher* is what Walkerdine (2003) calls an 'impossible subject position' that is nonetheless constantly 'held up as possible.' The *good enough* teacher discourse is further maintained through the production of curricular materials, as discussed here.
6. Figure 5 is a photograph of some of Taylor's TpT© lessons. It was her idea to spread them out as they are in the image. She, too, seemed surprised at the amount of the floor in her classroom they covered, as she ran to get Mary to show her.

References

Apple, M. [1986] 1988. *Teachers and Texts: A Political Economy of Class and Gender Relations in Education*. New York: Routledge.

Apple, M. 2001. *Educating the Right Way: Markets, Standards, God, and Inequality*. New York: Routledge.

Ball, S. J. 2012. *Global Education Inc.* New York: Routledge.

Ball, S. J., and A. Olmedo. 2013. "Care of the Self, Resistance and Subjectivity Under Neoliberal Governmentalities." *Critical Studies in Education* 54 (1): 85–96. doi:10.1080/17508487.2013.740678.

Baltodano, M. 2012. "Neoliberalism and the Demise of Public Education: The Corporatization of Schools of Education." *International Journal of Qualitative Studies in Education* 25 (4): 487–507. doi:10.1080/09518398.2012.673025.

Barad, K. 2007. *Meeting the Universe Half Way: Quantum Physics and the Entanglement of Matter and Meaning.* Durham, NC: Duke University Press.

Bartky, S. 1990. *Foucault, Femininity, and the Modernization of Patriarchal Power. From Feminism and Foucault: Paths of Resistance, L. Quimby & I. Diamond.* Lebanon, NH: University Press of New England. (Reprinted in McCann, C. R. and S. Kim. eds. 2013. *Feminist Theory Reader: Local and Global Perspectives.* 3rd ed. New York: Routledge.)

Bartlett, L., M. Frederick, T. Gulbrandsen, and E. Murillo. 2002. "The Marketization of Education: Public Schools for Private Ends." *Anthropology & Education Quarterly* 33 (1): 5–29.

Bennett, J. 2010. *Vibrant Matter: A Political Ecology of Things.* Durham, NC: Duke University Press.

Biken, S. K. 1995. *School Work. Gender and the Cultural Construction of Teaching.* New York: Teachers College Press.

Braidotti, R. 2000. "Teratologies." In *Deleuze and Feminist Theory*, edited by I. Buchanan, and C. Colebrook, 156–172. Edinburgh: Edinburgh University Press.

Brown, W. 2015. *Undoing the Demos: Neoliberalism's Stealth Revolution.* Brooklyn, NY: Zone Books.

Casey, L. M. 2013. "The Will to Quantify: The 'Bottom Line' in the Market Model of Education Reform." *Teachers College Record* 115 (9): 1–7. Accessed July 2, 2014. http://www.tcrecord.org.proxy-remote. galib.uga.edu/library. ID Number: 17107.

Coffey, A., and S. Delamont. 2000. *Feminism and the Classroom Teacher: Research, Praxis, Pedagogy.* New York: Routledge Farmer.

Connell, R. 2008. "The Neoliberal Parent and Schools." *Our Schools, Our Selves* 18 (1): 175–193.

Costigan, A. T. 2013. "New Urban Teachers Transcending Neoliberal Educational Reform: Embracing Aesthetic Education as a Curriculum of Political Action." *Urban Education* 48 (1): 116–148.

Davies, B. 2005. "The (im)Possibility of Intellectual Work in Neoliberal Regimes." *Discourse: Studies in the Cultural Politics of Education* 26 (1): 1–14. doi:10.1080/01596300500039310.

Davies, B., and P. Bansel. 2007. "Neoliberalism and Education." *International Journal of Qualitative Studies in Education* 20 (3): 247–259. doi:10.1080/09518390701281751.

Deleuze, G., and F. Guattari. [1980] 1987. *A Thousand Plateaus: Capitalism and Schizophrenia.* Translated by Brian Massumi. Minneapolis, MN: University of Minnesota Press.

Dolphijn, R., and I. van der Tuin. 2012. *New Materialism: Interviews & Cartographies.* Ann Arbor, MI: Open Humanities Press.

Duncan, J. 2007. "New Zealand Free Kindergartens: Free or Freely Forgotten?" *International Journal of Qualitative Studies in Education* 20 (3): 319–333. doi:10.1080/09518390701281926.

Foucault, M. [1976] 1990. *The History of Sexuality, Volume 1: An Introduction.* Translated by R. Hurley. New York: Vintage Books.

Foucault, M. [1984] 1997. The Ethics of the Concern of the Self as a Practice of Freedom. In *Michael Foucault Ethics: Subjectivity and Truth.* Edited by Paul Rabinow and translated by Robert Hurley et al. (Vol 1 *of Essential works of Foucault, 1954-1984*), 281–301. New York: The New Press.

Foucault, M. [2004] 2008. *The Birth of Biopolitics.* Edited by Michel Senellart and translated by G. Burchell. New York: Palgrave MacMillian.

Gabriel, R., and J. N. Lester. 2013. "Romance Quest of Education Reform: A Discourse Analysis of the *Los Angeles Times'* Reports on Value-Added Measurement Teacher Effectiveness." *Teachers College Record* 115 (12): 1–32.

Gill, R. 2008. "Culture and Subjectivity in Neoliberal and Postfeminist Times." *Subjectivity* 25 (1): 432–445. doi:10.1057/sub.2008.28.

Giroux, H. A., and P. McLaren. 1988. "Teacher Education and the Politics of Democratic Reform." In *Teachers as Intellectuals: Towards a Critical Pedagogy of Learning*, edited by H. A. Giroux, 158–176. New York: Bergin & Garvey Publishers.

Goldstein, D. 2014. *The Teacher Wars: A History of America's Most Embattled Profession*. New York: Doubleday.

Goodings, L., and I. Tucker. 2014. "Social Media and the Co-production of Bodies Online: Bergson, Serres and Facebook's Timeline." *Media, Culture & Society* 36 (1): 37–51. doi:10.1177/0163443713507813.

Grumet, M. R. 1988. *Bitter Milk: Women and Teaching*. Amherst: University of Massachusetts Press.

Harvey, D. 2005. *A Brief History of Neoliberalism*. New York: Oxford University Press.

Ivinson, G., and E. Renold. 2013. "Valleys' Girls: Re-Theorising Bodies and Agency in a Semi-Rural Post-Industrial Local." *Gender and Education* 25 (6): 704–721. doi:10.1080/09540253.2013.827372.

Klein, N. 2007. *The Shock Doctrine: The Rise of Disaster Capitalism*. New York: Picador.

Kumashiro, K. K. 2012. *Bad Teacher! How Blaming Teachers Distorts the Bigger Picture*. New York: Teachers College Press.

Luke, C. 1992. "Feminist Politics in Radical Pedagogy." In *Feminisms and Critical Pedagogy*, edited by C. Luke, and J. Gore, 120–137. New York: Routledge.

Maher, F., and M. K. Tretreault. 2000. "Knowledge Versus Pedagogy: The Marginalization of Teacher Education." *Women's Studies Quarterly* 28 (3/4): 194–201. doi:128.192.114.19.

May, T. 2005. *Gilles Deleuze: An Introduction*. New York: Cambridge.

Miller, J. I. 2005. *Sounds of Silence Breaking: Women, Autobiography, Curriculum*. New York: Peter Lang.

Munro, P. 1998. *Subject to Fiction: Women Teachers' Life History Narratives and the Cultural Politics of Resistance*. Philadelphia, PA: Open University Press.

Nias, J. 1989. *Primary Teachers Talking: A Study of Work as Teaching*. New York: Routledge.

Ong, A. 2006. *Neoliberalism as Exception*. Durham, NC: Duke University Press.

Peck, J. 2013. "Explaining (with) Neoliberalism." *Territory, Politics, Governance* 1 (2): 132–157. doi:10.1080/21622671.2013.785365.

Phillips, B. J., J. Miller, and E. F. McQuarrie. 2012. "Dreaming in Pictures: Pinterest and the Visual Imagination." Presentation at the American Academy of Advertising Conference.

Saltmarsh, S. 2007. "Cultural Complicities: Elitism, Heteronormativity and Violence in the Education Marketplace." *International Journal of Qualitative Studies in Education* 20 (3): 335–354. doi:10.1080/09518390701281934.

Sleeter, C. E. 2008. "Teaching for Democracy in an Age of Corportocracy." *Teachers College Record* 110 (1): 139–159.

St. Pierre, E. A. 2004. "Care of the Self: The Subject and Freedom." In *Dangerous Coagulations?: The Use of Foucault in the Study of Education*, edited by Bernadette Baker, and Katharina E. Heyning, 325–358. New York: Peter Lang.

Steger, M. B., and R. K. Roy. 2010. *Neoliberalism: A Very Short Introduction*. New York: Oxford.

Taguchi, H. L. 2012. "A Diffractive and Deleuzian Approach to Analysing Interview Data." *Feminist Theory* 13 (3): 265–281. doi:10.1177/1464700112456001.

Taubman, P. T. 2009. *Teaching by Numbers: Deconstructing the Discourse of Standards and Accountability in Education*. New York: Routledge.

Walkerdine, V. 2003. "Reclassifying Upward Mobility: Femininity and the Neo-liberal Subject." *Gender and Education* 15: 237–248. doi:10.1080/09540250303864.

Walkerdine, V., and J. Ringrose. 2006. "Femininities: Reclassifying Upward Mobility and the Neo-liberal Subject." In *The Sage Handbook of Gender and Education*, edited by B. Francis, and L. Smulyan, 31–46. Thousand Oaks, CA: Sage.

Watkins, M. 2007. "Thwarting Desire: Discursive Constraint and Pedagogic Practice." *International Journal of Qualitative Studies in Education* 20 (3): 301–318. doi:10.1080/09518390701281900.

Weiler, K. 1988. *Women Teaching for Change: Gender, Class, and Power*. South Hadley, MA: Bergin & Garvey Publishers.

Appendix

Thank you so much for agreeing to speak with me! I am excited to begin working together, and I am particularly interested in knowing more about the working lives of women elementary school teachers. If at any time you are uncomfortable answering any of the questions presented, please feel free to decline to answer. Please know that I have been a teacher myself and have the most possible respect and appreciation for your time and responses to the following questions.

Background Information:
- How/When did you decided to become a teacher?
- Thinking back on how you thought teaching would be when you initially decided to teach and the reality you live now, what are some of the main differences?
- Did you ever want to be anything other than a teacher? Tell me about the process of deciding to become a teacher and the struggles/joys around that decision.

The Life of a Teacher:
- What is something you just never have the time left over to do that you'd like to get done?
- What are some things that you have to do that you feel take away from what you'd like to be doing as a teacher?
- Remember a time recently when you've felt appreciated (either by a colleague, a student, an administrator, etc). What did they say or do that made you feel as though you are appreciated?
- Remember a time recently when you've felt underappreciated at work. What happened (what was said or not said/did or not done) that made you feel this way?
- What is the most frustrating part of teaching for you right now?
- What are your other responsibilities (outside of work)?
- Walk me though a typical day in your life.
- What do you love to do when you have free time?
- Who would you say are your main sources of support when you are struggling with balancing it all or when you are having a horrible day?
- What is the most frustrating part of trying to balance work and your other obligations?
- What comes to mind as something you are struggling with right now in balancing all of your roles?
- How do you make time for yourself?
- What do you enjoy doing when you have a free afternoon or evening?
- What does an excellent day look and feel like?
- When do you feel most accomplished?

Dexter time: the space, time, and matterings of school absence registration

Linnea Bodén (iD)

Working with a posthumanist approach, this article explores how the computer software Dexter, used for the registration of students' absences and presences, is part of the production of different practices of time, place, space, and matter in Swedish schools. The empirical material engaged with comes from two schools, and the students involved are in grades 7–9. The article creates knowledge on how the digital registration of students' presences, absences, or late arrivals is dependent upon material-discursive practices. The "bodily presences" of students are continually destabilized in relation to Dexter, showing that school absences and presences are (re) shaped depending on relations of spacetimematter.

A beginning: space, time, and computer software

Well, Max just said something about that: "I don't understand, in the morning ten minutes is like five seconds. In the evening, it's much slower." (Interview with Camilla, mother of Max, 9th grade, Sandö school)

When thinking about school absence and late arrivals, time clearly becomes a center of attention. The quote is about time and how time feels different during the morning on the way to school than in the evening. It is also, I would claim, a quote about having or not having breakfast, about toothbrushes, hair gel, school buses, the distance to the bus stop, hallways, classrooms, bodies being or not being in place, the schedule, and spare time at night. Or as Max himself expresses it:

You know, when the timetable for the bus was a bit kooky [i.e., it didn't match the start of the school day], you were forced to be late. And then the teacher had already registered it all in Dexter [computer software for the registration of the absences and presences of students] and we get an unexcused absence. (Max, student)

The 10 minutes that was five seconds in the morning can thus also be about having a late arrival registered.

In this article, I argue that absences or being late is not only about time but also about students being at school or not. Time, presence, and absence are always entangled with places and spaces, such as the distance to the bus stop or the hallway and different materialities: toothbrushes, buses, schedules, and computer software. Consequently,

I address how qualitative research can engage with such relations, both empirically and theoretically. New educational arrangements including digital technologies have made relations between space, time, and matter critical to educational practices (Bright, Manchester, & Allendyke, 2013; Duncheon & Tierney, 2013; Fenwick, Edwards, & Sawchuk, 2011), which means that actions in educational settings do not happen *in* space and time but can instead be theorized as *of* spacetimematters (Barad, 2007; Juelskjær, 2013). By exploring how computer software is part of producing different practices of time, place, space, and matter in schools, the aim of the article is to create knowledge on how students' absences/presences and on time/late arrivals are shaped and reshaped.

The approach of this article is posthumanist, where posthuman theory is:

> both a genealogical and a navigational tool … to explore ways of engaging affirmatively with the present, accounting for some of its features in a manner that is empirically grounded without being reductive and remains critical while avoiding negativity. (Braidotti, 2013, p. 5)

In educational research, posthumanism has often been understood as a symbolic decentring of the human subject, rather than a radical questioning of how (human) subjectivity as such is produced (Pedersen, 2010). Even though the focus for this article is not the production of subjectivity, this remark is important. To be able to research educational practices like school absence, a radical investigation of the relations – the intra-actions[1] – that produce absenteeism needs to be undertaken. Based on this, I will try to follow how "[s]pace, time, and matter are intra-actively produced in the ongoing differential articulation of the world" (Barad, 2007, p. 234) in relation to students' absences and presences in school. This means that space and place are not static or already existing, but always in the process of becoming. What is at issue is thus not time and space as relative (in relation to each other or to themselves) but rather that "intra-actions themselves matter to the making/marking of space and time" (Barad, 2007, p. 180). Space, time, and matter are thus continually constituted through intra-actions.

Returning to the opening quotation, it can be claimed that the space and time of Max's home are embedded in material-discursive relations (cf. Barad, 2007). Depending on those relations, 10 minutes are *both* "five seconds" and "much slower." As Massey (1999, p. 283) claims, space "is the product of relations, which are active practices, material and embedded, practices which have to be carried out, space is always in a process of becoming." Because each minute of potential unpunctuality will be registered digitally when arriving at school, time in the morning goes quickly whereas spare time at night seems slow and never-ending. One sees here an ongoing (re)shaping of relations of time and space that contrasts with time considered as a succession of repetitive and equal periods unrelated to bodies, materials, places, and spaces, in which a complex enactment is reduced to a linear progression (cf. Barad, 2007, p. 234; Duncheon & Tierney, 2013). Materialities and places are not passive entities, but always already a part of the production of practices of space and time in *spacetimemattering* (Barad, 2007).

Spacetimemattering in educational research

The idea that social (and material) actions are not only taking place but are making both place and space has come into social theory from geography, as space and place have become central concepts in studies of social, cultural, economic, and political relations (Gregory, 1994; Hubbard, Kitchin, & Valentine, 2004; Hubbard & Kitchin, 2010).

However, according to Gulson and Symes (2007), the take up off spatial theory in education has initially been slow (see also Allen, 2013; McGregor, 2004). Space and time *have* been given attention in educational research (recent examples: Alm, 2010; Grave, 2011; Skolverket, 2013), and the idea that the physical environment affects learning and teaching in schools is almost an axiom. The same applies to notions on time and temporalities, where studies have emphasized how students that "manage" their time well are more likely to succeed educationally (see for example Duncheon & Tierney, 2013). Still, studies focusing on, for example, how classrooms are designed and used (Fenwick et al., 2011) are often located within a positivist paradigm. And studies focusing on students' time management skills often view time as either linear and objective (in line with positivist assumptions) or as a social construction (Duncheon & Tierney, 2013). These points of departure tend to overlook how materialities and technologies are part of producing space and time.

However, evolving (posthumanist, I would add) theories open up for thinking on how materialities and technologies increasingly blur the borders of both educational spaces and temporalities (Duncheon & Tierney, 2013). To accomplish this, what needs to be researched is "the recursive interplay between the spatial and the social, the product of the complex ongoing relations" (McGregor, 2003, p. 363). From this point of view, schools can be understood as specific configurations of space and time that are continually remade (McGregor, 2003) and where relations of power, class, and gender (Allen, 2013; Gordon & Lahelma, 1996; Hopkins, 2010; O'Donoghue, 2007; Reimers, 2014; Shilling, 1991) are played out. This understanding can open up insight into the spatial and temporal dimensions underpinning educational processes and practices (Gulson & Symes, 2007), with studies focusing on how educational spaces and temporalities enable or disenable learning, create inclusion or exclusion, and open up or close down educational practices (Duncheon & Tierney, 2013; Fenwick et al., 2011). By creating new knowledge on the relations between space, time, matter, and technology, this article aims to contribute to what can be described as an under-researched area within educational studies: how (technological) artifacts in schools are part of, as well as produce, educational spatialities and temporalities.

Following the spacetimematterings of schools absence and presence

This main section of the article will introduce Dexter and the setting of the study. Subsequently, I will unfold some of the empirical engagements. The different sections necessarily overlap, but will focus on different practices of place/space, time, and matter in relation to Dexter and absences/presences.

The setting of the study

Dexter is the software for the registration of students' absences and presence in use in the Sandö school[2] (students in grades 3–9) and at the Björnäng school (students in grades 7–9). Teachers and school staff are able to log on to the system to report student absences and presence, but also to write student reports and e-mail students and parents. School staff are the only ones who interact with the system directly. However, a text messaging service is connected to Dexter and when a teacher registers an unexcused absence or a student arriving late for class, parents receive a text message on their phones. Messages are sent as soon as a registration is complete, at half-hour intervals – day and night – but only at the first registration, which means that parents will not receive more than one message a day. Since all absences registered in Dexter are transferred automatically into the computer system for grading, the only registration that is allowed is "bodily absence"; that is, a student's physically not being at the lesson. Teachers can make a note about someone being present without participating, but what is written in the notes will not be transferred to the system for grading, or become part of the messages to parents.

Dexter is used in many Swedish schools.[3] In the schools studied, the word "Dexter" has transformed from being solely the name of the software to being part of the everyday language related to school absence/presence. In an interview, one of the parents described her conversations with her daughter: "I got one Dexter today, I usually say. … Yes, I got Dexter today, and then she knows that we received a text message concerning … I guess that's what we call it at home." In a similar way, students frequently asked teachers if they "got Dexter" when they arrived (late) to class. When Zehbija (8th grade, Björnäng school) entered the classroom one afternoon, she asked "Hey, did we get Dexter?" and the teacher Britt answered her, laughing: "Yes, you got thirty seconds." In a similar way, teachers described how they would "dextra" the lesson – a Swedish transformation of the name of the software into a verb meaning "to do" the registration. Dexter seems to have become an integral part of the way parents, students, and teachers relate to school absence.

Like McGregor (2004), I am hoping to disrupt notions of what belongs to the "inside" and the "outside" of the school and its classrooms in relation to school absence. It can be claimed that the school is a constant aspect of students' homes by virtue of the text messages. In an interview, the mother of Evelina (8th grade, Björnäng school) described Dexter as part of her everyday life:

> I have a daughter with some trouble getting away to school in the morning, sometimes. So last week, I received five Dexters. That's not that funny. (Mother of student)

At the same time objects and practices that are primarily associated with the home or the society outside school constantly becomes part of the school (like the timetable of the bus Max took to school). The teacher Anna at the Sandö school describes how the text messages do not only affect the parents, but also teachers work: "We have decided on not registering a late arrival if it is less than five minutes, because of the messages sent to parents." The limits of what belongs to the school and what belongs to the students' homes are thus constantly blurred in relation to the software, and what happens inside the classroom is not separate from what is conceptualized as being outside it (McGregor, 2003).

In the article, I have therefore worked with notes made in classrooms, schoolyards, hallways, teachers' offices, canteens, gymnasiums, cafeterias, and so on of the two schools, as well as notes made on public transport rides on my way to/from the schools, at parent meetings and information meetings at the Educational Office, and more. In total, I spent around 110 hours at these different locations/events. To be able to create knowledge on the relations between Dexter and the ones affected by the practices surrounding the system, I also carried out four student group interviews at one of the schools (with 18 students in grade 9); interviews with teachers from both schools; intraviews[4] with Dexter and teachers (in total seven teachers and one student assistant participated in the interviews/intraviews); as well as interviews and group interviews with five parents from both schools. Students, teachers, and parents were asked about their relations to school absence and we discussed absenteeism, late arrivals, the formal school rules concerning the registration of absences and late arrivals, Dexter, the text messages sent through the system, and so on. Even though the empirical material I engage with in this article is produced in/with two schools, I have not focused on what distinguishes the schools from each other. Since the aim of the article is to create knowledge on how practices of absences/presences are shaped and reshaped in relation to digital registration, what becomes important is rather to focus on the relations between Dexter and events of spacetimematter in the educational settings, which will be shown in the following empirical engagements.

School places, school spaces

When looking at my notes from an afternoon at the Björnäng school, it became apparent that Dexter had become an ally to help teachers make students attend school activities even if the teacher had no possibility of knowing who was "bodily present":

> It's crafts lesson. Everyone is concentrated, quietly working at the sewing machines. Someone is humming, and two of the boys are helping each other. It's a very peaceful lesson, and the teacher Britt even says she doesn't have to bring the computer to the craft lessons, but can do the registrations afterwards, because there are seldom any unexcused absences or late arrivals.

> At the end of the lesson, Danielle asks what happens if she doesn't go to the gymnasium to watch students from one of the city's high schools do a music performance. Britt answers, "If you don't go, it becomes truancy, it becomes Dexter." Danielle questions her and asks how the teachers will know that the students weren't there. Britt responds, "Mats [the homeroom teacher of the class] will keep on eye on that, the homeroom teachers know."

> Later the same afternoon I follow the students to the show. The entire school is gathered in the gymnasium and the students are sitting and standing on the floor, climbing up the wall bars or moving around in the large room. The room is dark, with only some spotlights onstage. There isn't a chance for anyone to know who is there and who isn't. No one is doing the absence registration.

It can be claimed that the teacher is using the software as a threat to be able to control students' bodies, in relations between place and time. At the same time, resistance by students occurs, as Danielle seems to have noticed the limitations of Dexter in relation to particular places. However, when decentring the human meaning-making in this and similar events, it is possible to theorize Dexter as more than a system of control (and resistance), to instead view it as part of the relational material and embedded practices that produce places, spaces, and temporalities.

The quiet and peaceful atmosphere at the crafts lesson is in line with dominant discourses on how orderliness in schools enhances learning (see for example US Department of Education, 2014). The crafts classroom becomes "closed, coherent, integrated as authentic, as 'home,' a secure retreat" (Massey, 2005, p. 6), a distinctive, bounded, and timeless (or right-on-time) area that represents the ordinary of the everyday. In sharp contrast to this, the gymnasium and the music performance become, literally, the unknown and the dark that need to be – but at the same time cannot be – controlled by Dexter. A spatial dualism is created, between the classroom as a meaningful school area and areas like the gymnasium (when it is not used for PE) as outside the limits of what counts as good schooling (i.e., the meaningless). Some places are produced as indisputably good for learning, which makes Dexter seem unnecessary as the students are likely to be at the right place at the right time. Consequently, presence at other places becomes possible to question – as Danielle does – and important to defend – by the teacher mentioning that "it becomes Dexter" if students do not show up.

Well-known and demarcated areas (like classrooms) have sometimes been referred to as *places*, whereas the unknown "out-there" has been described as *spaces* (where places, cultures, and events are played out). However, critical approaches to theories on place and space have argued that places – just like spaces – are complex and shaped by particular power arrangements (Hubbard & Kitchin, 2010; Massey, 2005). A questioning of the distinction between space and place is called for since they are both "constructed through an ongoing and recursive ordering process, which involves things, people and events" (McGregor, 2004, p. 352). Refusing the distinction between the classroom as a place "in-here" and the gymnasium as a place "out-there," it can be claimed that both the classroom and the gymnasium are destabilized in relation to numerous intersecting material-discursive relations, of which Dexter is part. The classroom is destabilized in relation to the absences and presences of students' bodies, as no digital registration can be done in that particular place, because of the lack of a computer. And the gymnasium is destabilized, as the registration is impossible to perform. But, it is also a destabilization of Dexter in relation to the places/spaces which contradicts the notion of the software being a tool of control; the software is not really necessary in the classroom, and in the gymnasium it is too dark and the students are too many and too mobile for registrations to be possible. The impossibility of registering the activity in the gymnasium might even produce the event as something exterior to educational practice.

Presence after the present

How places and spaces are produced in relation to Dexter, and how this consequently (re) shaped school absences became manifest in the following episode, which started in the staffroom at the Sandö school:

> Leif enters the room with a folded bit of paper that he hands over to his colleague Agneta. Agneta looks at the paper, filled with names, and soon understands that it is a list showing the absent – or rather the present – students from the crafts lesson the same morning. The teacher was ill, so the fill-in teacher (who is unable to log on to Dexter) has written the names of all the present students, handed the list over to Leif who is supposed to hand it over to Agneta who will "dextra" the lesson.

> When we arrive at the teachers' office – after crossing the school yard, walking through the hallway on the ground floor, up the stairs and through another hallway – Agneta sits down in front of the computer, places the paper next to the keyboard, logs on to Dexter and chooses the headline in the drop down menu that says, "Register absence – Fill-in teacher." Agneta and I notice that the crafts lesson isn't registered since the symbol of the lesson is red on the overview of the schedule of the week. She continues the registration by comparing the names of students on the computer screen with the names written on the paper. She finishes by ticking the boxes in front of the names of the missing students and throws the paper in the paper bin.

The paper has to be taken through rooms and buildings and the absence of students is carried – in a very literal sense – in the hands of the teachers. Thinking about the paper as well as the computer software in terms of how they intra-act with the teachers enables an understanding of how these matters become necessary for the registration. One could claim that there would not be any present or absent students from this particular lesson without the paper or without Dexter. Through these intra-actions, school absence is materialized.

The paper is carried, and eventually ends up in the teachers' office, where the software is programmed to send a text message to parents of each absent student. Hence, the absence of students emerges several hours after the lesson. Presence in the classroom is not evident until the registration is done, in the teachers' office, which means that presence is not produced when it takes place (in the present) but afterward. A complex relation of spacetimematter is created, as the absences and presences travel through the school building and simultaneously through time, making it difficult to actually say when or where the absence occurs. This means that the absences or presences of the students do not exist solely in the classroom when the fill-in teacher writes the note or in the teachers' office as Agneta does the registration. It is a becoming that changes directions and significations as it is produced in different places at different times. As a student, it is not sufficient to attend the crafts lesson; what eventually counts as being present is what is registered in the computer software. There is an interesting tension between the requirement of the bodily presence of "the now" on the one hand – a constraint that is seemingly fixed and distinct – and the spatially and temporally floating movement that eventually produces presence (and following this, what is finally transferred to the grading system). In these material-discursive engagements, school absence in some sense becomes detached from the bodies of students, making it necessary to move the focus from individual students to how spatial practices are ordered in space and time (Fenwick et al., 2011).

Late arrivals in between clocks and closed doors

Repeatedly in the empirical engagements, the relations between materialities (like the paper above) and what was registered became important, in relation to absence and presence in general and to late arrivals in particular. That clocks were described as essential may come as no surprise. However, what made them substantial in relation to late arrivals was less expected:

> There isn't one, there is no lower limit. But I won't do less than five [minutes] because it has to do with clocks, so you can't do it. Yes, it's about the synchronisation of clocks, and we're not doing this to mess with people so to speak. (Interview with teacher Malin, Björnäng school)

As long as the school is dealing with clocks, time cannot be trusted. Whether they are clocks placed on the walls in the corridor, in the teachers' office, canteens and class rooms, or watches on the wrists of teachers and students (but more commonly on the students' mobiles phones) or on every computer screen where the registrations were performed, timepieces – the most taken for granted measurement of time – instead become the obstacle that produces time as inexact. Time almost becomes timeless. The intra-actions between the timepieces at the schools do not facilitate being on time but rather makes it more difficult. This has to be taken into account according to Malin, because a late arrival is not registered "to mess with people." The in-betweens of time, the different places/spaces where the clocks are placed and the matter of clocks themselves lead to questions about what can be registered and thus considered as a late arrival. However, the problems with synchronization show how relations of space, time, and matter always have loose ends and potential elements of change (Massey, 2005).

Still, five minutes as a limit kept returning throughout my empirical encounters. It emerged as a moderate limit, not too much and not too little to register. But, it became clear that five minutes was both more and something else than merely 300 seconds:

> Well, that's difficult, I have five minutes as a limit, you have closed the door, you have like started off the class, and then I have registered five minutes. But I haven't registered three, two, one or something like that. But I feel like if you close the door and begin the class and five minutes have passed, I can, I have made the registration. (Interview with teacher Maria, Sandö school)

The started or not-started lesson/briefing and the opened or closed door seem to order and structure time and space as well as bodies and artifacts in a specific way that relates back to social and material practices. It would be tempting to describe a closed door as a representation of a started lesson. However, drawing on posthumanist theorizing, in line with St Pierre (2013) and van der Tuin (2011), I question this representational logic and ask what practices materialities like a door produce in intra-actions, rather than seeing a door as already codified and inscribed with meaning (Grosz, 2005). The closed door and the practice of closing the door seem to reproduce the binary between the inside and the outside, where the classroom becomes associated with being on time at the right place while the outside, behind the door, becomes a space of lateness. The classroom is thus defined in relation to what is "out there"/ "in here" (Massey, 2005) and is always dependent on relations between an outside and an inside (Clarke, Harrison, Reeve, & Edwards, 2002). The door of the classroom for arts at the Sandö school was always locked, and the teacher had to open it for students on their way in (independent of their being late or not) as well as on their way out. The arts teacher Sanna explained to the class that that is the reason for waiting until everyone is outside the door before opening it – "Otherwise I'll get lots of late arrivals." The binary gets substantiated when these practices are related to what can be registered digitally. Only full minutes can be registered and there are no "in-between" options that allow for a registration to take into account the complexities of the school setting, where doors sometimes can only be opened from the inside.

The teacher Maria describes it as hard to know whether to register a student's arrival as late or not. "Well, I try to be precise. I have wondered, well, two minutes, would you take that [i.e., register that] or would you decided upon a limit, or how does it work?" When I asked her about her limits, and she answered "five minutes … you have closed the door," it became obvious that being late was not only about being in the classroom at the exact time the lesson was supposed to start. She stated that when "we all have just gotten into the classroom and everybody starts gathering their things, I haven't felt the need to register it," but it is different "if you have started the briefing." The student Madde (9th grade, Sandö school) had a similar description: "You know, five minutes, it's different you know, maybe the class has started and we have started to go through things and so. You know, one two minutes is just unnecessary, I think." Time seems to be something other than a measurement that can be estimated using clocks, rather it relates to temporal and situational practices like starting the briefing, and to materialities like a closed door. Time can thus be described as being far from a linear distinctively progressive unit. Rather, past events (for example, if someone has closed the door or not) and future events (for example, what will be registered) are implicated in one another and in the present (Barad, 2012, p. 44). What is produced as school absence thus contains affective traces of the past and of the future (see Renold & Ivinson, 2014).

At last: space–time–computer software

The empirical engagements of spacetimematterings in relation to the digital registration of school absence have created knowledge on how the registration of students' presences, absences, or late arrivals are dependent upon myriads of local and situational practices: the relations between classrooms and other areas, the papers with students' names that need to be carried through the school, closed or open classroom doors, the synchronization of clocks, the informal but widespread use of five minutes as a guiding precept in relation to late arrivals, and so on. By engaging in the seemingly mundane practices of the ordinary school day, the article shows how the combination of posthuman theory and empirical engagements produce new knowledge on how spatial, temporal, material, and technological events continuously affects education. These insights extend beyond the new understandings created of the digital registration of school absence discussed in this article and contribute to pushing the field of educational researching and writing forward.

Focusing on the different examples in the article highlights different properties of spacetimematterings and the practices produced in relation to Dexter: how places/spaces of absence/presence in relation to students bodies are continually (de)stabilized in relation to Dexter, how time and presence become detached from the present, and how materialities affect what is produced as absence or late arrival. What is common among these examples is that they are all moving moments that constitute school absences as fluid and as always dependent on intra-actions and relations. A consequence of this is that what is registered or not might be thought of as affected by serendipity. I would however claim that thinking about this in terms of randomness risks belittling the complexity of the material-discursive relations that constantly make the connections between time, space, and matter appear as absenteeism. What becomes important enough to register or not – what is produced as a "real" absence or late arrival – is fully dependent on these entanglements. And more radically, any simple connection between school absence and student bodies comes into question.

The anthropocentric and individualistic discourses, where school absences and school refusal behaviors are viewed as caused by maladjusted individuals and each student in the end is assigned both responsibility and blame, can thus be questioned (see for example Stroobant & Jones, 2006, for a critical examination of discourses alike). Nevertheless, when all these temporalities meet with Dexter, what is fluid, transitional, and variable has to be transformed into something stable and invariable since what is finally counted as absence is what is digitally registered. Either a student is in the classroom at the right time or s/he is not, and bodily presence is the only thing that matters, in both senses of the word. Full minutes are what can be registered and all the entanglements between spaces, times, and matters that in the empirical engagements seemed to create five minutes then disappear. When transferred to binary code, five minutes are always 300 seconds and time is reduced to a measurement of a temporal succession. Again, the software can be seen as rigid and as a system of unmitigated control of educational practices, but what then becomes important to notice is that *also* temporary practices are produced in relation to Dexter. The movement of the paper through the educational spaces, the distrust in clocks, and problems with locked doors all appear in relation to the software. The porosity of space and time, school absence, and Dexter becomes more apparent when the text messages are sent to parents. There is no causal relation between the time an absence takes place – and let us temporally assume that the absence takes place at the time a student is bodily absent from the classroom – and the time the parents receive the message. As has been shown, this depends for instance on when (and if!) the list of names ends up in the teachers' office or when the teacher does the registration.

The wavelike motion in time and space that seems to be created in relation to Dexter – from school absence and late arrivals as fluid, to fixed and back to fluid again – however does not change the fact that Dexter is a powerful agent that in intra-actions of spacetimematterings produces presences, unexcused absences, and late arrivals. Regarding the software as a neutral tool to be used to merely deter and to track school absences would be to underestimate both the possibilities and the difficulties of Dexter. In relation to school absence, Dexter is producing educational spaces and temporalities as before/in/after the presence of the present. It produces five minutes as a spatial and material practice rather than as a measurement of an elapsed amount of time. It produces Dexter time.

Acknowledgments

My sincerest thanks to Eva Reimers, Ann-Marie Markström, and Karin Gunnarsson for challenging discussions of the article, to Klara Arnberg, Helena Hill, and Linn Sandberg for encouraging comments at an early stage of the writing process, and to Paulina Semenec for her helpful generosity. I would also like to thank the two anonymous reviewers for productive remarks and Constance Ellwood for the proof reading.

Notes

1. The concept of intra-action is ontologically different from the more commonly known interaction, where interaction presupposes a pregiven split between the components while intra-action points at the mutually constitutional nature of the entanglements of the event.
2. All the names of places and people are pseudonyms. However, the name Dexter is not. Because of the widespread use of Dexter, using the actual name will not compromise confidentiality.
3. Over 80 % of municipalities in Sweden use similar software (Bodén, 2013).
4. The intraviews in my study can be described as a methodology used to question the anthropocentrism of the conventional qualitative interview. I performed the intraviews together with Dexter and teachers, where the software was regarded as an equally important "speaker" (cf. Bodén, 2014).

ORCID

Linnea Bodén ⓘ http://orcid.org/0000-0002-4197-304X

References

Allen, L. (2013). Behind the bike sheds: Sexual geographies of schooling. *British Journal of Sociology of Education, 34*(1), 56–75. doi:10.1080/01425692.2012.704719

Alm, F. (2010). *Uttryck på schemat och intryck i klassrummet: En studie av lektioner i skolor utan timplan [Expressions on the schedule, impressions in the classroom: A study of lessons in schools without a set timetable]* (Unpublished doctoral dissertation). Institutionen för beteendevetenskap och lärande [Department of Behavioural Sciences and Learning], Linköping.

Barad, K. (2007). *Meeting the universe half way: Quantum physics and the entanglement of matter and meaning.* Durham: Duke University Press.

Barad, K. (2012). Nature's queer performativity. *Kvinder, Køn og Forskning, 21*(1–2), 25–54. Retrieved from https://tidsskrift.dk/index.php/KKF/article/viewFile/51863/95446

Bodén, L. (2013). *Absence on the computer screen. A study on digital systems for the registration of presence and absence in Swedish compulsory schools.* Unpublished manuscript.

Bodén, L. (2014). The presence of school absenteeism: Exploring methodologies for researching the material-discursive practice of school absence registration. *Cultural Studies ⇔ Critical Methodologies.* Advance online publication. doi:10.1177/1532708614557325

Braidotti, R. (2013). *The posthuman.* Cambridge and Malden, MA: Polity Press.

Bright, G., Manchester, H., & Allendyke, S. (2013). Space, place and social justice in education: Growing a bigger entanglement. *Qualitative Inquiry, 19*, 747–755. doi:10.1177/1077800413503794

Clarke, J., Harrison, R., Reeve, F., & Edwards, R. (2002). Assembling spaces: The question of 'place' in further education. *Discourse: Studies in the Cultural Politics of Education, 23*, 285–297. doi:10.1080/0159630022000029786

Duncheon, J. C., & Tierney, W. G. (2013). Changing conceptions of time: Implications for educational research and practice. *Review of Educational Research, 83*, 236–272. doi:10.3102/0034654313478492

Fenwick, T. J., Edwards, R., & Sawchuk, P. (2011). *Emerging approaches to educational research: Tracing the sociomaterial*. Abingdon: Routledge.

Gordon, T., & Lahelma, E. (1996). 'School is like an ant's nest': Spatiality and embodiment in schools. *Gender & Education, 8*, 301–310. doi:10.1080/09540259621548

Grave, B. S. (2011). The effect of student time allocation on academic achievement. *Education Economics, 19*, 291–310. doi:10.1080/09645292.2011.585794

Gregory, D. (1994). *Geographical imaginations*. Oxford: Blackwell.

Grosz, E. (2005). *Time travels: Feminism, nature, power*. Durham and London: Duke University Press.

Gulson, N. K., & Symes, C. (2007). Knowing one's place: Space, theory, education. *Critical Studies in Education, 46*(1), 97–110. doi:10.1080/17508480601123750

Hopkins, P. E. (2010). *Young people, place and identity*. Abingdon: Routledge.

Hubbard, P., & Kitchin, R. (2010). *Key thinkers on space and place* (2nd ed.). London: SAGE.

Hubbard, P., Kitchin, R., & Valentine, G. (2004). Editor's introduction. In P. Hubbard, R. Kitchin, & G. Valentine (Eds.), *Key thinkers on space and place* (pp. 1–15). London: SAGE.

Juelskjær, M. (2013). Gendered subjectivities of space time matter. *Gender and Education, 25*, 754–768. doi:10.1080/09540253.2013.831812

Massey, D. (1999). Spaces of politics. In D. Massey, J. Allen, & P. Sarre (Eds.), *Human geography today* (pp. 279–294). Cambridge and Oxford: Malden.

Massey, D. (2005). *For space*. London: SAGE.

McGregor, J. (2003). Making spaces: Teacher workplace topologies. *Pedagogy, Culture & Society, 11*, 353–377. doi:10.1080/14681360300200179

McGregor, J. (2004). Spatiality and the place of the material in schools. *Pedagogy, Culture & Society, 12*, 347–372. doi:10.1080/14681360400200207

O'Donoghue, D. (2007). 'James always hangs out here': Making space for place in studying masculinities at school. *Visual Studies, 22*(1), 62–73. doi:10.1080/14725860601167218

Pedersen, H. (2010). Is 'the posthuman' educable? On the convergence of educational philosophy, animal studies, and posthumanist theory. *Discourse: Studies in the Cultural Politics of Education, 31*, 237–250. doi:10.1080/01596301003679750

Reimers, E. (2014). Discourses of education and constitutions of class: Public discourses on education in Swedish PBS television. *Discourse: Studies in the Cultural Politics of Education, 35*, 540–553. doi:10.1080/01596306.2013.871228

Renold, E., & Ivinson, G. (2014). Horse-girl assemblages: Towards a posthuman cartography of girls' desire in an ex-mining valleys community. *Discourse: Studies in the Cultural Politics of Education, 35*, 361–376. doi:10.1080/01596306.2014.888841

Shilling, C. (1991). Social space, gender inequalities and educational differentiation. *British Journal of Sociology of Education, 12*(1), 23–44. doi:10.1080/0142569910120102

Skolverket [The Swedish National Agency for Education]. (2013). *En tidsgeografisk studie av strukturen i lärares vardag [A time-geographical study on teachers' working days]*. Stockholm: Fritzes.

St Pierre, E. A. (2013). The appearance of data. *Cultural Studies ⇔ Critical Methodologies, 13*, 223–227. doi:10.1177/1532708613487862

Stroobant, E., & Jones, A. (2006). School refuser child identities. *Discourse: Studies in the Cultural Politics of Education, 27*, 209–223. doi:10.1080/01596300600676169

US Department of Education. (2014). *Guiding principles: A resource guide for improving school climate and discipline*. Washington, DC: Author.

van der Tuin, I. (2011). Gender research with 'waves': On repositioning a neodisciplinary apparatus. In R. Buikema, G. Griffin, & N. Lykke (Eds.), *Theories and methodologies in postgraduate feminist research: Researching differently* (pp. 15–28). London and New York, NY: Routledge.

Diffractive pedagogies: dancing across new materialist imaginaries

Anna Hickey-Moody, Helen Palmer and Esther Sayers

ABSTRACT

We theorise an interdisciplinary arts practice university course and consider the forms of educational imaginary challenged by our curriculum. We argue for the disruptive and generative potential of what we call diffractive pedagogy as an example of the type of learning that can take place when materiality and entanglement are considered as vital constituents. Through self-expression and interweaving across disciplinary boundaries, the potential to produce, embody and theorise simultaneously can be realised. Student bodies do not exist in isolation from one another, or from the environment. It is indeed impossible to separate the dancer from the dance, the teacher from the student, and the bodies from the environments and objects to which they relate. This being true, our student body reproduced our teaching bodies as abject, as messy and peripheral to their imaginings of university education. Materially, student bodies remade the limits to which their consciousness was imaginatively drawn. Through our embodied work, unconscious change began the processes of affecting students' imaginaries of university education.

Women, as a class, have provided thought for far too long with images or metaphors for whatever vice or virtue. (Gatens 1996, 135)

Ontological indeterminacy, a radical openness, an infinity of possibilities, is at the core of mattering. (Barad 2012a, 2012b, 16)

These quotes identify two issues that are central to our approach to bodies: art and pedagogy. Firstly: that what is uncomfortable, unthought, indeterminate, is unconsciously feminised. Secondly: that this process of feminising the new puts finite boundaries on what might be made to matter. In this paper, we reflect conceptually and philosophically on the kinds of political and pedagogical problems that may arise when university curricula are opened up to arts practice-based learning. We consider the ways in which the bodies involved in such generative processes of mattering can become controlled by fear such that what is made to matter can become (self-)policing. But we also argue that embodied creative processes employed in pedagogical contexts can challenge and extend those engaged in learning, allowing them to find modalities and forms of expression other than those that reproduce stereotypical constructions of their identity or dominant tropes of representation. We are thus concerned both with the preconceptions and the complexities of representation that can arise in arts-based educational programmes, and with the potential of *non*-representationalist, 'diffractive' thinking (on which we will expand later) for approaching the materiality of making and learning through art.

To address these joint concerns, we consider the ways in which movement, form, materiality and gesture might be reimagined through dance and film, constructing and performing identities in relation to, for instance, urban landscapes, gendered bodies or unequal power relations. For example, rigid ideas and preconceptions of British Muslim femininity, which operates as a particularly powerful trope and image at these times, can be undone by critical, aesthetic engagements with lived contexts and the power relationships embedded in everyday life, challenging social perceptions of the silenced or subservient woman. While anxieties may sometimes arise about whether or not contemporary movement practices, such as those found in dance and film, are entirely congruent with a religious identity, such practices can also offer a different lens on femininity, providing a means of critically reflecting on and even developing religious identities. As we discuss further below, experimental practices mean embracing the unknown and sitting with the discomfort that the unknown can bring.

Creative practices allow for the remaking of reductive and historically determined images, figures or metaphors that are routinely assigned to differently gendered, differently abled, and diversely classed and raced bodies. Building on a feminist investment in the agency of materiality, we think through the problem of the body as a site of learning, raising questions about how diverse bodies might fit in those environments that have traditionally suspended the body altogether, such as the university. As Probyn writes in her article 'Teaching Bodies',

> We may often teach potentially 'messy' topics like embodiment or sexual identity. At the same time the zone of contact between student and teacher is heavily policed by ourselves and our institutions. So while we offer material that potentially sets off lines of flight, we then have to continually re-territorialize the very bodies that have been set in motion through our teaching. It's a situation that is bound to veer towards abstraction, and at times a lifeless rendition of hot subjects. (2004, 35)

Learning in higher education is popularly thought to pertain to the transfer of abstract historical and theoretical knowledge (Coffey 2013), and this process typically occurs in ways that largely ignore the physicality of learning. Attempting to change this in a student ('consumer')-driven higher education climate can be extremely difficult, in ways that seem to relate to an imagining of 'legitimate' education as pertaining solely to the transfer of abstract, historically reified thought. The body, coded as feminine, or the material, remains relegated to the abject (Kristeva 1984a, 1984b).

Conversely, arts-based curricula call on students to rethink, re-feel and remake their understandings of their bodies, together with their imaginings of *what a learning body might be*, by working practically and inventively through movement and gesture. This process of invention can be facilitated through movement practices undertaken individually, in pairs, or in small class groups. For example, to explore the theme of freedom and control, students might be asked to create a freedom image and a control image, with these images becoming a score for two movements, a freedom movement and a control movement. Students can be supported by staff to adapt or rework these movements across scales (giant and tiny freedom and control movements) and levels (low, medium and high freedom and control movements). Through choreographic scaffolds, students might be encouraged to devise a solo freedom and control dance, teaching these to a partner in order to build a freedom and control duet. Each duet might have to include certain elements such as a run, a roll, a reach or a weight share, as well as both students' freedom and control dances. The pairs could then be asked to put themselves together in groups of four to make a longer dance, building on the visual and choreographic material they have collectively generated.

Across such series of embodied creative processes, students might also be asked to create images and dances that are subsequently filmed and/or to develop original sounds-capes, built on recording the sounds of their bodies moving in space. An approach such as this, involving a series of creative productions and translations, may be met with reluc-tance by some, in particular when faced with the task of using their bodies to explore the broad directives of freedom and control. A pedagogical system that presents repeated structures and patterns of abstract discourse is often more familiar to students, and when asked to improvise within a choreographic structure, they can sometimes fail to see the logic of this, feeling that they are not learning anything of value, or at least unsure as to the value of the process with which they are being asked to engage. Working in small groups is often challenging for students across a range of disciplines, but in arts-based education in particular, this can cause a number of logistical and perceptual pro-blems as they navigate the encounters of their bodies, their movement through space, and their relationships to their own bodies and those of others in both movement and still-ness. Students are of course constructed at least in part by the system in which they have been educated, and in western educational settings, they are typically taught to work towards their own learning goals individually. Some may feel anxieties about the openness of a practice-based task, while others will be excited to have creative space to play.

Student apprehensions in relation to their own learning often point towards precon-ceptions about how university teachers should teach, as well as the kinds of knowledges that universities should impart. But this can shift through practices that change imaginings of what legitimate knowledge looks (and feels) like. Vehicles for learning that involve experimentation and creation, underpinned by those feminist philosophical imaginaries that see matter as generative, can be received with mistrust at first. Through no fault of their own, students often value preconceived and representational models of thought and expression. We feel that such a disembodied, *re*productive, rather than productive, philosophical imaginary requires reconfiguring. There must be ways to allow for embodied and creative learning processes that are open-ended, nomadic (Braidotti 1996; Roy 2003) and affirmative. Yet the difficulty of this task leads us to reflect more deeply on why exper-imentation, and the inclusion of the body in the curriculum, matter.

Mattering

The turn to matter within feminist thought has foregrounded the generative qualities of materiality and of working with the body. Feminist and new materialist scholarship together demonstrate the co-implication of bodies and subjectivities within the process of moving and making. It is important to note this co-implicated and relational nature of the 'matter' of the new materialisms, as well as the fact that this field embodies a profound movement beyond a Cartesian mind–body dualism. Both conceptual shifts are pedagogically significant in that bodies are endowed with agency and complexity, and resist being posited as inferior to language or discourse. Barad's neologism *intra-activity* allows us to see this:

> The notion of *intra-action* (in contrast to the usual 'interaction,' which presumes the prior existence of independent entities/relate) represents a profound conceptual shift. It is through specific agential intra-actions that the boundaries and properties of the 'components' of phenomena become determinate and that particular embodied concepts become meaningful. (2003, 815)

Intra-activity is a concept grounded in philosophies of immanence. There is no 'beyond' the body; rather, the focus shifts to a 'between' located *in, with*, and *through* the body. As enacted 'material-discursive phenomena' (Barad 2003, 821), bodies are inseparable from discursive practices. Colebrook's position, whilst different to Barad's in significant respects, nevertheless highlights the way that the body produces itself through matter, and is useful in conjunction with Barad's theory of intra-action in terms of the infusion of concepts with material meaning. Colebrook advocates a feminist 'critical vitalism' (2005, 53), which refuses the idea that matter requires thought to grant it meaning. She reminds us of the link between the modern notion of dynamism and the Greek *dynamis* or potentiality, which was always on its way to actualisation or *energia* (58). 'Bodies matter, not because they cause our being, but because the living of them *as material* – as is the very nature that is our own – is made possible only through regarding ourselves as subjects, as beings who have some recognizable, repeatable, and accountable identity' (68). Here we see a dual understanding of the verb 'to matter', which has become an important facet of new materialist thought. Bodies matter *as matter*; they matter because they are important but they exist through their material *mattering*. Bodies therefore *are* discursive practices themselves, and they are inseparable from the environments in which they move, shape and express themselves. A dance move performed by a body is a meaningful, particular and embodied concept. It is a discursive practice that can be read as we read a text, and does not need to become text in order for this to happen. As Minh-ha (1989) points out below, becoming does not require transitivity. This does not mean that it expresses nothing; rather, the language it uses does not require translation to be understood.

There is evidence from multiple disciplinary sources that embodied, aesthetic experience can produce subjectivities in very direct ways. Diverse artistic practices can demonstrate this. For example, Coleman (2009) writes about the becoming of female bodies through their experiences of media images. Coleman argues that subjectivities are not merely affected but rather produced through girls' relationships with such images. Minh-ha, on the other hand, writes about the 'intransitive' nature of writing as becoming:

> To write is to become. Not to become a writer (or a poet) but to become, intransitively. Not when writing adopts keynotes or policy, but when it traces for itself lines of evasion. (1989, 18)

In a similar vein, non-representationalist or 'diffractive' forms of writing and reading have been championed as specifically feminist tools through van der Tuin's work – see for example her reading of Chantal Chawaf (van der Tuin 2014). As this work shows, diffraction has been taken up and developed by feminist scholars who have transformed it from a scientific model into an analytic tool and then, further, a methodology for dismantling patriarchal structures. Haraway (1997) and Barad (2007) both discuss diffraction as a dynamic, non-linear method of reading and writing in which stable epistemological categories are challenged, temporalities are disrupted and disciplines are complexified. More specifically, Barad develops Haraway's use of diffraction as a metaphor for rethinking the geometry and optics of relationality into a 'mutated critical tool of analysis' (2003, 802 n.3).

Diffractive analysis, then, can operate as an alternative method of analysis that pays attention to both relationality and material agency. Taguchi details what she terms a diffractive analysis in terms of a 'transcorporeal process of becoming-minoritarian with the data', where 'the researcher is attentive to those bodymind faculties that register smell, touch, level, temperature, pressure, tension and force in the interconnections emerging in between different matter, matter and discourse, in the event of engagement with data' (2012, 267). This 'data' might be quantitative, or equally it could be a text or a dancing body. A diffractive reading, then, resists the hierarchisation of one type of meaning over another. As van der Tuin (2014) explains, diffractive methodologies can aid feminism because the modes of perception and creation are shifted and women's bodies and subjectivities are no longer produced by or for men.

Such feminist potential need not only be perceived in the diffractive acts of writing and reading. We argue that dance is an analogous process that may also be read diffractively. Elsewhere Hickey-Moody (2009a, 2009b, 2009c, 2013) has written about young people's individual and group subjectivities *becoming* through dance practices. Extending Minh-ha's statement above, we recognise that to dance is also to become. Not to become 'a dancer', but to become, intransitively. This happens because dancing allows pasts to fold back into presents in unexpected ways, bodies are pushed to become other than who they have been, and corporeal forms are changed physically and emotionally. Movement practices can remind us that: 'Bodies, ultimately the instruments that write dance, are living testimonies to the fact that all texts are a composition of different times' (Hickey-Moody, 2009a, 2009b, 2009c, 62). As non-representational, non-linear, spatiotemporally complex practices, the link between dancing and writing has been made across multiple disciplines and times. A famous example of such a trans-disciplinary link is Valéry's (1958) alignment of prose with walking, poetry and dancing, which demonstrates the self-styling, self-making and self-creating aspect of dance.

Bringing theoretical perspectives together through arts practices informed by feminist approaches to materiality on the one hand, and ideas of the body-becoming popularised through the work of Deleuze and Guattari (1987) on the other, can generate frames for thinking about the body as productive of subjectivity. Producing and experiencing images and moving the body changes how people feel about, and see, their bodies (Featherstone 2010). This focus on the embodied, experiential production of subjectivity is not new. The work of generations of feminist theorists is particularly valuable in this respect. This includes, but is not limited to, Blackman (2008a, 2008b, 2012), Gallop (1988), Grosz (1994), Gatens (1996) and Barad (2012a, 2012b). However, in spite of substantive literature accounting for the fact that bodies are produced, with the notable exceptions of Gallop (1988) and Ellsworth (1997), bodies in higher education tend to be thought about as being governed (Gilmour 1991) rather than being remade or regenerated. This pervasive discourse on governance needs to be countered. Taking into account the level of embodied confidence required for students to give their body license to co-create their own movements, phrases and creative concepts, and consequently the difficulties many of them face in meeting this challenge, movement-as-learning is a central empirical focus for contemporary feminist-materialist pedagogy.

Nowhere in the creative process do students more directly embody the entanglement of matter and meaning (Barad 2007) than when they use their bodies to generate expressive movement, and nowhere do they struggle more in permitting themselves to produce their own subjectivities than through a creative act. Many young people in Britain are negotiating complex self-constructions of multi-faceted identities, sometimes navigating a path between family tradition and contemporary urban life. Those who are British-born and come from migrant families, for example, are often very aware of their 'journeys from invisibility to visibility and from the periphery to the core of social life' (Hoque 2015, back cover). Students in general often need to experience a sense of belonging, to be and feel visible and to 'own' their learning pathways. However, students in higher education often arrive at their institutionalised learning experience wanting, or at least expecting, to be governed or well-schooled in modes of disembodied learning that are based on a disavowal or suppressing of the body. This is learned through a pre-university education system that is purported to 'spoon feed' students so that they can pass exams (Smith 2008; Samah, Jusoff, and Silong 2009). The proposition of unlearning this attitude to knowledge acquisition can be embedded in the use of dance as a methodology for teaching and learning creative processes in higher education. This is highly challenging for some students, as they are asked to engage with significant processes of *unlearning* in order to participate. An educational and social imaginary that produces students who are so uncomfortable with using their bodies to learn in the classroom needs to be redressed.

In *Material Thinking*, Carter (2004) explains that 'the language of creative research is related to the goal of material thinking, and both look beyond the making process to the local reinvention of social relations' (10). Building on the change that Carter advocates through creative processes of *Material Thinking*, Barrett (2007) proposes that 'artistic practice be viewed as the production of knowledge or philosophy in action' and specifically suggests that '[t]he emergence of the discipline of practice-led research highlights the crucial inter-relationship that exists between theory and practice and the relevance of theoretical and philosophical paradigms for the contemporary arts practitioner' (1). 'Making' produces new thought, but such thought is often disavowed and devalued through processes of feminisation and abjection. The reluctance to learn through dance can demonstrate some of these processes, in particular for young people who understand dance as always sexualised. For example, expressive movement performed by a female dancer is often seen in the first instance as inextricably linked to sexualisation and provocation, which is problematic for those young women whose commitment to a religious identity mitigates precisely against such sexualisation or objectification. Substantive pedagogical work needs to be undertaken with all students to explain that moving the body might not be explicitly sexual or necessarily provocative. It might, like walking or sitting, be very pedestrian.

New materialist thought enables us to build on some of the now established debates around creative practice as research, and to question the lived limits of educational imaginaries in university classrooms. The inseparability of theory and practice, and indeed of theory and matter, is a clear example. New materialism posits matter as indeterminate, constantly forming and re-forming in unexpected ways (Coole and Frost 2010), and thus abandons any idea of matter as inert and subject to predictable forces. Matter is agentive and is always becoming. Matter 'feels, converses, suffers, desires, yearns and remembers' and, since 'feeling, desiring and experiencing are not singular characteristics or capacities of human consciousness' (Dolphin and van der Tuin 2012, 16), new materialism offers a re-definition of animacy or live-ness as well as of human-non-human relations. The implications of such a revisioning are that knowledge is immanent, contingent and produced through human-matter intra-actions. Barad explains that

> … what is needed is a robust account of the materialization of *all* bodies – 'human' and 'non-human' – including agential contributions of all material forces (both 'social' and 'natural'). This will require an understanding of the nature of the relationship between discursive practices and material phenomena; an accounting of 'nonhuman' as well as 'human' forms of agency; and an understanding of the precise causal nature of productive practices that take account of the fullness of matter's implication in its ongoing historicity. (2012a, 2012b 66)

Bodies and things are not separate, and their inter-(and intra-)relationships are vital both to how we come to know ourselves as human and to how we interact with our environments. The ways in which students can be called upon relate to each other and themselves in our arts practice classrooms can draw upon memory, culture, religion, and politics via methods that may be radically different from those through which students are typically invited to see themselves and relate to others in theory based learning environments.

Barad's theories of entanglement demonstrate that we only exist in relation to our own environment; that 'the very ontology of the entities [that is, the objects under investigation, the inquiring scientist and the apparatus] emerges *through* relationality: the entities do not preexist their involvement' (Kirby 2011, 76). Barad's agential realism is both an epistemological and an ontological practice, incorporating both the human and the non-human and transcending the opposition of realism and social constructivism. In order to demonstrate how matter comes to matter in specific circumstances or practices, we must ask what possibilities exist for agency within material-discursive phenomena. For Barad (2003, 825), agential separability is a welcome alternative to the unsatisfactory differentiation between the geometries of absolute exteriority on the one hand (determinism), and absolute interiority (or free will) on the other. Matter is dynamic and active in its own iterability; the result is an 'ongoing topological dynamics of enfolding whereby the spacetimematter manifold is enfolded into itself (Barad 2007, 177; Deleuze 1993). Despite the supposed implications of the term 'separability', on Barad's account there is in fact no separation between the measuring and the measured, the observer and the observed. Following Barad, but also drawing on Deleuze and Guattari, Taguchi posits a 'collective-body-assemblage researcher subjectivity' which produces 'a different kind of knowing produced in a co-constitutive relation between matter and discourse where it is impossible to pull apart the knower from the known' (2013, 715).

In a pedagogical space, then, the distinction between the teacher and the taught can be equally problematised. We understand the 'taught' here to be both the teaching 'material' (the curriculum; the course content; reading matter; theory) and the learning subjects. All are mutually implicated and embodied. Barad draws attention to scientific apparatus as phenomena *itself* and 'not preformed interchangeable objects that sit atop a shelf waiting to serve a particular purpose' (2003, 816). Neither are teachers or teaching materials simply preformed; teachers, students, objects and spaces are equally material phenomena and similarly entwined with one another. The movements made by students engaged in arts practice learning might involve extant or emergent material interventions such as taped lines across the floors and walls, strokes made by paintbrushes, lines of musical notation, or soundwaves. The material-discursive entanglements or intra-actions that are the condition under which agential separability emerges allow for a future which is 'radically open at every turn' (826). This radical openness is precisely what students can feel as a challenge. Indeed, this is why it is often more generative to give a brief to students that is deliberately open, consisting only of the requirements to express freedom and control, for example, whilst including a number of particular bodily movements.

As a way of exploring this entanglement and co-constitution of matter and subjectivity, new materialism has emerged as a methodology, a theoretical framework and a political positioning and emphasises the complex materiality of bodies immersed in social relations of power (Dolphin and van der Tuin 2012). Inventive methods (Lury and Wakeford 2012), including arts-based (Jagodzinski and Wallin 2013) and visual methods (Pink 2007; Rose 2012), are increasingly being mobilised to explore the agency of matter and advance vitalist frameworks. Drawing on such approaches, practice-based creative arts curricula, in particular, are able to mobilise the intra-actions of theory with practice so as to develop new approaches to materialist pedagogy and research. Here the agency of matter is positioned as both pedagogical and resistant. Matter teaches us through resisting dominant discourses and showing new ways of being. Bodies resist dominant modes of positioning, political actions defy government rule, sexuality exceeds legal frameworks – resistant matter shows us the limits of the world as we know it, and prompts us to shift these limits.

Re-making bodies

Creativity, in relation to learning, is understood by us as that activity that produces something new, such as an idea or a tangible output. This is most likely to occur when courses are transdisciplinary and pedagogically multi-modal, offering a means to engage with and give voice to a multiplicity of learner subjectivities. Combining theory with practice can shift the focus onto students' experience of creative practice across a range of contexts (Dewey 1934; Greenland 2000; Craft, Jeffrey, and Leibling 2001; Burnard 2012). In this way, students can be invited to work, think and make within and across a range of spaces such as the art studio, computer lab and performing arts spaces. Introductory sessions can be used to encourage students to identify and reflect on the nature of creativity and creative learning through analysis of their biographical experiences. This can then be built upon through engagement in subsequent course activities, lectures and workshop discussions, and focused reading. The translation of abstract, textual knowledge into creative experimentation in turn needs to be modelled in taught sessions. Nevertheless, it can be understandably difficult for students – particularly those who are unfamiliar with creative processes – to trust themselves to new learning environments that involve developing experimental practices. Issues of confidence and ownership of their own creative practice/body/action can plague the student experience, even though those teaching and working with them may offer enthusiastic encouragement. Specific strategies need to be developed so as to counter this lack of confidence, such as the use of tape, as mentioned above, to allow students to record a trace of their movements through a space, helping them produce a drawing of their actions. This kind of activity gives tangible purpose to movement, and can help to build confidence, not least when the activity requires a student to share their movement with others (such as a partner who records the direction of travel with the tape).

In our view, it is also important to involve students in researching the very notion of creativity and to introduce them to key theoretical concepts that explore different aspects of creativity. This needs to be complemented with practical elements to allow students to explore creative production progressively and through a range of different methodologies, including, for example, visual, audio, film, and performance-based media. In this way, students can make links between processes in different fields and expand their own conceptual and procedural understanding of creative learning and practice. Again, guidance through a series of exercises in which different forms of movement are explored can support the emergence of such understanding. As indicated above, providing parameters through a theme can better afford creative and experimental responses to delimited tasks: thus, the contrasting ideas of freedom and control can provide a focus for several weeks of work using paint, movement, and drawing as exploratory media. Mobilising this transdisciplinary approach invites a range of aesthetic explorations that extends beyond one particular artistic form. One experimental methodology and line of enquiry might begin with creating a visual object to demonstrate the meanings that students attribute to key words or concepts. From this starting point, movement phrases can be devised during sessions in which that visual object is used as a catalyst. A lengthy warm up can encourage the use of the body as an expressive tool while certain group 'rules' can be set to counteract feelings of self-conscious exposure, which are almost inevitable in work of this kind (such rules might, for example, state that no one is to look at another during the exercise; that everyone should concentrate on their own movements; and that there should be no talking and no laughing at anyone else). In this way, students can learn through their subjective experience to push themselves beyond the immediate discomfort of something new and challenging, but not to be objectified by it. From such a starting point, movements might be developed over several weeks and eventually filmed (by the students) and set to sound compositions.

Developing student understanding using this kind of approach can be difficult, as students often prefer to be led or guided rather than to work with, and develop, their own ideas. As they engage more fully in this process, however, certain factors will begin to influence their decision-making when engaging in an activity such as filming. Some students might choose a narrative sequence in which the identity of performers is revealed, for example, while others might use techniques of abstraction in order to conceal the identity of the dancers. Preserving the freedom to make such decisions is important as this enables students to explore their movements in ways that can sit comfortably with their developing identity constructions, thus avoiding situations in which the curriculum and expected outcomes determine a particular approach that could be uncomfortable or counter-productive for some.

This kind of curriculum is about creativity in the context of learning. It involves developing a theoretical understanding alongside engaging with the processes of creativity through action. Often teachers at university level face mixed cohorts, in terms of prior experience, so that the questions of what to teach, and what level to teach to, are ever present. In the case of education students in particular, it is questionable how useful it would be for them to acquire specific or traditional art-making techniques such as learning to paint, work with clay or produce digital imaging. A broad understanding of what creativity is and does is of more use. It is to this end that we suggest that arts-based curricula (particularly when deployed in education departments) ought to employ a combination of media such as the moving image, sound, movement and conceptual thinking, even if such progressive strategies can be alienating for those who expect a traditional curriculum. In our view, the difficulty with conservative or 'traditional' fine art curricula is that they do not sufficiently allow either the traditional student or the student new to art to become distinctive. A curriculum that focuses on an embodied understanding of creativity seems to be the most productive way forward in terms of developing students' sense of singularisation, expression and becoming. As Dewey (1934) argues, aesthetic experience develops imagination that allows us to challenge old perceptions with new ones. By creating aesthetic experiences of their own, students become better equipped to imagine new possibilities for creativity and learning.

While it can certainly be more straightforward to create learning experiences in the arts and education that offer students discrete instruction in, say, film, music, dance or the visual arts, we suggest that a sustained creative experience across the four art forms is more valuable. Such an integrated approach fosters a better understanding of the ways in which creative processes inform one another, rather than separating these domains of thought and practice into discrete methodological bubbles. The teaching of creativity also needs to exceed its own boundaries and to 'leak across' and inform other aspects of students' learning experience. This can be difficult to achieve given the constraints of timetabling, room booking, staff availability and the more general structures that force education to be contained into individualised pockets of time, though one can usually find ways of working within even severely constrained environments. The materiality of those less-than-ideal spaces will itself inflect practice and work made. Adopting a transdisciplinary process, one can set specific yet flexible goals for students, such as making one artefact together using four different media, which in turn might serve as a prompt for a movement scenario developed in dance workshops, which might subsequently be filmed and overlaid with a soundtrack. In turn, this might become the basis and inspiration for a piece of textual interpretation that is written up and subsequently performed.

Rather than following traditional lecture or seminar formats, embodied practices such as dance classes need to be active, participatory and collective experiences in which everyone present is expected to take part. This format means that no one is allowed to 'sleep at the back'. Rooms of an adequate size and comfort are required for any performance-based sessions, but due to limits on space and complexities of timetabling, this is sometimes impossible; so one has to adapt to the limitations of spaces available. Practical and circumstantial environmental issues of architecture, heat, space and materiality (sometimes all too concrete) profoundly affect the ways in which students engage with learning, particularly when that learning is challenging and both physically and conceptually outside of their comfort zone. The materiality of learning matters and comes to make matter. It is the very materiality of experience here that tends to affect the students' abilities, willingness and motivation to respond openly and creatively to tasks set. The negotiation of challenge and reward is an important aspect of the creative process (Csikszentmihalyi 2009). It can be a struggle to devise a curriculum that contains enough challenge to be engaging but not so much as to be alienating. Students can also be uncomfortable with the requirement that everyone should join in, and one has to explore ways of teaching movement that can be achieved in ordinary classrooms, for example, keeping off the floor if it is a cold concrete surface. Rather than the room or the learner being at fault, a pedagogy that fails to adapt to the space and the learner requires further attention; all learning is material, after all.

When the environment is cold and uncomfortable, the body makes decisions. That decision can be to stop attending class, to leave or to refuse to engage. In an efficiency-driven machine such as a contemporary university, insisting upon a suitable room as an essential component of teaching can be seen as non-essential. We want to insist that taking matter seriously and attending to the corporeal in order to make learning effective is an important issue; where the environment is difficult or inadequate, it requires pedagogical solutions to mitigate against the negative effect of discomfort. The physicality of creative learning in higher education has thrown up urgent issues concerning students' and teachers' material existence and the environments in which we work and interact. On the approach we propose here, creative practices are themselves conceived as modes of understanding, in which students negotiate the physical aspects of making alongside what they want to express or represent. At the same time, this dimension of learning and teaching is conjoined with a textual and theoretical understanding of the role of creativity within the processes of learning.

In developing our approach, we have had to take into account the way that students themselves often expect to receive institutionalised learning experiences that are governed, structured and didactic. This seems to be especially the case for those who have not had a particularly creative education and who are used to teaching styles that rely on a directive approach to knowledge 'transfer'. Students who lack the confidence to work creatively tend to seek greater clarification and confirmation that they are doing it 'right', not doing it 'wrong'. When asked to choreograph their own movements, students may find it hard to begin, shooting furtive glances across the room, waiting, looking around, until some of the more confident members of the group start moving, in a sense modeling a response to the instruction to create a movement. Supported by their peers' involvement, most students in a group will in the end join in, working on their own separate actions, but some will continue to remain at the edge of the room: 'Miss, I don't know what to do.' Encouragement, ideas, scaffolding from staff slowly bring such students in, and eventually tentative steps and a physical, action-based response will follow.

To learn creatively, students have to unlearn their drive to find the *right* answer, as this suppresses their own ideas and the alternative possibilities that they might come up with. Any teacher wants students to establish connections and divergences in thinking and doing, generating what Braidotti would call 'materially embedded cartographies' (2013, 13). Through these cartographies, they may come to challenge the domination of conscious rationality. This requires in-depth transformations of students-as-subjects in terms of their processes of becoming, processes that are themselves differentiated by factors such as gender, race and sex. Insofar as it involves negotiating social subjectivities, students' work can take on a socio-cultural dimension in its production of collaborative creations that become, to use Braidotti's (2013) words, 'politically informed cartographies of the present' (12). To elaborate, if we take the example of young women who may be used to operating on the periphery of society, where conscious rationality has placed them, this kind of learning experience can enable them to re-imagine their subjectivity. More specifically, it can offer them a positive vision of the subject as an affective and dynamic individual while simultaneously allowing them to create affinities both with each other and with the material processes of dance, film, painting and sound, as well as with the textual and theoretical materials through which they are encouraged to come to a better understanding of the role of creativity in learning. Such an approach means supporting students in sustaining inter-connectedness as social subjects who are self-reflexive and 'not parasitic on the process of metaphorization of "others"' (12). This can be difficult, especially if students are unaccustomed to generating work other than on the basis of direct instruction from their teachers. Students need to 'own' their work before they can become active learning subjects; thus teachers need to find more effective ways to provide students with a language through which they can speak and express themselves. Only then will they be able to take on this ownership and develop the confidence to express themselves. Embodied creative practices are therefore usually slow to develop and some students will hesitate in constructing their own discourses and/or occupying more self-reflexive positions.

In thinking about these processes of teaching through arts-based curricula, the philosophical concept of 'difference' (Irigaray 1993; Braidotti 2002, 2012) is particularly useful because it helps interrogate the conceptual formations or roots of identity and power – not so much in terms of difference *between* cultures, as in terms of differences *within* the 'same' culture. An arts-based curriculum can serve to challenge pre-existing ideas of what constitutes the self, especially in relation to ethnicity and religion, through its attempts to construct 'an embedded and embodied form of enfleshed materialism' (Braidotti 2013, 13). Such an enfleshed materialism arguably transcends or at least cuts across the particularities of religion or culture. This kind of thinking about and through the materiality of curricula might raise questions such as: *how can creativity operate trans-culturally in a pluri-ethnic society at a time of increasing racism and xenophobia?* This is a question, it seems, without an easy answer. It is a question to which we still work to respond.

In researching arts-based teaching through our own teaching practice, we have been very aware that it is important that practice *as* research is democratic, inclusive and that everyone has the opportunity to participate. Ethical questions can be raised about curricular practices that make some students uncomfortable, for example, in the case of those students who are unaccustomed to dance in an academic context and who are uneasy about taking part because of their preconceptions of what dance involves. Teaching those who are not specialists or experts in given disciplines requires a different way of imagining one's teaching and curricula in order to generate alternative thinking around the form of delivery, content, pace, scaffolding and environment so as to ensure that students feel able to participate. Here we might draw on helpful examples of dance projects in community settings where embodied learning is achieved by equipping people with movement so that they can feel confident in their work. Innovative pedagogies that take account of the participant/learner and how they engage with the arts are being developed by About Face Theatre Company, Frontlinedance and Infuse Dance in the UK, by Restless Dance Theatre in Australia, and by The Olimpias in America.

The use of movement in the context of educational studies, rather than more established dance environments, often exposes misunderstandings about what constitutes 'dance' and teachers may be called upon to refute stereotypes of 'pop' dancing which are highly gender specific and sexualised. Contemporary movement practices that constitute performance curricula require students to move in space, but these practices are very different from popular methods for moving the body commonly referred to as 'dance', in that they are far less stylised. For such work to be effective, it is essential to dismantle some of the preconceptions of dance, in particular for students who are critical, for whatever reason, of those forms of dance that constitute the body as sexual object and agent. By returning to the ideas of space, movement and gesture, this resistance can be worked with and productively overcome. For example, the 'dance' at a folk dance festival or in a popular film clip will typically feature specific, often complex movements that are often passed down from generation to generation, or taught by a choreographer, an 'expert'. In similar ways, students in educational studies programmes can be asked to develop their own movements and to teach these movements to each other. Through the process of engagement with dance movement that is not necessarily historically determined and not explicitly sexualised, new and meaningful knowledges can be produced. After all, all bodies move.

This kind of creative practice allows students to explore ways of mapping routes through space and to create collaborative cartographies of bodies. At its most generative it becomes a practice of live theorisation: the thinking in action that takes place as students come to understand concepts about which they have read and then formulate (or materialise) their own. An understanding of the concepts of freedom and control, for example, will be produced and processed very differently when mapped through movement, painting, music and filming as compared with only reading a theoretical chapter in a sedentary position. A text set as a preliminary reading can be difficult to decipher, but through creative practice and some discussion students can come to understand their own creative processes and in turn make sense of theoretical writing *about* creativity. Students will typically oscillate between thinking and materiality as they theorise through practice.

Finally, the fact that many students in education departments are female is a significant factor in the particular case of learning through dance. McRobbie (1991, 192) highlights the affirmative role which dance can play for girls: 'Its art lies in its ability to create a fantasy of change, escape, and of achievement for girls and young women who are otherwise surrounded by much more mundane and limiting leisure opportunities.' McRobbie's presentation of dance as an emancipatory outlet for working class girls leads us to question why dance as an expressive practice in the pedagogical sphere is sometimes met with difficulty and reluctance. Of course, the different cultural backgrounds of students will lead to different answers to this question. The movement practices that we tend to teach do not subscribe to a popular kind of feminine embodiment. Dancing, for us, is not like becoming-Madonna; rather it is a process and practice of exploring one's own body in simple and not explicitly gendered ways. For female students of varying social, cultural and religious backgrounds who may never have visited nightclubs and for whom dancing in public is inextricably linked to the provocative, sexualised type of dancing mentioned above, any emancipatory or even purely expressive function of dance can be obscured. In order to allow for a different type of expression or communication through dance, it is necessary to try to develop a trans-cultural sensitivity and demonstrate that the movement of a body or a limb need not translate as sexualised or as asking to be seen, but rather, can be simply expressive. Through gesture, concepts can be materially embodied, without recourse to a linguistic medium, and with minimal reference to any frameworks of preconceived cultural assumptions.

Educational imaginaries and diffractive pedagogy

In *The Philosophical Imaginary*, Le Doeuff (1980, 114) maps the binary distinction between masculine and feminine onto the oppositions of externality and internality. This opposition, as well as a disassociation or disconnection between the materiality of a woman's body and the objects of the external world, can be seen in the perceived inhibitions of at least some female students, whose learning experiences have been a central focus of this discussion. Young women who are invited to move in classroom contexts may well be reluctant to express themselves through external bodily movement or to enter into a relation with external spatiotemporal materiality. In ways that complicate and contest the historical binary between modes of spatiality (external, rational, male) and temporality (internal, subjective, female), this discussion has sought to rethink the materiality of the body as an 'active, sometimes recalcitrant, force' (Alaimo and Hekman 2008, 5), such that the female gesture is felt only *through* and *with* other objects and beings (Irigaray 1989, 134).

> Bodies in social groups are not just bodies. They require an identity to make sense of their lives and to operate as human beings in a social setting. Human bodies in social groups require viable identities, but they can only obtain those identities from the social script extant in the society in which they live. (Hekman 2005, 113)

As researchers and as teachers, we are implicated in the enmeshing of bodies and environments, creation and thought, scripts and identities. In the reflections that we have presented here, drawn from our diverse experiences as practitioners and teachers, we have thought about feminist practices, arts-based teaching, and arts practice as research in terms of material-discursive entanglement (Barad 2007; Taguchi 2012; Childers 2013). Feminist theory matters and has an affective relationship with the bodies of researchers and practitioners. Rather than viewing theory as something to be read or applied, we suggest that theory is better approached as intra-agential matter: 'feminist research is a material-discursive becoming, a knowing through being, an ontology of methodology' (Childers 2013, 605). Building on this methodological proposition, we see our students as creating, producing and theorising through the production of movement.

In this paper, our goal has been to move towards a new materialist feminist arts pedagogy that opens up new educational imaginaries. We hope to have shown some of the disruptive and generative potential of diffractive pedagogy as an example of the type of learning that can take place when materiality and entanglement are considered as vital constituents. Through uncharted, embodied self-expression and interweaving across multiple media and boundaries, the potential to create, produce, embody and theorise simultaneously can be realised. Student bodies, however, do not exist in isolation from one another, or from their environments. The inseparability of self from environment is what Alaimo and Hekman (2008) calls trans-corporeality (238). Our aim here has been to demonstrate that the diffractive pedagogical practice of teaching and learning through dance embodies precisely this trans-corporeal subjectivity. It is indeed impossible to separate the dancer from the dance, the teacher from the student, and the bodies from the environments and objects to which they relate. This being true, a student body can reproduce our teaching bodies as abject: as messy and peripheral to their imaginings of university education. But at the same time, student bodies can materially remake the limits to which their consciousnesses were initially drawn. Through embodied work, unconscious change through corporeal practice can begin the process of affecting students' imaginaries of university education.

Disclosure statement

No potential conflict of interest was reported by the authors.

References

Alaimo, S., and S Hekman. 2008. *Material Feminisms*. Bloomington: Indiana University Press.
Barad, K. 2003. "Posthumanist Performativity: Toward an Understanding of How Matter Comes to Matter." *Signs: Journal of Women in Culture and Society* 28 (3): 801–831.
Barad, K. 2007. *Meeting the Universe Halfway: Quantum Physics and the Entanglement of Matter and Meaning*. Durham: Duke University Press.
Barad, K. 2012a. "On Touching: The Inhuman That Therefore I Am." *Differences* 23 (3): 206–223.
Barad, K. 2012b. *What Is the Measure of Nothingness? Infinity, Virtuality, Justice*. Osfildern: Hatje Cantz.
Barrett, E. 2007. "The Exegesis as Meme." In *Practice as Research: Approaches to Creative Arts Enquiry*, edited by E. Barrett, and B. Bolt, 159–164. London: I.B. Tauris.
Blackman, L. 2008a. *The Body: Key Concepts*. Oxford: Berg.
Blackman, L. 2008b. "Affect, Relationality and the Problem of Personality." *Theory, Culture and Society* 25 (1): 23–47.
Blackman, L. 2012. *Immaterial Bodies: Affect, Embodiment, Mediation*. New York: Sage.
Braidotti, R. 1996. *Nomadic Subjects: Embodiment and Sexual Difference in Contemporary Feminist Theory*. New York: Columbia University Press.
Braidotti, R. 2002. *Metamorphoses: Towards a Materialist Theory of Becoming*. Cambridge: Polity.
Braidotti, R. 2012. "The Notion of the Univocity of Being or Single Matter Positions Difference as a Verb or Process of Becoming at the Heart of the Matter." In *Interview with Rosi Braidotti, New Materialism: Interviews & Cartographies*, edited by Rick Dolphijn, & Iris van der Tuin, 19–37. Michigan: Open Humanities Press.
Braidotti, R. 2013. *The Posthuman*. Cambridge: Polity Press.
Burnard, P. 2012. *Musical Creatives in Practice*. Oxford: Oxford University Press.
Carter, P. 2004. *Material Thinking: The Theory and Practice of Creative Research*. Carlton: Melbourne University Publishing.
Childers, S. M. 2013. "Promiscuous (Use of) Feminist Methodologies: The Dirty Theory and Messy Practice of Educational Research Beyond Gender." *International Journal of Qualitative Studies in Education* 26 (5): 507–523.
Coffey, J. 2013. "Bringing the Body into the Sociology of Youth." *Tasa Youth*. Accessed June 12. http://tasayouth.wordpress.com/2013/08/26/44/.
Colebrook, C. 2005. "How Well Can We Tell the Dancer from the Dance? The Subject of Dance and the Subject of Philosophy." *Topoi* 24 (1): 5–14.
Coleman, R. 2009. *The Becoming of Bodies: Girls, Images, Experience*. Manchester: Manchester University Press.
Coole, D., and S. Frost. 2010. *New Materialisms: Ontology, Agency, and Politics*. Durham: Duke University Press.
Craft, A., B. Jeffrey, and M. Leibling, eds. 2001. *Creativity in Education*. London: Continuum.
Csikszentmihalyi, M. 2009. *Creativity: Flow and the Psychology of Discovery and Invention*. London: Harper Collins.

Deleuze, G. 1993. *The Fold: Leibniz and the Baroque*. London: Continuum.

Deleuze, G., and F Guattari. 1987. *A Thousand Plateaus: Capitalism and Schizophrenia*. Minneapolis: University of Minnesota Press.

Dewey, J. 1934. *Art as Experience*. New York: Perigree Books.

Dolphin, R., and I. van der Tuin. 2012. *New Materialism: Interviews and Cartographies*. Michigan: Open Humanities Press.

Ellsworth, E. 1997. *Teaching Positions: Difference, Pedagogy, and the Power of Address*. New York: Teachers College Press.

Featherstone, M. 2010. "Body, Image and Affect in Consumer Culture." *Body & Society* 16 (1): 193–221.

Gallop, J. 1988. *Thinking Through the Body*. New York: Columbia University Press.

Gatens, M. 1996. *Imaginary Bodies: Ethics, Power and Corporeality*. London: Routledge.

Gilmour, J. E. 1991. "Participative Governance Bodies in Higher Education: Report of a National Study." *New Directions for Higher Education* 1991: 27–39.

Greenland, P. 2000. *Hopping Home Backwards – Body Intelligence and Movement Play*. Leeds: JABADAO.

Grosz, E. 1994. *Volatile Bodies: Toward a Corporeal Feminism*. Bloomington: Indiana University Press.

Haraway, D. 1997. *Modest_Witness@Second_Millenium.FemaleMan_Meets_OncoMouse: Feminism and Technoscience*. New York: Routledge.

Hekman, S. 2005. "Constructing the Ballast: An Ontology for Feminism." In *Material Feminisms*, edited by S. Alaimo, & S. Hekman, 53–85. Bloomington: Indiana University Press.

Hickey-Moody, A. C. 2009a. *Unimaginable Bodies: Intellectual Disability, Performance and Becomings*. Rotterdam: Sense.

Hickey-Moody, A. C. 2009b. "Becoming-Dinosaur: Collective Process and Movement Aesthetics." In *Deleuze and Performance*, edited by L. Cull, 163–180. Edinburgh: Edinburgh University Press.

Hickey-Moody, A. C. 2009c. "Little War Machines: Posthuman Pedagogy and its Media." *Journal of Literary and Cultural Disability Studies* 3 (3): 273–280.

Hickey-Moody, A. C. 2013. *Youth, Arts and Education*. London: Routledge.

Hoque, A. 2015. *British-Islamic Identity: Third Generation Bangladeshis from East London*. London: IoE Press, Trentham Books.

Irigaray, L. 1989. "The Gesture in Psychoanalysis." In *Between Feminism and Psychoanalysis*, edited by T. Brennan, 127–138. London: Routledge.

Irigaray, L. 1993. *An Ethics of Sexual Difference*. London: Cornell University Press.

Jagodzinski, J., and J. Wallin. 2013. *Arts-Based Research: A Critique and a Proposal*. Rotterdam: Sense.

Kirby, V. 2011. *Quantum Anthropologies: Life at Large*. Durham and London: Duke.

Kristeva, J. 1984a. *Powers of Horror: An Essay on Abjection*. Columbia: New York.

Kristeva, J. 1984b. *Revolution in Poetic Language*. Columbia: New York.

Le Doeuff, M. 1980. *The Philosophical Imaginary*, London: Continuum.

Lury, C. and Wakeford, N. 2012. *Inventive Methods: The Happening of the Social*. Routledge: Abingdon.

McRobbie, A. 1991. *Feminism and Youth Culture: From Jackie to Just Seventeen*. Basingstoke: Macmillan.

Minh-ha, T. 1989. *Woman, Native, Other*. Bloomington and Indianapolis: Indiana University Press.

Pink, S. 2007. *Doing Visual Ethnography*. London: Sage.

Probyn, E. 2004. "Teaching Bodies: Affects in the Classroom." *Body and Society* 10 (4): 21–43.

Rose, G. 2012. *Visual Methodologies: An Introduction to Researching with Visual Materials*. London: Sage.

Roy, G. 2003. *Teachers in Nomadic Spaces: Deleuze and Curriculum*. New York: Peter Lang.

Samah, S. A. A., K. Jusoff, and A. D. Silong. 2009. "Does Spoon-Feeding Impede Independent Learning?" *Canadian Social Science* 5 (3): 82–90.

Smith, H. 2008. "Spoon-Feeding: or How I Learned to Stop Worrying and Love the Mess." *Teaching in Higher Education* 13 (6): 715–718.

Taguchi, H. L. 2012. "A Diffractive and Deleuzian Approach to Analysing Interview Data." *Feminist Theory* 13 (3): 265–281.

Taguchi, H. L. 2013. "Images of Thinking in Feminist Materialisms: Ontological Divergences and the Production of Researcher Subjectivities." *International Journal of Qualitative Studies in Education* 26 (6): 706–716.

van der Tuin, I. 2014. "Diffraction as a Methodology for Feminist Onto-Epistemology: On Encountering Chantal Chawaf and Posthuman Interpellation." *Parallax* 20 (3): 231–244.

Valéry, P. 1958. *The Art of Poetry*. Translated by Denise Folliot. Princeton, NJ: Princeton University Press.

Selfies, relfies and phallic tagging: posthuman part-icipations in teen digital sexuality assemblages

Emma Renold ⓘ and Jessica Ringrose

ABSTRACT

Inspired by posthuman feminist theory, this paper explores young people's entanglement with the bio-technological landscape of image creation and exchange in young networked peer cultures. We suggest that we are seeing new formations of sexual objectification when the more-than-human is foregrounded and the blurry ontological divide between human (flesh) and machine (digital) are enlivened through queer and feminist Materialist analyses. Drawing upon multimodal qualitative data generated with teen boys and girls living in urban inner London and semi-rural Wales (UK) we map how the digital affordances of Facebook 'tagging' can operate as a form of coercive 'phallic touch' in ways that shore up and transgress normative territories of dis/embodied gender, sexuality and age. We conclude by arguing that we need creative approaches that can open up spaces for a posthuman accounting of the material intra-actions through which phallic power relations part-icipate in predictable and unpredictable ways.

Introduction: girls, over-embodiment and the cyber relationship cultures of young sexualities

> The body is transformed, on the one hand, into an assemblage of detachable parts, on the other, a threshold of transcendence of the subject. This paradoxical mixture of loss of unity and multiplications of discourses constitutes the core of contemporary body politics (Braidotti, 2011, p. 63)

These are challenging sociopolitical times for educational researchers exploring the sexual cyber cultures of teen girls in an era where everyday lives are technologically mediated to unprecedented degrees of intimacy and intrusion (Braidotti, 2013, p. 89). Fear and fetish dominate representations of the contemporary sexual landscape for girls, in what we have theorized elsewhere as the phallocentric stolen becomings of the sexual girl-child (Renold & Ringrose, 2011). Anxiety and fear manifest over the premature hypersexualization of girls (Egan, 2013; Renold, Ringrose, & Egan, 2015) and in the contemporary and historical sexual abuse scandals via an omnipotent predatory man/becoming-man (fleshed and digital) who traverses past, present and future (Campbell, 2016; Jewkes & Wykes, 2012). These fears are escorted by the fetishization of the DIY (do-it-yourself) body beautiful that demands, commodifies and celebrates constant modification to an ever-morphing ideal type (Lazar, 2011). As predicted by Walkerdine (1998, 1999) the over-embodied, over-exposed girl has come of age (Driscoll, 2002), and nowhere is her sacrificial ontology to the phallic symbolic more marked than in her entanglement with the scopic biotechnological landscape of image creation and exchange in young networked peer cultures in the era of the sexy 'selfie' (Albury, 2015; Sastre, 2014; Senft & Baym, 2015; Warfield, 2015). In a globalized era, where the female body remains a focal point of advertising campaigns and reality make-over television underage girls who self-produce 'sexually explicit' images of their bodies are caught up in a complex set of moral, legal and protectionist debates (Albury, 2015; Gill & Elias, 2014; Hassinof & Shepherd, 2014; Karaian, 2014; Ringrose & Harvey, 2015; Ringrose, Harvey, Gill, & Livingstone, 2013). Girls and women negotiate new 'technologies of sexiness' in these postfeminist media contexts in ways that greatly complicate neo-liberal notions of rational consent or individual humanist agency (Evans & Riley, 2014). Moreover, femininity operates not only as a series of body parts – cut, cropped and cast out across cyber-socialities, but each body part *part-icipates* in localized global phallocentric networks, that require on-going transformations to be capitalizable.

Directing our feminist gaze to understanding the invasive force relations of contemporary digital corporeal culture in young people's everyday lives we wish to explore how phallocentric power relations work, through mapping three territorializing phallic tagging assemblages that teen girls and boys are caught up in and captured by. The first two assemblages, 'digital tagging as phallic touch' and 'compulsory coupledom' map a series of coercive digital tagging practices that we see as exerting phallic force relations from the profane (i.e. requests for, or the creation of, photos of girls' bodies) to the mundane (i.e. the repetitive tagging of a heterosexual 'relfie' – a relationship selfie). The final assemblage, 'Jak's breasts' explores the distribution of dis/embodied body parts (i.e. selfies of an older girls' cleavage) and maps their tagged part-icipation through Facebook comment exchanges that trouble heteronormative and generational territories of gender, sexuality, and age. We explore the affective potentialities and blockages inside and across our phallic assemblages so as to avoid the Oedipal plot of phallocentric theory (Irigaray and Deleuze and Guattari in Lorraine, 2008) which has everything tied up in ways that straight jacket our intellectual endeavors to map the messy and complex realities of living mediated lives and extended relational selves.

Putting the posthuman phallic in assemblage theory

Our entry point to foregrounding and theorizing the phallus in this paper is to acknowledge yet move beyond psychoanalytic castration theories based on lack (Lacan, Freud). In traditional psychoanalytic readings, as Berlant (2012, p. 64) summarizes, desire is heralded as *the* primary drive, and becomes an object to be possessed and pursued, either 'by having it or not having it; being (bearing or symbolizing) it or not.' In this paper, we are inspired by the writings of Deleuze and Guattari (1984/2004) where desiring-machines are everywhere. One of the central shifts from psychoanalytic thinking for Deleuze and Guattari, is that desire is not understood as lack and does not belong to the subject. Desire makes connections (hence their language of the machinic), but it is not oriented toward or directed by something (i.e. the Imaginary) and does not sit outside the social-technological, in fantasy. Desire is productive, it produces the real in dynamic sociomaterial-semiotic affective assemblages. However, and central to this paper, desire still yields to and is captured by something that looks like a Lacanian phallocentric Oedipal complex, converting the flows, territorializing them and assigning them to molar categories of sexuality, gender, age, race and so on. It is these territorializing practices that we attend to in our analysis below, where we work creatively with our multimodal qualitative research,[1] forming sexuality assemblages (Fox & Alldred, 2013) to glimpse and map the affective 'ontological intensities' (Deleuze & Guattari, 1987) of those often imperceptible micro-moments of (territorializing) forces and (de-territorializing) becomings (for further new educational materialist and posthuman methodological scholarship see, Coleman & Ringrose, 2013; Fox & Alldred, 2013; Snaza & Weaver, 2015; Taylor & Hughes, 2016; Taylor & Ivinson, 2013).

In order to explore the complexities of the prosthetic self and the technolocally mediated body, Deleuzo-Guattarian assemblage theory has been vital. Assemblage theory decenters the subject, to show how it is made up of and criss-crossed by multiple external forces, of the non-human, inorganic and technological kind. It thus enables us to map the dynamic processes of an extended and 'unfolding subjectivity outside the classical frame of the anthropocentric human subject, relocating it into becomings and fields of composition of forces and becomings' (Braidotti, 2002, p. 229). Assemblage theory also enables us to explore how 'images, representations, and significations (as well as bodies) are aspects of ongoing practices of negotiation, reformation and encounter' (Bray & Colebrook, 1998, p. 38) – practices that are always already intra-acting (as opposed to viewing bodies and images as separate entities, interacting). Our concept of 'part-icipation' draws attention to these intra-active process.

Indeed, our approach resonates with Braidotti's posthuman notion of 'organs without bodies'. She stresses that organs (like an image of a breast) are not simply dislocated and split off from the female body, which is reminiscent of older feminist theories that critiqued the symbolic representations of objectified female body parts (Bordo, 2003, see also Bray & Colebrook, 1998). Rather, Bradotti's 'organs without bodies' are in a symbiotic relationship where there is no simple ontological divide between human and machine. Exploring the weighty materializations of images and bodies entangled in digital time-space enables us to see new formations of more-than-human sexual objectification. This re-thinking of human embodiment via a posthuman lens helps us explore the affective arresting connections of the intra-acting (Barad, 2007; Lenz Taguchi & Palmer, 2013) force relations at play in the distribution, detachability and hybridization of girls' bodies and body parts (i.e. girls' bodily part-icipations in sexuality assemblages). We explore these dynamics further below through the practices of digital 'tagging'.

The digital affordances of phallic tagging

Digital social networking plugs individuals into a powerful techno–social–cultural 'relational affective assemblage' through a range of devices and platforms (Coleman & Ringrose, 2013, p. 133). Mobile digital technology devices and networks extend the affective capacities of the human body also dissolving the virtual/real digital/material and online/offline binaries (Clough, 2010; Van Doorn, 2011). Thus, it is not discrete human individuals plugged into digital networks, but intra-acting cyborg-subjectivities plugged into dynamic and shifting assemblages where the phone, the digital applications, and human bodies are all actants (Haraway, 1991; Latour, 2005). Social networking sites are thus a set of nonhuman machinic force relations and architectures which mediate the performance of generalizable and particular visual cyber subjectivities in a digitally networked 'affective public' (Papacharissi, 2009, 2015).

Dana boyd summarizes how mobile digital media platforms are characterized by common elements of: 'Persistence: the durability of online expressions and content; Visibility: the potential audience who can bear witness; Spreadability: the ease with which content can be shared; and Searchability: the ability to find content' (boyd, 2014, p. 11). 'Tagging' (a feature of Facebook since 2009) is by now a ubiquitous digital affordance on social media. Tagging images or online posts enlivens all of the digital affordances discussed by boyd – it increases the visibility opening up the prospective audience of address and surveillance and it 'spreads' images to others enabling circulation around a network (Jenkins, Ford, & Green, 2013). Even though images can be un-tagged, the image can persist since the image can be taken through the tagging. Tagging also facilitates searchability because it can link information about someone to posts. Tagging of images happens in all sorts of banal ways where several individuals are linked to an image or onto posts and status updates on Facebook. It also, however, allows for the possibilities of linking oneself to others in ways that are coercive and for images to be potentially manipulated. Tagging is thus a mode of digital connectivity (Van Dijck, 2013) a way of linking ones online persona or profile to another's, mediating and extending the affectivity of the body (Clough, 2010).

Here, we wish to consider the digital affordance of tagging in relation to young people's digital sexual cultures on social networks, where tagging was a primary way to connect others to conversations and images which referenced dominant or 'molar' (Deleuze and Guattarri 1987) representations of sex/y. Exploring the circulating 'life' of online images entails understanding the digital mediation beyond conventional notions of humanist agency (Kember & Zylinska, 2015). In particular, we explore the production of sexy 'selfies' (see Albury, 2015; Senft & Baym, 2015) and relationship selfies or 'relfies', to re-think 'live' gender and sexual relations in teen peer groups. We apply Braidotti's anti-oedipal twist on the scopophillic production of bodies and subjectivity to consider how digital tagging can operate through formations of phallic force relations where touch is sexualized and unwanted. Indeed, we are beginning to conceptualize how tagging operates as a vector of *posthuman digital touch*. Blackman

(2012) offers a very useful discussion of how technologies work as a form of affective touch; she argues communication technologies such as radio, the telegraph, cinema and the telephone were all historically understood to 'transmit ideas beliefs and emotions through … immaterial forms of contact, which were equated to a form of "mental touch"' (2012, p. 65). Our interest is when digital touch in, through and beyond the screen (Warfield, in press) operates as *phallic touch with potentially coercive impacts*.[2] Below we show how cyber ontologies of machinic decentered subjectivities enabled through digital tagging entangle across different territories with complex material effects for the young people in our research and their bodily part-icipations. Importantly, these intra-acting processes can also displace conventional boundaries, binaries and categories of sex/gender/sexuality, queering normative sexual regulation, as we explore.

Digital tagging as phallic touch: capture, currency and selfie 'exposure'

The first set of tagging episodes below emerge from data generated with young people in a school located in an economically deprived borough of South East London with high levels of immigrant populations. One fifth of the students at the school are white British, with the other major groupings being predominantly Black Caribbean and Black African. Almost half of the school population speak English as an additional language, and there is a higher than average proportion of young people with additional learning needs. The neighborhood had high levels of reported gang related activity, and young people discussed street violence, including being robbed as commonplace. Indeed the practices of tagging and digital capture so ubiquitous across young people's social networking sites needs to be situated within the physical and digital technologies of racialized surveillance built in to the material architectures of the school and wider community: from cameras in every corridor and street poised and ready to capture, identify and shame, through to the high metal fences topped with barbed wire that surround the school, and which positions young people as both 'at risk' and 'risky to others' (Silk, Andrews, & Thorpe, 2016).

In previous analysis, we have explored how some boys were deploying the digital affordance of tagging as a means of investing in a classed and racialized culture of masculine performativity (Harvey & Ringrose, 2015; Harvey, Ringrose, & Gill, 2013). Image exchange and distribution of girls' body parts accrued value and became part of longer list of attributes, from muscularity and fighting competencies to owning branded clothing and consumer goods which seemingly enabled boys to gain accumulative ascendance in competitive masculine peer group hierarchies. We wish to develop this analysis to foreground the processual and more-than-human nature of boys' digital sexual exchange in ways that demonstrate the materiality of these practices which we theorize as coercive non-consensual phallic touch. We begin with the capture and distribution of girls' profile pictures via 'friends-of-girl-friends' and 'ex-girl-friends' to images of hybrid constructions of the 'known-un-known' so as to flesh out the ways in which the distributed sexual subjectivities of girls via their sexualized body parts metamorphose across more-than-human digital social networks.

This first example gets at tagged images of girls in boys' social networks (both on Facebook and BBM[3]) who are 'friends of friends' – so not known through physical social interaction, rather solely through their digital social network. Ty (pseudonym) relates his own process of tagging 'sexy' images from girls' profile pics:

Ty (13): I can tag it if I like the picture I could tag myself in it and then it will come to my profile. I could make it my profile picture … it all leads to ratings because, 'he's got that girl on Facebook' and 'she's nice and how did he get her', they just want to find out, things like that.

Interviewer: And what do the girls think if you tag yourself in their pictures?

Ty: Nothing, sometimes they will un-tag you, if they don't want you to tag them. But by the time they get to know that you are tagged in it, you could have made it your profile picture already. They can un-tag you from it but then you have still got the picture.

Attaching oneself to a 'sexy' image of a girl via the process of 'tagging' oneself is a commonplace technologically mediated way of attempting to actualize rewards through 'ratings' for teen boys in their daily digital performances of heteronormative masculinities. Ty is 'getting' a 'nice (hetero-sexy) girl' and thus forming a nonconsensual digital sexual union. For us, this practice gets at what we see as coercive non-consensual phallic touch as Ty's digital subjectivity intra-acts ('I can tag myself in it') with the girls' tagged image to accrue value and sexual social status. A more-than-human analysis would also enable us to trace the metamorphosing image that moves in and out of the human (subject) and nonhuman (object), from an 'it' ('I can tag it') to 'that girl' and 'that picture' to a 'her' ('how did he get her?') and in subject–object assemblages in which she/it has the potential to 'know' and 'un-tag.' The force relations move swiftly through this phallic tagging assemblage in which digital affordances of the technology allow Ty to capture 'it' ('come to me'), enter 'it' (be 'in it') and where resistance ('they don't want you') is futile because he produces and owns 'it' ('you've made it your profile'). Moreover, any self (i.e.) agency on 'it'/'her' part is futile because he has now 'got the girl/got the picture.' The flow of invasion, capture, merger, ownership and display are a powerful set of phallic force relations that trouble the human agentic self-contained subject in the production, ownership and distribution of the sexy 'selfie', as we explore in two further examples below.

The next assemblage is by now a classic and much media hyped version of sexual tagging as a form of 'revenge porn' (Salter, 2015) where sexually explicit images sent privately to a partner are 'exposed' to a public audience online through processes of uploading images without consent and identifying the person possibly through the tagging mechanism. Here 15 year old teen girls discuss how 'naked' photos of an ex-girlfriend were distributed across Facebook when the relationship ended:

Carey:	There were naked pictures of her on Facebook.
Indigo:	She was in the year below us.
Alexandra:	Yeah she was in year nine. I think she sent pictures to someone and then he exposed her on Facebook and then tagged his friends to her naked pictures.
Carey:	She is talking about the person who moved schools …
Irina:	She sent it to her boyfriend
Rebecca:	And he showed his friends and they told everyone basically.
Interviewer:	And so can you tell me why you think she would send a picture to her boyfriend?
Alexandra:	He probably asked for it.
Interviewer:	So what do you think goes through their mind when they ask you for a picture that is of you naked?
Irina:	Obviously sex.
Interviewer:	So they are thinking of sex?
Irina:	Well obviously they are like show things and you know what boys do and what they are like and the next thing they will ask you for is sex. (15 year old girls, all names are pseudonyms)

Here, we see similar coercive flows of possession and display through the capture and merger of a girls' naked image and how naked (with the intra-action of the interviewer) becomes-sex ('obviously sex'). A more-than-human sexual shaming materializes via the phallic tagging which the boyfriend disseminates to 'his friends.' No longer in-relationship, her body is no longer privately owned, but cast out and then broadcast for wider phallic consumption and public shaming via endless ritualized speculation (Salter, 2015). A posthuman lens foregrounds the material and affective dynamics which connect rather than disconnect the digital image from the embodied girl and the intra-action of her digital dispersal across cyberspace with her physical departure when she 'moved schools.'

The final assemblage in this section brings together both the tagging practices from the two examples above which explored the coercive capture of identity and body parts, to explore a related form of phallic tagging in which girls could again be 'exposed' through being tagged in images that are part-self (i.e.), part other:

Skylar:	I look through my brother's phone a lot and in his pictures, like if the girl is rude or something or they have had an argument, he will expose her. Well he says he's going to but he don't normally. And they have this … thing about asking girls to write their name
Mercedes:	On their body somewhere, then take a picture. They don't say write on your privates whatever, they just say write it anywhere, but then girls do […]
Cherelle:	Yes, but obviously they expect them to write it on their/
Ashley:	They are expecting it to be a dirty picture and then the best one gets to go as my display picture.
Jodie:	But they don't show their face, they just their body part.
Interviewer:	So does this happen at this school where somebody has put this up as a display picture, these kinds of photos?
Mercedes:	Yeah, but we know who it is even if they don't show their face.
Cherelle:	Some people make it up and like we get tagged in school. Say like someone sent it to them and they like their skin colour is the same as someone else's they will say it is a different person and then they get tagged and called random names.
Interviewer:	So they could get a naked photo from anywhere and they tag it as somebody who it isn't?
Skylar:	As someone else, yeah.
Jodie:	Because boys add random girls, they probably don't even know who it is their selves. (13 year old girls, all names are pseudonyms)

Skylar describes how some boys ask for images of headless 'dirty' 'body parts' of girls with the boys' names written on them. These practices form part of the everyday digital power-plays of sexual exchange, ranking ('rating') and ownership ('the best one gets to go as my display picture'). She illuminates how girls' who comply and send an image of a sexual body part can then potentially be subject to the threat of 'exposure' and/or creation of a part-them/part-other sexual selfie if they are 'rude' or 'have had an argument' with the boy. What we want to draw attention to here is the affective gendered dynamics of 'exposure' in the production and distribution of these sexually explicit 'selfies', at once coercive and shift-able, since girls' identities can be connected to and potentially tagged in naked photos 'from anywhere'. We see these are bodily part-icipations circulating in ways that flow between the known (e.g. in which bits of bodies are identifiable as 'them') and unknown (e.g. bits of bodies from unidentified 'other' girls when 'boys add random girls'). This metamorphosis of becoming-random gets at the ways in which phallic touch can invade to erase, enhance and essentially f**k with girls' digital identities by skillfully merging them with the sexual body parts of other 'random' women and girls. Indeed, the capture and re-mastering of images seems to create a known-unknown hybrid cyborg selfie (or is it then a felfie or fake selfie[4]) of sexual sub/objectification par excellence – a phallic assemblage of collective currency for boys and a territorialization of girls' sexual becomings. However, see the third section of this paper for what (else) a headless sexual selfie can do!

Compulsory coupledom: relfies and the time-slips of more-than-human unions

For our next phallic tagging assemblage we turn to the semi-rural postindustrial landscape of an eco-nomically deprived welsh valleys' town. This is a community where gendered historical legacies loom large in what girls and women are expected to do and be (e.g. girlfriends, wives, mothers). The phallic image is thus not the sexually explicit detached body part that galvanizes 'sext' media moral panics (Hasinoff, 2015), but a relationship selfie or 'relfie'[5] of a 'smiley couple'; Callum (boy) and Cerys (girl). This relfie is tagged by another boy (Ryan), to Callum's facebook profile, the male half of the 'smiley couple', repeatedly over three years. It attracts over '300 comments' including the colloquial penetrative statement, 'get in there, Callum', which (hetero)sexualizes their togetherness. These digital 'comments' create specific intensities that complicate the 'like economy' of Facebook (Gerlitz & Helmond, 2013).

Beyond mere 'like' valuation (or not) of the post, we see the qualitative thrust of the comments which repeatedly heterosexualize Callum and Cery's friendship. The digital comments continually *re-vive*, create new 'liveliness' (Kember & Zylinska, 2012) via the digitally tagged connectivity of the posthuman relfie in the social media sexuality assemblage, as explained below.

This episode of relfie tagging emerged from a long interview between three friends, Cerys, Rees and Branwyn (age 15, all names are pseudonyms). These three were united in their abject status as working class 'high-achievers' in a 'low-achieving' school. The tagging discussion also followed lengthy and vivid descriptions of being subject to a range of physical gendered and sexual violence in school, including having stones thrown at them and yogurt smeared on their bags, and being routinely taunted as 'gay' and 'sluts and slags' for being 'stuck up' 'swots' – practices that when disclosed to teachers were met with the response, 'it's cos they fancy you'. Indeed, the girls talked animatedly of how 'past relationships' entangled with current relationships in problematic ways. Indeed, it is important to note that for these young people, resisting and refusing heterofamilial bonds in their school and community was risky, dangerous, and, ultimately, a rupturing of phallic belongings to heteronormative future imaginaries (Renold & Ivinson, 2015).

The conversation below follows from talk on how girls' 'relationships get brought up all the time' and how boyfriend-girlfriend relationships are regulated by their peers and in the wider community. It is here that the complexity and full force of the ways in which compulsory coupledom is intensified through digital networked cultures that the specific practices of tagging emerges:

Cerys:	(…) they'll like bring up the photo of me and one of the boys up again, like from my past relationship (3 years ago)
Interviewer:	What sort of photos?
Cerys:	Not like a photo like that (laughter) just like a normal photo like
Interviewer:	Just like as a couple like?
Cerys:	Yeah
INT:	Yeah ok
Rees:	They're on the carpet, just like (two tilted heads together smiling at the camera)
Cerys:	It's like a normal it's like a normal photo
Rees:	How many comments are on it, it's like 300 comments
Cerys:	It's got like 300 comments on it because
Rees:	Because they keep also
Cerys:	Over the years they always keep/
Rees:	They keep bringing it up. Every 2 months, it's … you just see the photo
Interviewer:	What is there that … why that photo?
Cerys:	It's just me and Callum smiling it's like … an old couple photo and now it's like, it gets brought up like every bunch of months and then Callum's just like 'oh Cer they've brought it up again Cer they've brought it up again, I've seen it again it's like' 'yeah I know'
Interviewer:	So … why what's going on there what what are the comments that are being attached to it every couple of months?
Cerys:	It's just I don't know it's sort of it's a thing to wind up Callum it is
Interviewer:	How's that work? How do you wind someone up by showing them a picture of them and their ex-girlfriend?
Branwyn:	Because they're commenting on it. It's like everyone can see it then

Cerys:	Yeah
Branwyn:	When it comes like up on your newsfeed
Cerys:	So like everybody that they're your friends like annoying friends and Callum's friends
Branwyn:	It's like embarrassing the boy … but it's like also bringing Cerys into it as well
Cerys:	Yeah … yeah and then it's like when he walks past me he goes oh Callum still likes you Callum still loves you and I just walk past and I go 'oh does he that's nice' and then Callum just laughs with me because he can see like the reaction that he's that … cos like me and Callum have the same reaction every time when Ryan comments

We begin to learn that it is Ryan and his mobile phone that has been doing all the tagging, pushing Callum and Cerys together, in a form of heterosexual harassment that needs to be situated in the wider context of how these girls, investing in school and future life beyond the valleys, are directly targeted:

Cerys:	The boys didn't like it that we had like other friends … it's like all of us has had past relationships – all of us has had at least one relationship with people like those boys
Branwyn:	Yeah
Cerys:	But only Ryan, only Ryan is the one … only Ryan is the one that hasn't … only Ryan has … hasn't let it go
Branwyn:	I think he'd like to control me now because when I tried to move on he was mailing me things like … I think he was trying to scare me or something or like trying to make me realise that I want him back or something
Cerys:	Yeah he tried that with Imogen

Ryan, we find out, uploads 'hundreds of photos' of his current and ex-girlfriends that he re-tags over and over – a practice which Branwyn (ex-girlfriend of Ryan) describes as a form of 'scary' coercive 'control.' Indeed, so powerful perhaps is the desire to 'couple-up' and heterosexualize boy–girl friendships that images of past relationships are resurrected. Here, we see the tagged relfie of an 'old smiley couple' with its appendage of additional sexualized comments being used to 'wind up' not only the 'couple' Callum and Cerys, but any boy-girl relationships that queer heterosexualization. We see this as a form of phallic tagging that re-winds and traverses linear space-time, in a community that refuses severed heterosexual unions (including abusive unions, see Renold & Ivinson, 2015). The 'smiley-couple' refie thus operates as a form of coercive posthuman phallic tagging where past relationships repeatedly pop up to penetrate and invade Other attachments and non-(hetero)normative relationship cultures.

What (else) can tagged cleavages do? Headless selfies, phallic ruptures and Jak's breasts

'Do we have only one point of exit from the kingdom of the phallus? On the contrary …' (Braidotti 1994, p. 53)

In this final section, we interject with a final assemblage to dislodge and liquidate what Irigaray (1985, p. 107) might call 'the mechanics of solids' in young people's digital phallocentric power plays. This section extends our theory of phallic tagging by focusing specifically on one of the rare moments (despite media speculation) of one young women's (age 18 or 19) unsolicited tagging of her cleavage to another younger (age 15) boy's profile. Through this example, like Chen (2012), we are keen to stress the animated vitality and dynamicism of movement through mapping what (else) the phallus can do. We explore, taking inspiration from Johnson's words, 'what now mocks and rocks the phallocentric system' (Johnson, 1995, p. 7) – that is, how might phallic tagging assemblages release and open up transgressions and transmorgifications of girls' (and boys') territorialized becomings.

As we described above, one of the ways that girls sought to minimize the possibility of identification of their sexual images in social networks was sending images that digitally edited out their heads, either through blurring techniques or cropping it off. These images were produced and circulated on social networks, including the BBM game where boys made a broadcast that proposition girls to send them images displaying the boys' name on a 'body part'.

In the earlier example the girls discussed their fears that they would be tagged in headless selfie images (fake selfies or 'felfies', see above) that were not of them. The headless images of body parts resonates with Braidotti's notion of the *organs without bodies*, where particular parts, for instance the breasts, operate as a prized organ – that is, breasts are over-invested in phallic bound energies, to the extent that the body becomes reducible to the organ as over-determined signifier of feminine sexual difference.

Two such images appeared on one of the 15 year old boys, Jak's Facebook page, in which an 'older girl' that Jak figured was '18 or 19' tagged him in. The first image is a headless photo with fingers opening up a sweatshirt to show an extreme close up of breast cleavage with 'Jak owns' written across the top of the breasts in black marker pen. The exchange, between Jak and his boy peers, that appears below the image reads as follows:

Looooooooool it's a fat man (boy 1)

lool cut dat non sence (Jak)

cut dat nigga talk lool (boy 1)

looool karrrr (Jak)

The second headless image is similar, but taken from further away so that the breasts, waist and arms are visible. The vest top is gone and the hoody sweatshirt is unzipped to the maximum point without showing the bra. The breasts are pushed up in a very tight bra to maximize the cleavage, again with Jak written in black marker across the chest and top of the breasts. The comments below this image are:

Looool went in Jak! (boy 2)

hahahahh ma lil goon on dis (boy 3)

Duknoooooo0 fam B-) (Jak)

Someones get gassed wid dis pic – comedy va (boy 4)

lool yee do a bakflipp (Jak)

lol (boy 4)

In previous writing (Ringrose & Harvey, 2015) about such images, we explored how girls who posted or sent sexy selfies were constructed as 'shameless', 'slaggy', and lacking in 'self- respect' particularly if images were unsolicited. Our focus was on the sexual objectification and slut-shaming of girls who send sexually explicit photos, which contrasted with the value and capital accrued by boys and young men 'owning' these images, in a peer economy of lad culture 'ratings.'

Considering this very same practice of the 'headless' cleavage selfie in the Canadian context, Karaian (2014) argues that removing the head erases the identity and a picture becomes just a picture not a disciplinary tool. She argues that the girl posting the picture can be seen as claiming her right to the erotic in a culture where girls are denied their sexual agency. What we wish to contribute to these analyses is to go beyond the Foucauldian binary of discipline/resistance and a humanist approach to individual, rational agency, desire and rights. Instead we are interested in how a posthuman approach privileges attention to the image of the cleaveage, as material actant. Our focus here is on the agentic potentiality of the tagged cleavage in a multi-modal multi-directional assemblage of digitized skin, ink, symbol and text, which name, shame but perhaps also queer. We argue that this is an assemblage that produces a cleavage both materially tagged (on skin) and digitally tagged (on Jak's mobile phone screen, Facebook page and news feed). It is also a *tagging* of Jak (unsolicited and imposed) in ways that invade and rupture the normative part-icipation of boy-solicited images of sexually explicit girl body parts. Indeed, we want to argue that this is no simple act of 'self-sexualization' (Lamb, 2010) or expression of a 'phallic-girl' femininity (McRobbie, 2008), nor are girls simply rationally reclaiming their sexual 'rights' to 'resist' objectified and girl-shaming erotophobic culture (Karaian, 2014).

Much has been written about the historical association of the pen as a metaphorical penis and thus the material and symbolic phallocentricism of knowledge (Gilbert & Gubar, 1979). The use of the black marker pen(is) ink-ing Jak's name across a semi-anonymous cleavage to create a digitized boy-tagged cleavage-selfie could in some ways operate as a twenty-first century re-claiming of digital sexual agency. However, we would suggest something more-than-human is emerging when the materiality of the digital in its complex multi-modal assemblage is dissected. We want to create a further data assemblage that complicates the sexual shame versus agency dichotomy so prevalent in discussion of sexually explicit body part selfies.

We speculate that Jak's unease in this event is perhaps due to the unsolicited nature in which a digital image of a tagged cleavage appears on Jak's personal newsfeed. Medussa like, (Cixous, 1976) this posthuman image (flesh-on-screen-digital) scores and permanently fixes Jak's name in ink without his consent and for others to view. Re-routing the directionality is certainly one central rupture in the phallocentric culture of the normative practices of boys' requesting girls' send them sexually explicit images. But what else might be going on here? If we take a de-centered and distributed approach to Jak's digital subjectivity, we also see space-time-body contractions as Jak-in-ink is reduced to text and transported without his consent across a voluptuous digitized cleavage. Perhaps we are also seeing what could be described as Jak's becoming-breast, the materialization of his infantilization (shrunk in text) *and* sexual capture and commodification (text on breast) for comedic value and exploitation (note the other boys comments, 'someone's get gassed wid dis pic – comedy va'). He is also perhaps becoming-dildo, captured and used for sexual shame and pleasure. Indeed the intra-action between infant and sexual commodity in Jak's becoming-breast is reminiscent of the character Gulliver in Swift's *Gulliver's Travels* (1726/2012) in Brobdingang. In this fictional land of the giants, Gulliver shrinks to the size of a pea in the land and is used and abused as an object of female consumption as he oscillates between reified baby-doll and human dildo (see Boucé, 2001).

While the latter reading might be a creative diffraction (Barad, 2007) too far, it does gesture towards how the symbolic and material might intra-act and unfold into endless possibilities which rupture (if only to be quickly re-territorialized) the phallic status quo. Indeed, the final rupture we want to pay attention to is in the queering of Jak's becoming-breast when we explore how the image intra-acts with his peers' comments that the image is of a 'fat man.' A new materialism reading would foreground not only the queer implications of a semiotic-textual union in which Jak has been tagged to what his friends suggest is a pair of 'man-boobs' and thus written across the chest/ sexually commodified by a man. It would also consider a reading which explores the direct relationality of the event itself – that Jak has been given a pair of 'boobs' with his name on – they are, very simply, Jak's breasts.

Conclusion: cartographic urges, utopian visions and polemics

When it comes to girls and sexuality, social science research finds itself increasingly caught up in territorializing representational regimes which stifle, obfuscate and silence critical scholarship that attempts to imagine girls' digital sexual cultures otherwise. It is an on-going struggle to communicate empirical research 'findings' that acknowledge yet deterritorialize the binary machines which posit Cartesian splits of mind and body, dichotomous offline-online social worlds, risky 'victims' and abusive 'perpetrators', and heteronormative gender bifurcations which tether masculinity to boy bodies and femininity to girl bodies. It is thus perhaps no surprise that many researchers intellectually and affectively bathe in and are released by recent developments advanced through posthuman feminisms and are enticed by the provocations of new feminist materialism educational scholarship and practice (see Taylor & Hughes, 2016).

In many ways our trajectory in this paper follows Braidotti's (1994, p. 56) triple manifesto for contemporary posthumanist scholarship, which suggests first that we *develop and hone our cartographic urges.* For us, this entails mapping the trapping effects of the patriarchal symbolic and phallocentric regimes which criss-cross young people's peer cultures in ways that territorialize desire. In line with this task we mapped out how phallic tagging can operate by offering an analysis of entangled and intra-acting bodily part-icipations in a series of sexuality assemblages. We drew on examples from the (hetero)sexually profane (the sexually explicit sexting nudes and headless selfies) to the (hetero)sexually mundane (the sexually implicit hetero relfie of a 'smiley couple'). We considered how young teens navigate multiple versions of posthuman networked digital relationalities through mapping how phallic force relations via digital tagging (or *phallic touch*) channeled energies back into familiar material manifestations of control and capture of girls' social networking images.

However, we also demonstrated how feminist inspired posthuman assemblage theory can illuminate the complex ambiguities of what else a digital affordance like tagging enables. The intra-acting complexities between the collective audience and profiles of the social network jointly create the value or parodied purchase of a post in ways that are unstable and shifting. The *tagging* cleavage as agentic actant *rather than* captured body part is a case in point. We can consider the cleavages and their capacities differently – they do not work in the expected ways—the cleavage becomes manly ('man-boobs'), they are funny (LOL) and Jak does not control their presence on his profile page nor the comments posted about the images from his friends. We see the possible cracks where phallocentric flows are re-routed and overthrown through the intra-action of image and comment in Jak's becoming-breast and becoming-dildo, despite Jak's attempts to recoup the tagged cleavage as proof of the girl as 'slaggy' and 'shameless' (see Ringrose & Harvey, 2015).

Working at the in-between spaces of the often imperceptible micro-moments of rupture gives us to tools to follow the *utopian drive* of Braidotti's second suggested goal of posthuman feminist scholarship. We see the space where Jak-and-the-cleavage becomes otherwise. Cartesian binaries fall away and interpretations that Jak and his friends as sexist; that the girl who tags her own breasts is a victim of a 'pornified' society; that girls are only valued for commodifying their body parts; OR alternatively, that cleavage-selfies are clear cut evidence of girls' individual sexual agency, all begin to break down. Mapping the multiplicities of what else the phallus can do, through Deleuzeo-Guattarian assemblage theory, keeps the potentialities of affective force relations in flow – potentialities that are often imperceptible through humanist phenomenological cartographies so prevalent in the social sciences.

Opening up space for a posthuman accounting of the material intra-actions through which phallic power relations shift and fold in on themselves follows Braidotti's third suggestion that feminist researchers cultivate their own *polemical touch*. What this means for us is that we cultivate the 'desire to get everyone talking' about these issues – not in the stale and taken for granted ways with which we are familiar, rather in a more dynamic accounting of how phallic assemblages might work in unknown unpredictable ways. Holding on to the uncertainties and the power of the not-yet (Manning, 2013) is, for us, a necessity in the over-coded world of young sexualities.

Notes

1. Jessica's data were generated from a project exploring digital sexual communication among economically and racially marginalized young people in London funded by the National Society for the Prevention of Cruelty to Children (see Ringrose, Gill, Livingstone, & Harvey, 2012). The project worked in-depth with a total of 35 young people aged 13–15 in two school communities in inner city, multicultural, London schools. Jessica Ringrose and Laura Harvey collected the online and in-person data discussed in this article. The methodology included conducting initial focus groups where we asked young people to 'walk us through' their online and mobile phone practices. Young people were then invited to 'friend' our Facebook research account. We conducted weekly observations of account activity on selected Facebook profiles for three months and conducted in-depth individual follow-up interviews with 22 young people. Renold 's data was generated across two intersecting pilot projects over a 2 month period. Working with a wider research team, including Victoria Edwards, Ian Thomas and Cat Turney, she explored young people's gender and sexual well-being through participatory and creative multi-media methods in rural and urban locales. Project 1 included facilitating weekly 'feminist lunch clubs' and Project 2 included mapping the experiences of digital sexual harassment in young peer cultures (both funded by Cardiff University). The data explored in this paper was generated in an unstructured friendship group 'interview' with two girls and one boy (white welsh, age 15) who lived in an ex-mining south wales' valleys town.
2. For further analysis of resistance to phallic touch and cybersexism through explorations of teen feminist 'posthuman affect' see Renold and Ringrose (in press) and Ringrose and Renold (2016).
3. Blackberry Messenger.
4. According to the Urban Dictionary, a 'Felfie can quickly be summed up as a "fake selfie" or a photograph taken of ones self that is not actually of the person they say it is. It is commonly used by males and females who send photos out to

a person (male or female) of themselves revealing parts of their body in the hope that they may receive one in return. Felfies usually do not show the persons face as this would be a give away. They are generally used so that the person receiving the "felfie" will be aroused and think that the person sending the photo has a better body than they actually do.' http://www.urbandictionary.com/define.php?term=Felfie.

5. 'A relfie ... is a "relationship selfie," or when you take a selfie that includes a relationship partner or someone else you are close to' http://www.scienceofrelationships.com/home/2014/6/23/what-does-your-relfie-say-about-your-relationship.html.

Acknowledgements

The authors would like to thank all of the young people who participated in the research projects. An earlier version of this paper was presented as 'Doing digital gender: mapping posthuman phallic force relations in teen girls' sexuality assemblages' at the Utrecht University *Doing Gender Annual Research Lecture*, Utrecht, the Netherlands March 2015. We would like to thank the organizers for inviting us and the audience who offered lively and productive feedback on the paper.

Disclosure statement

No potential conflict of interest was reported by the authors.

Funding

This work was supported by the Cardiff University and the National Society for the Prevention of Cruelty to Children (NSPCC).

ORCID

Emma Renold (iD) http://orcid.org/0000-0001-6472-0224

References

Albury, K. M. (2015). Selfies, sexts and sneaky hats: Young people's understandings of gendered practices of self-representation. *International Journal of Communication, 9*, 1734–1745.

Barad, K. (2007). *Meeting the Universe Halfway: Quantum physics and the entanglement of matter and meaning*. Durham, NC: Duke University Press.

Berlant, L. (2012). *Desire/love*. Brooklyn, NY: Punctum Books.

Blackman, L. (2012). *Immaterial bodies: Affect, embodiment, mediation*. Thousand Oaks, CA: SAGE.

Bordo, S. (2003). *Unbearable weight: Feminism, western culture and the body* (2nd ed.). Berkeley: University of California Press

Boucé, P. (2001). Gulliver phallophorus and the maids of honour in Brobdingnag. In *XVII-XVIII. Bulletin de la société d'études anglo-américaines des XVIIe et XVIIIe siècles* (vol. 53, pp. 81–98). Retrieved from http://www.persee.fr/web/revues/home/prescript/article/xvii_0291-3798_2001_num_53_1_1599

boyd, D. (2014). *Its complicated: The social lives of networked teens*.New Haven, CT: Yale University Press.

Braidotti, R. (1994). Interview: Feminism by any other name (with Judith Butler). *Differences: A Journal of Feminist. Cultural Studies, 6*(2–3), 30–61.

Braidotti, R. (2002). *Metamorphoses. Towards a materialist theory of becoming*. Cambridge: Cambridge University Press.

Braidotti, R. (2011). *Nomadic subjects: Embodiment and sexual difference in contemporary feminist Theory* (2nd ed.). New York, NY: Columbia University Press.

Braidotti, R. (2013). *The posthuman*. London: Polity Press.

Bray, A., & Colebrook, C. (1998). The haunted flesh: Corporeal feminism and the politics of (dis)embodiment. *Signs: Journal of Women in Culture and Society* 24, 35–67.

Campbell, E. (2016). Policing paedophilia: Assembling bodies, spaces and things. *Crime, Media and Culture* [ifirst]. http://dx.doi.org/10.1177/1741659015623598

Chen, M. Y. (2012). *Animacies: Biopolitics, racial matterings and queer affect*. London: Duke University Press.

Cixous, H. (1976). *The laugh of the Medusa* (K. Cohen & P. Cohen, Trans.). *Signs, 1*, 875–893.

Clough, P. (2010). The affective turn: Political economy, biomedia and bodies. In M. Gregg & G. J. Siegworth (Eds.), *The affect theory reader* (pp. 206–225). Durham, NC: Duke University Press.

Coleman, B. & Ringrose, J. (Eds.). (2013). *Deleuze and research methodologies*. Edinburgh: Edinburgh University Press.

Deleuze, G., & Guattari, F. (1984/2004). *Anti-oedipus: Capitalism and schizophrenia*. London: Continuum.

Deleuze, G. & Guatarri, F. (1987). *A thousand Plateaus capitalism and Schizophrenia*. (Translated from the French by Robert Hurley, Mark Seem, & Helen R. Lane). Minneapolis, MN: University of Minnesota Press.

Driscoll, C. (2002). *Girls: Feminine adolescence in popular culture and cultural theory*. New York, NY: Columbia University Press.

Egan, R. D. (2013). *Becoming sexual: A critical appraisal of the sexualisation of girls*. Boston, MA: Polity Press.

Evans, A., & Riley, S. (2014). *Technologies of sexiness: Sex, identity and consumer culture*. New York, NY: Oxford University Press.

Fox, N., & Alldred, P. (2013). The sexuality-assemblage: Desire, affect, anti-humanism. *The Sociological Review, 61*, 769–789.

Gerlitz, C., & Helmond, A. (2013). The like economy: Social buttons and the data-intensive web. *New Media & Society, 15*, 1348–1365

Gilbert, S., & Gubar, S. (1979). *The Madwoman in the attic: The woman writer and the nineteenth-century literary imagination*. New Haven, CT: Yale Nota Bene Press.

Gill, R., & Elias, A. S. (2014). 'Awaken your incredible': Love your body discourses and postfeminist contradictions. *International Journal of Media and Cultural Politics, 10*, 179–188.

Haraway, D. (1991). *Simians, cyborgs and women: The reinvention of nature*. New York, NY: Routledge.

Harvey, L., & Ringrose, J. (2015). Sexting, ratings and (mis)recognition: Teen boys' performing classed and racialised masculinities in digitally networked publics. In E. Renold, J. Ringrose, & D. Egan (Eds.), *Children, sexuality and sexualisation* (pp. 352–367). London: Palgrave

Harvey, L., Ringrose, J., & Gill, R. (2013). Swagger, ratings and masculinity: Theorising the circulation of social and cultural value in teenage boys' digital peer networks. *Sociological Research Online, 18*(4).

Hasinoff, A. (2015). *Sexting panic: Rethinking criminalization, privacy, and consent*. Champaign, IL: University of Illinois Press.

Hassinof, A. & Shepherd, T. (2014). Sexting in context: Privacy norms and expectations. *International Journal of Communication, 8*, 2932–2415.

Irigaray, L. (1985). *The sex which is not one*. Ithaca, NY: Cornell University Press.

Jenkins, H., Ford, S., & Green, J. (2013). *Spreadable media: Creating value and meaning in a networked culture*. New York: NYU Press.

Jewkes, Y., & Wykes, M. (2012). Reconstructing the sexual abuse of children: 'cyber-paeds', panic and power. *Sexualities, 15*, 934–952.

Johnson, C. M. (1995). Of dykes & deltoids: Irony and fetishism(s) in lesbian spectatorship of macho-woman films. *Spectator, 16*, 45–56. Retrieved from http://cinema.usc.edu/assets/099/15991.pdf

Karaian, L. (2014). Policing 'Sexting': Responsibilization, respectability and sexual subjectivity in child protection/crime prevention responses to teenagers' digital sexual expression. *Theoretical Criminology, 18*, 282–299.

Kember, S., & Zylinska, J. (2012). *Life after new media: Mediation as a vital process*. Cambridge, MA: MIT Press.

Lamb, S. (2010). Feminist ideals for a healthy female adolescent sexuality: A critique. *Sex Roles, 62*, 294–306.

Latour, B. (2005). *Reassembling the social: An introduction to actor-network-theory*. New York, NY: Oxford University Press.

Lazar, M. (2011). The right to be beautiful: Postfeminist identity and consumer beauty advertising. In R. Gill & C. Scharff (Eds.), *New femininities: Postfeminism, neoliberalism and identity* (pp. 37–51). London: Palgrave.

Lenz Taguchi, H., & Palmer, A. (2013). A more 'livable' school? A diffractive analysis of the performative enactments of girls' ill-/well-being with(in) school environments. *Gender and Education, 25*, 671–687.

Lorraine, T. (2008). Feminist lines of flight from the majoritarian subject. In C. Colebrook & J. Weinstein (Eds.), *Deleuze and gender* (pp. 60–82). Edinburgh: Edinburgh University Press.

Manning, E. (2013). *Always more than one: Individuation's dance*. Durham, NC: Duke University Press.

McRobbie, A. (2008). *The aftermath of feminism: Gender, culture and social change*. London: Sage.

Papacharissi, Z. (2009). The Virtual Geographies of Social Networks: A comparative analysis of Facebook, LinkedIn and ASmallWorld. *New Media and Society, 11*, 199–220.

Papacharissi, Z. (2015). *Affective publics: Sentiment, technology and politics*. Oxford: Oxford University Press.

Renold, E., & Ivinson, G. (2015). Mud, mermaid and burnt wedding dresses: Mapping queer belongings in teen girls' talk on surviving the ordinary traumas of gender and sexual violence. In E. Renold, J. Ringrose, & D. Egan (Eds.), *Children, sexuality and sexualisation*. Buckingham: Palgrave.

Renold, E., & Ringrose, J. (2011). Schizoid subjectivities? Re-theorising teen-girls' sexual cultures in an era of 'sexualisation'. *Journal of Sociology, 47*, 389–409.

Renold, E., & Ringrose, J. (in press). Pinballing and boners: Posthuman feminist intra-activist research assemblages in secondary school. In L. Allen & M. L. Rasmussen (Eds.), *The handbook of sexuality education*. London: Palgrave Macmillan.

Renold, E., Ringrose, J., & Egan, R. D. (Eds.). (2015). *Children, sexuality and sexualisation*. Buckingham: Palgrave.

Ringrose, J., Gill, R., Livingstone, S., & Harvey, L. (2012). *A qualitative study of children, young people and 'sexting'*. London: National Society for the Prevention of Cruelty to Children (NSPCC).

Ringrose, J., & Harvey, L. (2015). Boobs, back-off, six packs and bits: Mediated body parts, gendered reward, and sexual shame in teens' sexting images. *Continuum Journal of Media and Cultural Studies, 29*, 205–217. http://dx.doi.org/10.1080/103043112.2015.1022952

Ringrose, J., Harvey, L., Gill, R., & Livingstone, S. (2013). Teen girls, sexual double standards and 'sexting': Gendered value in digital image exchange. *Feminist Theory, 14*, 305–323.

Ringrose, J., & Renold, E. (2016). Cows, cabins and tweets: Posthuman intra-acting affect and feminist fires in secondary school. In C. Taylor & C. Hughes (Eds.), *Posthuman research practices in education* (pp. 220–241). London: Palgrave.

Salter, M. (2015). Privates in the online public: Sex(ting) and reputation on social media. Published online before print September 7, 2015. http://dx.doi.org/10.1177/1461444815604133

Sastre, A. (2014). Hottentot in the age of reality TV: Sexuality, race, and Kim Kardashian's visible body. *Celebrity Studies, 5*(1–2), 123–137.

Senft, T. M., & Baym, N. K. (Eds.). (2015). What does the selfie say? *Special Section, International Journal of Communication, 9*, 1588–1606.

Silk, M., Andrews, D., & Thorpe, H. (2016). *Routledge handbook of physical cultural studies*. London: Routledge.

Snaza, N. & Weaver, J. (Eds.). (2015). *Post-humanism and educational research*. New York, NY: Routledge.

Taylor, C., & Hughes, C. (2016). *Posthuman research practices in educational studies*. Buckingham: Palgrave.

Taylor, C., & Ivinson, G. (2013). Material feminisms: New directions for education. *Gender and Education, 25*, 665–670.

Van Dijck, J. (2013). *The culture of connectivity: A critical history of social media*. Oxford: Oxford University Press.

Van Doorn, N. (2011). Digital spaces, material traces: How matter comes to matter in online performances of gender, sexuality and embodiment. *Media, Culture and Society, 33*, 531–547.

Walkerdine, V. (1998). *Daddy's girl: Young girls and popular culture*. Cambridge, MA: Harvard University Press.

Walkerdine, V. (1999). Violent boys and precocious girls: Regulating childhood at the end of the millennium. *Contemporary Issues in Early Childhood, 1*, 3–23.

Warfield, K. (2015, June). The model, the #realme, and the self-conscious thespian: Digital subjectivities young canadian women, and selfies, *The International Journal of the Image, 6*, 1–16.

Warfield, K. (2015). Making the cut: An agential realist examination of selfies and touch. *Social Media and Society, 2*(2). doi: http://dx.doi.org/10.1177/2056305116641706

Learning with children, ants, and worms in the Anthropocene: towards a common world pedagogy of multispecies vulnerability

Affrica Taylor and Veronica Pacini-Ketchabaw

This article takes the naming of the Anthropocene as a moment of peda-gogical opportunity in which we might decentre the human as the sole learning subject and explore the possibilities of interspecies learning. Picking up on current Anthropocene debates within the feminist envi-ronmental humanities, it considers how educators might pedagogically engage with the issue of intergenerational environmental justice from the earliest years of learning. Drawing on two multispecies ethnogra-phies within the authors' Common World Childhoods' Research Collec-tive, the article describes some encounters among young children, worms and ants in Australia and Canada. It uses these encounters to illustrate how paying close attention to our mortal entanglements and vulnerabilities with other species, no matter how small, can help us to learn with other species and rethink our place in the world.

Introduction

In this article, we explore the kinds of learning that take place when chil-dren meet with ants and worms in their everyday, multispecies common worlds.[1] For a while now, we have been contemplating the pedagogical implications and affordances of repositioning children within the common worlds we co-inhabit and co-shape with a whole host of other species, enti-ties and forces (Taylor and Giugni 2012; Pacini-Ketchabaw 2013; Taylor 2013). In an attempt to move beyond education's traditional focus on child development and learning within an exclusively socio/cultural (in other words, exclusively human) context (Rogoff 2003), we deliberately reposi-tion children within the full, heterogeneous and interdependent multispecies common worlds in which we all live. In line with this shift beyond the social, or beyond the exclusively human, we also move away from the individual child-centred pedagogies that predominate in early childhood education. We focus, instead, on the collective manners and means through which children learn from engaging with other species, entities and forces in their immediate common worlds. We call these collectively engaged modes of learning 'common world pedagogies' (see Common World Childhoods Research Collective 2014).

This shift to common world pedagogies not only challenges human-centric assumptions about individual children's significant relations, it also challenges the assumption of human exceptionalism, including the assumption that only humans have the capacity to exercise agency (Plumwood 2007). In lieu of singling out children as the sole learning subjects and regarding their actions upon the world as the sole locus of agency, we follow Latour's (2004, 2009) notion of distributed or collective agency. We are interested in tapping into the relational and co-shaping learning that occurs when children and animals physically encounter each other in their common worlds. As we see it, the children are not the only orchestrators or actors in these interspecies worlds and encounters. Rather, the learning emerges from the relations taking place between all the actors – human and more-than-human alike.

Even though the child, worm and ant interspecies encounters we recount in this article are seemingly insignificant, small and ordinary events, we strategically frame them within the huge ethical questions posed by the Anthropocene. This is the term being currently adopted by earth systems scientists (Crutzen 2002, 2006; Steffen, Crutzen, and McNeill 2007) to describe the new geological epoch, or 'the new world' order (Zalasiewicz et al. 2010), in which overconsumptive and fossil-fuel-dependent human activities have 'permanently changed the planet' (Stromberg 2013). Inspired by Haraway's (2008, 2013) relational ethics and Hird's (2013a, 2013b) environmental ethics of vulnerability, we take up the challenge of learning to inherit and respond to this world that we have so fundamentally altered and damaged (Haraway 2011, 2013) by considering how we might address the conjoined issues of interspecies and intergenerational justice within the field of early childhood education. The issue of how best to respond to these challenges and how to address these issues is not easy, especially if we are to avoid reiterating the kinds of human-centric assumptions and actions that got us into this mess in the first place.

In the first section of this article, we explore some of the challenges, complexities and paradoxes thrown up by the naming of the Anthropocene and consider the implications for the field of education. Drawing on recent debates within the feminist environmental humanities, we reflect on some of the ethical considerations and pedagogical affordance of our relations with other species. We then move on to recount a number of minor events, or encounters between children and ants and children and worms. These are taken from the ongoing multispecies ethnographies we are conducting in early childhood education settings in Canberra, Australia, and Victoria, Canada.[2] These ant, worm, child encounters raise questions about our entanglements and mutual vulnerabilities with other species in these challenging ecological times. They also illustrate some of the ways that we might learn with, rather than about, other animals, in small ways and within our immediate and everyday common worlds.

Inheriting and responding to the Anthropocene

The term *Anthropocene* was first popularised by the Nobel Prize-winning scientist Paul Crutzen in his article 'Geology of Mankind', published in the journal *Nature* in 2002. Crutzen used it to describe a new geological epoch, emerging out of the Holocene, in which human activities have fundamentally and permanently changed the planet's biosphere. Crutzen and other earth systems' scientists, such as Will Steffen and John McNeill, argue that humans first started to become 'a global geophysical force' (Steffen, Crutzen, and McNeill 2007) in the industrial revolution, and that this anthropogenic force moved into what they call 'The Great Acceleration' at the end of the second world war. These scientists measure the accelerating multiple impacts of human activities, including the acidification of oceans, the depletion of the ozone layer, fundamental changes to the earth's carbon, phosphorous, and nitrogen cycles, climate change and the rapid loss of biodiversity as evidence of the Anthropocene. They point to the massive and exponentially increasing rate of species' extinctions, a phenomenon that has not been witnessed since the last ice age, as the strongest evidence of anthropogenic change.

This cumulative body of evidence of irreversible human-induced changes to the earth's interdependent geo- and bio-systems calls into question the sustainability of life on earth as we know it, including the survival of our own species (Colebrook 2012; Wolfe and Colebrook 2013). This is the radically altered world and uncertain future that we now inherit and bequeath to future generations. This realisation compels us to consider our ethical responsibilities, as educators, to tackle the pressing interrelated questions of interspecies and intergenerational justice in the Anthropocene.

We want to emphasise that we see this connection between intergenerational and interspecies justice as an inexorable one. The boundary-blurring 'natureculture' bio-philosophies of feminist science studies scholar Donna Haraway (2008, 2011, 2013), that situate multispecies relations with the complex mix of human and non-human, material and semiotic assemblages, have opened our eyes to the ways that humans and other species share entangled, cascading and enmeshed pasts, presents and futures. Haraway's work has provoked us to consider the profound ethical and ecological implications for children of these interspecies entanglements (see Pacini-Ketchabaw 2012, 2013; Taylor 2013; Taylor, Blaise, and Giugni 2013).

Beyond bio-philosophy, the interconnected sets of measurable and irreversible changes to earth systems that earth scientists are now naming as the Anthropocene make it indisputable that we live in a multispecies world in which 'natural and human forces' are complexly intertwined – so much so that 'the fate of one determines the fate of the other' (Zalasiewicz et al. 2010, 2231). It now seems quite apparent that the bifurcations of western epistemologies, which relegate 'nature' as a separate realm to 'culture', have become completely untenable. It is no longer plausible to separate the human from the so-called 'natural world', and it is no longer possible to deny that our fate, as a human species, is already bound up with the fate of other species (Rose et al. 2012).

Herein lie a number of potent paradoxes that the Anthropocene provokes us to confront. As an undeniably powerful, creative and destructive species, humans are both responsible for, and mortally vulnerable to, the life-threatening biospheric changes that we have brought upon ourselves and countless other species with whom our lives are entangled. At face value, the omnipotent belief that we are an exceptional species is reconfirmed by the declaration of the Anthropocene. But on the other hand, this same belief in human exceptionalism is self-sabotaging. It leads us to imagine that we can endlessly intervene to 'improve on nature', always find new techno-fixes to repair the messes we have created, and/or use up the earth's resources without suffering the consequences. It also leads us to disavow our own mortal entanglement in the same earth systems we so radically disturb. In other words, it is the fatally flawed belief in human exceptionalism, in the guise of omnipotence and radical nature/culture separatisms that has unhinged us and produced the imbroglio of disorderings that are now being named the Anthropocene.

We join with others in the social sciences, particularly those now working in the environmental humanities, in a call for a carefully considered ethical response to the Anthropocene (Gibson-Graham and Roelvink 2010; Scholars Concerned for Life in the Anthropocene 2010; Colebrook 2012; Rose et al. 2012; Haraway 2011, 2013; Rose 2011, 2013; Somerville 2013; Wolfe and Colebrook 2013; Gibson, Rose, and Fincher 2015). Along with them, we take this naming moment not only as an event that signals portending disaster, but as a wake-up call and a moment to fundamentally reconfigure our mindsets and our actions. It seems important that the naming of the Anthropocene should not become an excuse to exercise even more human domination and control, to scramble for yet another grandiose human techno-fix, or to construct yet another extraordinary and heroic human narrative of rescue and recovery (Haraway 2013). Rather, we want to seize this eventful naming moment as one of transformational opportunity. We therefore take it as a break point for interrupting business-as-usual, radically reimagining what it means to be human, revisiting the crucial question of agency, and risking finding new ways of relating to the world that we inherit and inhabit along with all other species. As educators, we are interested in how we might constructively and creatively implement these transformative opportunities from the earliest years of schooling.

In response to the naming of the Anthropocene, there are three key interventions we are advocating and enacting in the field of early childhood education. The first involves a simultaneous reimagining of agency and our place in the world. This intervention is prompted by recognising the ultimate folly of treating the world as a human stage and seeing ourselves as the only actors on it. We encourage those working with young children to consider what we might learn from other species about what is already happening in the world, both in relation to and beyond our participation in it (Scholars Concerned for Life in the Anthropocene 2010). This human-decentring intervention involves moving well beyond the current preoccupation with the developmental and learning needs of the individual child. It shifts the pedagogical focus from individual children to worldly relations. It fosters and supports children to pay attention to and be curious about the other creatures in their immediate worlds. It reinforces that the world is not just about us and acknowledges that we are not its only learners, scriptwriters, actors, movers, makers and shapers.

The second intervention involves 're-situating humans within ecological systems' (Gibson, Rose, and Fincher 2015) or what we are referring to, following Latour (2004, 2009) as common worlds. It challenges the mistaken assumption that we are exceptional and therefore separate from the rest of the world. The naming of the Anthropocene reminds us that it is this kind of exceptionalist and separatist thinking that supports the delusional belief that we are immune from the fallout of our destructive actions. To enact this intervention in early childhood education, we work with children in ways that explore exactly how our lives are already entangled with the lives of other species, in ways that stress that we do not just belong to our own human-kind, but that we are members of interconnected and interdependent multispecies common worlds.

The third intervention responds to another problem associated with dividing the world into culture (us and our concerns and activities) on the one side, and nature (or the environment) on the other. This is the problem of only considering human lives (or occasionally also the lives of other species admired for their 'intelligence') as worthy of ethical considerations and denying the ethical implications of our entanglement with all other species. By 're-situating nonhumans within ethical terms' (Gibson, Rose, and Fincher 2015), we want to support early childhood educators to find ways of encouraging children to develop a multispecies ethics. We are not only talking about learning to conduct ethical relations with those species that children have already formed attachments to – such as pets, familiar farm animals and those non-domestic animals that are often sentimentally and anthropomorphically portrayed in children's literature and popular culture, but also species that are not so easy to recognise and love.

Interspecies vulnerabilities

Pushing beyond recourse to human exceptionalism is no easy task. Cognizant of the inherent limits of our own all-too-human partialities, we can only hope that our efforts might be a little more than academic and gestural. In promoting a pedagogy that emerges out of real-life interspecies encounters, we aim for the modest goal of fostering a nascent, incomplete and somehow embodied appreciation of the ways in which more-than-human life forms and forces co-shape our common worlds. We want young children to sense and register, in more than cognitive ways, that it is never just about 'us'. And we also want to stay open to the possibility that other species and life forms shape us in ways that exceed our ability to fully comprehend.

We have been well assisted in this challenging task by Hird's (2010, 2012, 2013a, 2013b) insightful science and environmental sociologies, which extend Haraway's entangled species ontologies into microbial worlds. Based on her tutelage in Lyn Margulis's Massachusetts microbiology laboratory, and her own passionate engagement with bacteria in Canada's waste landfill sites (2013a), Hird's (2010) microontologies have helped us to take some early steps in thinking through the potent agency and worldly significance of the subterranean worlds of worms and ants. Hird (2013a) stresses that while humanism might predispose us to care selectively about some other animals that are 'big like us' and acknowledge that they have an auxiliary role to play, along with us protagonists, in 'the greatest show on earth', it usually fails to incite our interest in smaller life forms. Through engaging with and thinking through bacteria, she points out that the less glamorous, but nevertheless essential and real action takes place backstage. Human lives and actions might be big and spectacular, but it is the backstage metabolising work of microbes and bacteria that creates the conditions of possibility for these front-of-stage lives and actions (2013a). We could similarly point to the essential life-supporting work that is going on underground, where quadrillions of worms and ants are engineering the show that we, as humans, are simultaneously putting on and witnessing on the surface of the earth.

The point we are making here is that, despite the human predilection to reiterate human exceptionalism, including within many epic and heroic narrations of the Anthropocene, the fact is that our human lives are totally dependent on the lives of other, much smaller, often overlooked and sometimes invisible creatures, such as worms and ants. Their work in composting the earth to make it viable for other life forms not only predates our own relatively short, if spectacular, human life on earth, but will most likely postdate us as well.

Drawing on a microbial perspective, Hird suggests that we need to disengage ourselves from humanism's 'profoundly myopic' ontologies and ethics (2010, 36). She points out that even when we seek to include the nonhuman animal in the ethical realm from a humanist position, we still 'pivot on a comparison between the humans and (the) animal' (2010, 36). Hird (2012, 262) asserts that this is because humanist ontologies can only ever produce an 'Other-ethics based on face-to-face interaction', an ethics that constantly defaults to the human-as-type and relies on some kind of anthropomorphic recognition of ourselves in the other animal. In other words, while it is possible to extend a sense of ethical responsibility to the animal with appealing big eyes (like ours) and a cute face (like ours), it is not so easy to include those life forms which have no face at all – like bacteria and earthworms – within a fundamentally humanist ethical schema. She proposes a radically different kind of ethics, one that does not rely on the human as the default extender of ethical care, and which she calls an ethics of vulnerability (2012, 262). Within this 'inhuman' form of ethics, we are called into account for our vulnerability alone, not for our largess and capacity to care for others. The agency is completely reversed when we become beholden to the myriad of micro life forms we rarely see, let alone acknowledge, and yet which sustain the lives of all large animal species, including our own.

More recently, in an extension of these ideas and in stronger recognition of the Anthropocene, Hird (2013b, 105) has been writing about an 'environmental ethics of vulnerability' that is 'sensitive to human and nonhuman asymmetrical vulnerability to an unknowable future'. In other words, this environmental ethics of vulnerability is one that recognises that, although all species have inherited and are co-implicated in the environmental uncertainty and mess we now find ourselves in, it might well be that we humans are among the most vulnerable species of all.

Multispecies ethnography

In responding to the legacies of the Anthropocene within the field of early childhood education, our efforts to develop a multispecies ethics of environmental vulnerability require methods that allow us to focus upon the relationalities, interdependences and encounters between children and animals in their local common world environments. The longitudinal, situated, immersed, relationship-based, affect-attuned and observational methods of multispecies ethnography are well suited to this purpose (Kirksey and Helmreich 2010; Ogden, Hall, and Tanita 2013).

For the last two years, we have undertaken early childhood multispecies ethnographies in two sites: a wet forest in Victoria, British Columbia in

Canada, and a dry bushland area of Canberra, Australian Capital Territory. The multispecies ethnographic methods we have used have required us, as well as the children, to become more attuned to ways in which human and nonhuman alike affect and are affected by each other. They have allowed us to recognise how mutual vulnerabilities emerge not only in singular moments of multispecies encounter, for instance, when children, ants and worms meet, but that they are always already there. Whether we recognise these mutual vulnerabilities or not, our multispecies lives and futures are co-implicated simply because they are interdependent and entangled in mutually constituted and now fundamentally damaged worlds.

The multispecies ethnographic methods work with what Tsing (2013) refers to as 'more than human sociality', in which all of the actors learn about each other *in action* and researchers become companion participants in sticky webs of connection engaging in experimental and inventive practices. These inventive and experimental co-implicated research practices require new kinds of observational skills that are akin to what Latour (2004) calls 'learning to be affected'. Learning to be affected requires us to develop more-than-cognitive modes of attention – to become attuned to the multifarious ways that human and nonhuman bodies are moved, disconcerted and enlivened through their common world encounters. In our early childhood multispecies research contexts, this means paying attention not only to what the children are saying and doing, not only to how the children's bodies are being moved, affected and enlivened by the animals they encounter, but also paying attention to the movements and actions of the worms, ants, water, rain boots, fingers, sticks, rocks, mud, pebbles and dust. We push ourselves to learn to be affected by and think with all of the actors – in particular by and with the children's, the ants' and the worms' bodies, movements, disconcertments and preferences – even though, as Tsing (2013) points out, and we acknowledge, this is extremely hard work.

The hard work is not just about noticing the multitude of things that are going on for human and nonhuman others, but it is also about noticing what human and nonhuman others notice (Tsing 2013). Of course, this is never fully achievable. The limits to human intentionalities, observations and knowings are premised in multispecies ethnographies, precisely because they acknowledge that humans are not the only ones exercising agency and not the only animals noticing, observing, acting, knowing, affecting and being affected. We recognise that our efforts to notice by being there and being interested (Hird 2013a), by staying attuned and learning to be affected (Latour 2004), by asking questions and paying attention to the temporal and the transitive (Lorimer 2010), by using images as processes of 'collaborating and moving *with* the world' (Kind 2013, 429) and by pushing ourselves to think through and with multiplicity of more than human actors (Whatmore 2013) are always delimited by the partiality of our human apprehensions and ambivalences.

Challenging the humanist research conventions of the 'all-knowing-human-actor-as-researcher', we resist responding to the things we do notice during these multispecies encounters as objectified 'findings to be analysed'. Instead, we deliberately ask questions, open up possibilities, remain curious, but also admit that there is always more going on than we can ever know. Our intention is to evoke and provoke rather than represent or explain what might be going on in those encounters (Lorimer 2010).

As experienced early childhood ethnographic researchers, we are already quite skilful at engaging with children. But directly engaging with small beings such as ants and earthworms provides much greater challenges. To supplement our 'modest witnessing' (Haraway 1997) of the embodied encounters of ants, worms and children in our multispecies ethnographies, and to help us to take more account of ants' and worms' socialities (Tsing 2013) and more-than-human agencies (Whatmore 2013), we turn to ant and worm science texts. This engagement with science is not so much about extracting ideas in order to reconfirm our superior capacity for 'knowingness' (Hird 2013a; Probyn 2014) as it is about learning how best to respond to the multispecies relations and entanglements within which we are already implicated, including through relations of scientific enquiry.

In responding as best we can to these relations, we need to ensure we do not overlook the fact that the ants and worms that children meet in the forest or bush have their own particular biographies (Tsing 2013), and their own evolutionary trajectories and heritages that exist separate from as well as bound up with their relations with us (Haraway 2008, 25). We might be able to respond more creatively to worms and ants if we can glean from science an appreciation, albeit only partial and imperfect, of their impressive complexities and capacities. For instance, we might understand that if we accidentally sever a worm with a garden shovel, it may well be able to regenerate itself. We might recognise that an agitated ant running around in circles because we are about to step on it, is releasing scented hormones to communicate danger to other ants in the colony. We might reduce our conceited sense of human exceptionalism with the humbling recognition that the daily work of worms and ants provides the conditions of possibility for much life on earth, including ours. The knowledge, of course, also matter in our pedagogies.

Our engagements with the bush, the forest, the ants, the worms, the children, the art of noticing and the biological and earth systems sciences are not only research acts. These engagements are also inherently pedagogical. In the process of conducting multispecies ethnographies with young children and other species in their immediate common worlds, we are also constituting new kinds of multispecies pedagogies (Common World Childhoods Research Collective 2014). These more-than-human pedagogies exceed the logic of developmentalism, in which the individual child acquires age-appropriate knowledge in the process of becoming rational and autonomous.

Multispecies pedagogies explore the conditions of possibility for interspecies learning, not autonomous individual human development and learning. They are built upon relations, they stress interdependencies and they ponder the ethical and political implications of entangled human and nonhuman lives.

In the following sections, we offer a series of vignettes of child–animal encounters, assembled from the multispecies ethnographies we have been conducting in Victoria, British Columbia and in Canberra, Australian Capital Territory over the last two years. The vignettes draw upon a range of fragmented elements, including: fieldwork photographs; observational field notes; reflections on ant and worm sciences and biographies; and ethical ponderings prompted by the work of feminist scholars working in the environmental humanities.

Child–worm encounters

Earthworms constantly remind us of our vulnerabilities, particularly when we recall that they predate us by 600 million years, and even though they are our contemporaries, they will likely outlive us (Schwartz 2012). These invertebrate animals, once considered lower organisms, are deeply entangled with other species' lives and, more poignantly, are active members of the history of the world (Bennett 2010). Writings about earthworms date back to Aristotle, who suitably called them 'the Intestines of the Earth'. While earthworm taxonomy is still incomplete, taxonomists have identified more than 8000 species of earthworms from approximately 800 genera which live all around the world, except in regions with extreme climates, such as deserts and ice-covered areas (Edwards 2004). Earthworms are also quite diverse in

Figure 1.   Inspecting a worm. Author's photos.

size: 'no other terrestrial invertebrate has such a wide range of sizes between the smallest and the largest individuals' (Edwards 2004, 4).

> Earthworms abound on the wet west coast of British Columbia, and the children at this child care centre encounter them all the time in the gardens they tend, the forest we visit weekly, and even on sidewalks during their regular walks. The earthworms attract the children who are fascinated by the movements of these red wigglers (Figure 1). The children often pick them up with a stick or with their hands, while some of the adults around them try to contain their immediate disgust for the earthworms. Children, though, are focused on the earthworms' responses to these encounters as they wriggle beneath the soil or on their hands or stay still at the end of a long stick. The children interpret these responses in many different ways. Sometimes they jump and giggle as they comment on how the worms tickle their hands. Other times they are determined to find the earthworms 'a house' or name them or bring them to what they call 'safety' (Figure 2). Yet other times they simply spend long moments enjoying the worms' movements in their hands as they softly share their own stories with the worms.

Are the children, through these multiple encounters with worms, learning to take these sophisticated animals seriously? What possibilities reside in different forms of relating and intersecting with earthworms? Why are the children so curious about earthworms? Are the children becoming capable of a 'caring obligation', as Bellacasa (2010) calls these kinds of relatings, towards the worms through these ordinary encounters? How might these sticky beings, who are indispensable in our world, also become indispensable in our pedagogies?

As Darwin pointed out in the late 1800s, the work of worms is vital for maintaining soil fertility in ecosystems such as grasslands, forests and agriculture. As prolific eaters that work in symbiosis with bacteria, these vermicular invertebrates are able to breakdown dead plant and animal matter in soils and continuously turn soil over and preserve its structure, aeration,

Figure 2. Finding worms. Author's photos.

drainage and fertility (Edwards 2004). Through their work of consuming matter, fragmenting it and mixing it with mineral particles in soil to create water-stable aggregates, earthworms contribute significantly to soil formation. They can also move large quantities of soil from the deeper strata to form a stone-free layer on the surface of the soil. Through this significant work, earthworms leave cracks and crevices in the soil to maintain aeration, drainage and porosity. The burrows they create are coated with a mucous that forms a suitable environment for microbes. As earthworms digest the organic matter, the nutrients present in it are converted to a form that is more bioavailable to plants (Vergara 2012).

> The children and the educators now know where to find earthworms and they visit these places frequently in search of the vermicular creatures. In the forest, they like to visit what the children have named Worm River. The red wigglers abound at the bottom of this shallow stream. Carefully the children walk around them to ensure that their colourful rain boots avoid the earthworms. The children also know that digging in the forest will yield many treasures, including the earthworms they like to unearth, inspect and put back into the forest's rich soil. One of their favourite places to dig is the root of a huge, rotten cedar tree that has fallen down, where earthworms have been doing their work of decomposing (Figure 3). One of the classrooms has made the difficult decision to bring earthworms into a big tank in their yard (Figure 4). Here, children and worms are getting to know each other. The children refer to the worms in the tank as 'a family'. The ethics of having the earthworms in a tank became a regular conversation among the children and the educators; in the end, they agreed to transport the worms back and forth between the tank and their garden.

Multispecies pedagogies are filled with difficult decisions, unanswered questions and ethical conundrums. The children are learning to respond to the worms, and the worms are learning to respond to close encounters with

Figure 3. Digging for worms. Author's photo.

children. Responses from everyone, though, are unpredictable, unexpected and at times unwelcomed. These encounters are not about technique and exact calculation. Yet, here is where pedagogies become interesting and alive with possibility. The decisions made by the educators and children have (literal) consequences for making the earth. We are convinced that we need earthworms to participate in decomposing our practices.

Caring for the earthworms is a vital part of child–worm encounters. Yet, questions of life and death become real when children encounter earthworms.

> The children are much bigger than even the fattest earthworms they find in the forest. Although they like to care for them, find new houses for them or transport them to areas where they will not be stepped on, accidents happen … One morning during one of our visits to the forest, a child was tending a wiggly worm in Worm River. With a long stick, he picked up the worm to ensure other children running around through the water would not squash it. Through this transportation process, the worm fell from the end of the stick. Determined to complete the task, the child picked up the dancing worm with the stick again. This time, though, the unlucky worm broke in two (Figure 5).

In this encounter, the earthworm surprises the child by regenerating itself from the bisection, as if it were a plant (Xiao, Ge, and Edwards 2011). Might this 'magic', as the child referred to the moment, present possibilities for thinking about our vulnerabilities to the earthworm? This moment of regeneration might not be just for the earthworm, but also for the children. It might allow them to reimagine life as they know it. Moreover, might the earthworm regeneration be a way of displacing, as Haraway (1997, 12)

Figure 4.   Worms in tank. Author's photo.

Figure 5.   Broken worm. Author's photo.

writes, 'development, fulfilment and containment' in pedagogies to respond to the messy inheritances we bequeath to future generations?

Yet, how do we account for the consequences that regeneration has for the earthworm? The regeneration of specific parts will always depend on where the cut took place. The earthworm may or may not be able to replace its sexual organs, or yield a full head or a tail (Clark 2013). The cut has consequences, not only for the earthworm, but also for the children's life-worlds. It is also possible that a child might step on an earthworm by mistake or even intentionally. No easy response exists for either the earthworm or the children in these ordinary encounters. This is a case of learning to live *with* each other for survival and to always be mindful of each other's vulnerabilities.

Child–ant encounters

Just like earthworms, ants might be small, but they render big species like us humans quite insignificant in other scalar terms. They predate us by at least 100 million years and outnumber us by around 1.5 million to one (Ward 2010). They are the most numerous and species-diverse of all social insects. Apart from their primordial and ubiquitous presence in all parts of the world (except for the polar regions), they are probably best known for their extraordinary social organisation. Ants' high-level sociality is evident in their capacity for industrious collective work, which they undertake within complex systems of labour division, communication and cooperation. It is because of their capacity to act collectively that ants can effectively colonise and modify environments. One ant alone cannot make a huge impact on the world, but working collectively, ants become a powerful engine room of earth movers and shapers.

There are gravelly ant nests all through the dry sclerophyll bushlands where we walk on Wednesday afternoons. The children never lose their fascination for them. On every walk, they stop and stare intently at the miniature worlds of tiny pebbles and small holes that cover the surface of the underground ant homes (Figure 6). They are looking to spot the scurrying inhabitants as they dart in, out and about. In the cooler months, when the ants are more docile, the children squat down on the ground to inspect the nests at close range. They study the tiny component parts of this micro-landscape in minute detail, but always with an eye for the action. They often call out when they spot ants carrying dead insects and seeds into the holes. When the ants are sluggish, the children push small twigs down the holes to see if they can rouse them (Figure 7). They know that there are thousands of ants down there somewhere.

What is it about the small details of this miniature ant world that repeatedly grabs and holds the children's attention? Does all this close looking give them an inkling that there are complex and mysteriously unknown worlds beyond their own? Are they somehow registering that worlds exist within

Figure 6.   Inspecting an ant nest. Author's photos.

Figure 7.   Poking an ant nest with a stick. Author's photo.

worlds, and, if so, do they have a sense that these nested worlds are connected?

   In hot, dry environments, such as those that predominate in Australia, ants do the work of worms. They are the subterranean 'ecosystem engineers' that keep the soil structure healthy and porous by digging aerating tunnels and allowing precious rain to penetrate the ground (Evans et al. 2011). Like worms, they are extraordinary composters. Worker ants clean the surrounding surface environment and increase the nutrient base of the soil by depositing plant and animal waste in their tunnels for food storage. They are extremely efficient at doing this regenerative work. Each ant can carry more than 20 times its body weight (Ward 2010). Many ants also have close and mutually beneficial relationships with plants, usually involving the exchange of protection for nutrition. The most famous example of this is the well-documented symbiotic relationship between seed-gathering ants and acacia plants. The ants increase the dispersal and germination rate of the acacia seeds by carrying them down into their nests and effectively 'planting' them in the nutrient-rich soil. In return, the ants get to feast on the

Figure 8.   Waiting for the ants to climb on her hand. Author's photo.

acacia seeds' sweet outer top casing, called the elaisome, before the seeds germinate (Forest and Madden 2011, 2–3).

> As the weather warms up, so do the ants. They come out and about, doing their business. They get faster and feistier. The children quickly learn that when they stomp on the ground, the ants will come running out. As the agitated ants start to swarm over the top of the nest, protecting their territory, the children back off to a respectful distance. But they still can not resist prodding the nests with sticks, hoping for a rise, or perhaps the thrill of seeing a line of ants marching up the stick towards their hands.

It is interesting to note the ways in which both children and ants test their agency in this encounter and how this agency is determined not only by size, but also by speed and volume. By partaking in this provocative dance of relating, of threatening and protecting, of advance and retreat, what do the children learn about the relative power and affect that large and small creatures can exert upon each other?

> Sometimes, ants run up the children's legs or into their clothing and bite them. This is usually a form of retaliation against the children's provocations, or when the children simply do not notice that they are standing in the middle of a swarming ant nest. There have been some highly charged moments when

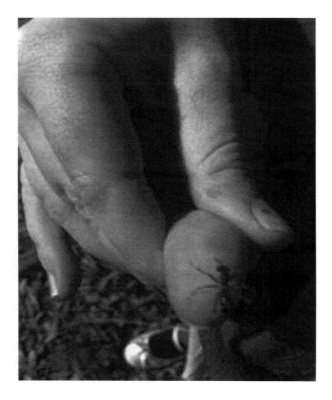

Figure 9.   Taking a closer look. Author's photo.

frenzied ants scurry and bite and panicked children scream and squash. These fight and flight, life and death moments are marked by the rush of alarm pheromones and adrenalin and by the smell of formic acid. But the children who calmly observe the ants rarely get bitten. This child is waiting patiently for an ant to walk onto her hand so she can take an even closer look at it (Figure 8). Her perseverance pays off. Both ant and child seem unfazed by their intimate encounter (Figure 9).

Both ants and children face a risk and pose a threat to each other in these embodied exchanges, albeit unevenly. Both register their mutual vulnerabilities. While the defensively swarming ants clearly recognise the children as a potential threat to their nests, the children are well aware that ants can bite them. They also know they can easily kill ants. This understanding presents an ethical dilemma for the children: to kill or not to kill the ants, before or if they bite them? It seems the children are on a number of different routes towards responding to the risks and vulnerabilities they share when they bodily engage with these small creatures. Their actions portend different kinds of learnings. The children who goad ants might learn that there are consequences to their actions and that even small creatures can become formidable foes. Those children whose feet inadvertently get in the way might learn the consequences of not paying attention to the lifeworlds of smaller creatures. Those who carefully seek intimacy with the ants might learn about the precarity of life through (literally) holding the responsibility for another life, and at the same time, through risking making themselves vulnerable to another species.

Conclusion: towards a common worlds pedagogy of multispecies vulnerability

When responding to the Anthropocene in this article, we have been very conscious of scale – the scale of the problems of the Anthropocene, the scale of children's immediate lifeworlds, the scale of worms' and ants' lifeworlds, and the scale of our own efforts to respond. We are well aware that we are engaging as very small players, along with very tiny animals, on a very small stage, with very small interspecies events, in the face of gargantuan planetary challenges. Our primary scalar strategy has been, and still is, to situate our research and the pedagogies we are developing within the geohistorical specificities of the immediate commonplace worlds that children actually inhabit along with other species (Taylor 2013) and to gradually unravel and trace the entangled threads that knit this particular common world into countless other worlds – and indeed, into the global commons.

Our modest efforts have been buoyed by Haraway's (2013) reminder that only 'partial recuperations' are possible and that responding to the Anthropocene is as much about paying close attention to everyday small things, contingent partialities and messy relationalities as it is about the geo-sublime proportions of carbon measurements, global warming and melting ice caps (Instone 2015). We have also been invigorated by what we have learnt from ants and worms. They have reminded us that, beyond the radar of the spectacular 'big action' we partake in on the surface of the planet, a proliferation of tiny earth movers, industriously working underground, taking collective action, are literally reshaping, shifting and making the earth.

As researchers, our abilities to notice and appreciate the complex minutia of interspecies reciprocities and co-shapings have been sharpened and refined by witnessing what happens when the bodies of muddy children and slippery worms touch each other in the wet forests of British Columbia, and when dusty ants and children congregate in the dry bushlands of the Australian Capital Territory. These seemingly minor, trivial and yet also mortally intense earthy encounters have shown us that learning how to respond and respect in multispecies common worlds can only happen in those embodied (and often fraught) moments when humans and animals actually meet and notice each other.

Our witnessing of such real-life encounters among children, ants and worms and our readings of Hird's (2010) microontologies have, in combination, helped us to conceive of ways in which we might bring very small animals into the realm of ethics within these common world pedagogies. We may have not been able to completely resist the temptation to default to a self-referential humanist ethics of largess and care for these little creatures, but at least the not-always-gorgeous encounters with faceless ants and worms, and an apprehension of their incredible collective potency, gave us some sense of the possibility for tapping into an ethics of our own vulnerability to other life forms on earth.

All of the above have helped us glimpse how we might learn with other species in the Anthropocene and work towards a common worlds pedagogy of multispecies vulnerability. What we are proposing goes beyond how early childhood pedagogues and researchers have addressed children's relations by focusing on their social-emotional development, or on the importance of the environment of relationships. Learning with other species would not exclusively follow human plans, wishes and desires. Everything becomes relevant in fostering and researching child–animal relations in the Anthropocene, human and otherwise. As Tsing (2013) writes, the challenge is bringing 'more-than-human socialities' into our understandings of pedagogies and research.

But we have to admit that this is no easy task and there have been limits to our work. These glimpses are hard to sustain. Taking the encounters among children, earthworms and ants as serious pedagogical moments has required us to work continually at decentring the human in our own thinking and practice. While it has been quite easy to recognise the agency of the ants and worms within the encounters (particularly those biting ants), we have found it nigh impossible not to position the children as the central actors, and difficult, at times, to resist the temptation to search for evidence of an ethics based in human-centric care for the other. Despite these limitations, we continue to argue for an ethico-political pedagogy of mutual vulnerability in the Anthropocene that recognises that learning through encounters with other species is not always harmonious and pleasant, is not always equal, and does not offer us 'moral certitudes or simple escape routes' from the mess we are in (Haraway 2011, 115). Perhaps the most we can claim is that these small interspecies pedagogical encounters are incremental, if fleeting, moments of 'multispecies achievements' (Haraway 2013), 'where multispecies players enmeshed in partial and flawed translations across difference redo ways of living and dying' and of reworlding damaged worlds together.

Disclosure statement

No potential conflict of interest was reported by the authors.

Notes

1. The notion of common worlds is central to our work. It is a term we borrow from Latour (2004, 2009). He first deployed it as a strategy for resisting the Great Divide between 'nature' (or the nonhuman) on the one hand and 'society' (or a separate human world) on the other. Common worlds are thus the undivided, heterogeneous, human and more than human collectives.
2. This research is conducted with ethics approval from the University of Canberra, ACT, and the University of Victoria, BC.

References

Bellacasa, M. P. 2010. "Ethical Doings in Naturecultures." *Ethics, Place & Environment: A Journal of Philosophy and Geography* 13 (2): 151–169.

Bennett, J. 2010. *Vibrant Matter: A Political Ecology of Things*. London: Duke University Press.

Clark, P. 2013. "Making Heads or Tails out of Severed Earthworms." *The Washington Post*. June. http://www.washingtonpost.com/wp-srv/special/metro/urban-jungle/pages/130604.html

Colebrook, C. 2012. *Extinction*. Open Humanities Press. http://www.living booksaboutlife.org/books/Extinction.

Common World Childhoods Research Collective. 2014. Common World Childhoods website. http://www.commonworlds.net/.

Crutzen, P. 2002. "Geology of Mankind." *Nature* 415: 23. doi:10.1038/415023a.

Crutzen, P. 2006. "The Anthropocene." In *Earth System Science in the Anthropocene*, edited by E. Ehlers and T. Krafft, 13–18. Berlin: Springer, e-book.

Edwards, C. 2004. "The Importance of Earthworms as Key Representatives of the Soil Fauna." In *Earthworm Ecology*, edited by C. Edwards, 3–11. New York: CRC Press.

Evans, T. A., T. Z. Dawes, P. R. Ward, and N. Lo. 2011. "Ants and Termites Increase Crop Yield in a Dry Climate." *Nature Communications* 2: 262. http://www.nature.com/ncomms/journal/v2/n3/pdf/ncomms1257.pdf.

Forest, F., and Madden, D. 2011. *Elaiosomes and Seed Dispersal by Ants. DNA to Darwin Case Study*. http://www.dnadarwin.org/casestudies/2/FILES/AntsSG2.0.pdf.

Gibson, K., D. B. Rose, and R. Fincher, eds. 2015. *Manifesto for Living in the Anthropocene*. New York: Punctum Books.

Gibson-Graham, J. K., and G. Roelvink. 2010. "An Economic Ethics for the Anthropocene." *Antipode* 41: 320–346.

Haraway, D. 1997. *Modest_Witness@Second_Millenium.FemaleMan©_Meets_OncoMouse™*. London: Routledge.

Haraway, D. 2008. *When Species Meet*. Minneapolis, MN: University of Minnesota Press.

Haraway, D. 2011. "Speculative Fabulations for Technoculture's Generations: Taking Care of Unexpected Country." *Australian Humanities Review* 50: 95–118.

Haraway, D. 2013. *Distinguished Lecture*. Arizona State University, Institute for Humanities Research [video]. http://ihr.asu.edu/news-events/news/2013-distinguished-lecturer-donna-haraway-reading-group.

Hird, M. J. 2010. "Meeting with the Microcosmos." *Environment and Planning D: Society and Space* 28: 36–39.

Hird, M. J. 2012. "Animal, All Too Animal: Toward an Ethic of Vulnerability." In *Animal Others and the Human Imagination*, edited by A. Gross and A. Vallely, 331–348. New York: Columbia University Press.

Hird, M. J. 2013a. "On Preparations: Learning and Teaching Materiality." Paper presented at Developing Feminist Post-constructivist Qualitative Research Methodologies in the Educational Sciences conference, at Stockholm University, Stockholm. June 2013.

Hird, M. J. 2013b. "Waste, Landfills, and an Environmental Ethic of Vulnerability." *Ethics and the Environment* 18 (1): 105–124.

Instone, L. 2015. "Risking Attachment in the Anthropocene." In *An Ethics for the Anthropocene*, edited by K. Gibson, D. B. Rose, and R. Fincher, 29–36. New York: Punctum Books.

Kind, S. 2013. "Lively Entanglements: The Doings, Movements and Enactments of Photography." *Global Studies of Childhood* 3 (4): 427–441.

Kirksey, S. E., and S. Helmreich. 2010. "The Emergence of Multispecies Ethnography." *Cultural Anthropology* 25 (4): 545–576.

Latour, B. 2004. *Politics of Nature: How to Bring the Sciences into Democracy.* Cambridge, MA: Harvard University Press.

Latour, B. 2009. *On the Modern Cult of the Factish Gods.* London: Duke University Press.

Lorimer, J. 2010. "Moving Image Methodologies for More-than-human Geographies." *Cultural Geographies* 17 (2): 237–258.

Ogden, A., B. Hall, and K. Tanita. 2013. "Animals, Plants, People, and Things: A Review of Multispecies Ethnography." *Environment and Society: Advances in Research* 4: 5–24.

Pacini-Ketchabaw, V. 2012. "Postcolonial Entanglements: Unruling Stories." *Child & Youth Services* 33: 313–316.

Pacini-Ketchabaw, V. 2013. "Frictions in Forest Pedagogies: Common Worlds in Settler Colonial Spaces." *Global Studies of Childhood* 3 (4): 355–365.

Plumwood, V. 2007. "Human Exceptionalism and the Limitations of Animals. A Review of Raimond Gaita's the Philosopher's Dog." *Australian Humanities Review*, 42. Online publication. http://www.australianhumanitiesreview.org/archive/Issue-August-2007/EcoHumanities/Plumwood.html

Probyn, E. 2014. "Women Following Fish in a More-than-human World." *Gender, Place & Culture: A Journal of Feminist Geography* 21 (5): 589–603.

Rogoff, B. 2003. *The Cultural Nature of Human Development.* Oxford: Oxford University Press.

Rose, D. B. 2011. *Wild Dog Dreaming: Love and Extinction.* Charlottesville, VA: University of Virginia Press.

Rose, D. B. 2013. "Multispecies Belonging in the Time of Extinctions." Public lecture, Australian Studies Research Network 2013 seminar series, at History House, Sydney, 10 May.

Rose, D. B., T. van Dooren, M. Chrulew, S. Cooke, M. Kearnes, and E. O'Gorman. 2012. "Thinking through the Environment, Unsettling the Humanities." *Environmental Humanities* 1: 1–5.

Scholars Concerned for Life in the Anthropocene. 2010. *Manifesto for Living in the Anthropocene.* http://www.ecologicalhumanities.org/manifesto.html

Schwartz, J. 2012. *Worm Work: Recasting Romanticism.* Minneapolis, MN: University of Minnesota Press.

Somerville, M. 2013. *Water in a Dry Land: Place-learning through Art and Story.* New York: Routledge.

Steffen, W., P. Crutzen, and J. R. McNeill. 2007. "The Anthropocene: Are Humans Now Overwhelming the Great Forces of Nature." *AMBIO: A Journal of the Human Environment* 36 (8): 614–621.

Stromberg, J. 2013, January. "What is the Anthropocene and Are We in It?" *Smithsonian.* http://www.smithsonianmag.com/science-nature/What-is-the-Anthropocene-and-Are-We-in-It-183828201.html

Taylor, A. 2013. *Reconfiguring the Natures of Childhood.* London: Routledge.

Taylor, A., M. Blaise, and M. Giugni. 2013. "Haraway's 'Bag Lady Story-telling': Relocating Childhood and Learning within a 'Post-human Landscape'." *Discourse: Studies in the Cultural Politics of Education* 34 (1): 48–62.

Taylor, A., and M. Giugni. 2012. "Common Worlds: Reconceptualising Inclusion in Early Childhood Communities." *Contemporary Issues in Early Childhood* 13 (2): 108–119.

Tsing, A. L. 2013. "More than Human Sociality: A Call for Critical Description." In *Anthropology and Nature*, edited by K. Hastrup, 27–42. New York: Routledge.

Vergara, S. E. 2012. "Worms." In *Encyclopedia of Consumption and Waste: The Social Science of Garbage*, edited by C. Zimring and W. Rathje, 1008–1010. Thousand Oaks, CA: Sage.

Ward, P. S. 2010. "Taxonomy, Phylogenetics, and Evolution." In *Ant Ecology*, edited by L. Lach, C. Parr, and K. L. Abbott, 3–17. Oxford: Oxford University Press.

Whatmore, S. 2013. "Earthly Powers and Affective Environments: An Ontological Politics of Flood Risk." *Theory, Culture & Society* 30 (7/8): 33–50.

Wolfe, C., and Colebrook, C. 2013. Is the Anthropocene … a Doomsday Device? Dialogue. The Anthropocene Project, Haus Der Kulturen Der Welt, January 2013. http://www.youtube.com/watch?v=YLTCzth8H1 M.

Xiao, N., F. Ge, and C. Edwards. 2011. "The Regeneration Capacity of an Earthworm, Eisenia Fetida, in Relation to the Site of Amputation along the Body." *Acta Ecologica Sinica* 31: 197–204.

Zalasiewicz, J., M. Williams, W. Steffen, and P. Crutzen. 2010. "The New World of the Anthropocene 1." *Environmental Science and Technology* 44 (7): 2228–2231.

A Walk in the Park: Considering Practice for Outdoor Environmental Education Through an Immanent Take on the Material Turn

Jamie Mcphie

David Andrew George Clarke

This article considers practice for environmental education from the perspective of the material turn by taking the reader along on an outdoor learning session in a park. We present a fictional walk where we encounter plants, trees, wasp-orchids, stones, walking sticks, plastic bags, people, weather, and kites, each of which has a story to tell that demonstrates ontological immanence and the material process of being alive. These stories help suggest some practical ways in which environmental education can be reoriented from an essentialist paradigm to one of becoming, tackling prevailing conceptions of the human mind as disembodied from the world.

In this essay/lesson, we articulate some practical applications of an approach to environmental education that embraces an ontological turn in contemporary Western philosophy. Ivakhiv (2014. p. 1) summarizes this turn as an "'ontopolitical' milieu of contemporary social, cultural, and environmental theory, critical realism, agential realism, nonrepresentation theory, enactive and embodied cognitivism, post-phenomenology, multispecies ethnography, integral ecology, and various forms of 'new materialism', 'geophilosophy,' and 'cosmopolitics'." These approaches, related to each other by their attention to non-dualist, new materialist, and immanent conceptions of reality, are discussed in the literature as salient to broad realms of investigation including science, politics, and education (Barad, 2007; Coole & Frost, 2010; St. Pierre, 2004).

More concisely, *the material turn* has been highlighted as being of particular significance to environmental education as a ready paradigm that decolonializes, dehierarchicalizes, and deterritorializes essentialist conceptions of the human relationship to the environment (Clarke & Mcphie, 2014, 2015). These properties are of particular importance in overcoming the limitations of sustainability education practice that straightforwardly seeks to tackle the *crisis of perception* of *disconnection* from *nature*. Identifying that the prevailing modernist malaise of *disconnection* is a mere presumption—resultant of underlying metaphysical assumptions—leads to a questioning of environmental education's *(re)connect to nature* practices. Mannion, Fenwick, & Lynch (2013) for instance, note how the popular focus on place-responsive education for socioecological justice education can be aligned with emerging posthuman debates that attend to the sociomaterial nature of reality. Noel Gough has sought to bring this understanding to environmental and outdoor education theory and research, stating that:

> posthuman/place relations are not about individual subjects autonomously forming and developing relations with the world but, rather, about realizing that these relations always already exist, and might be as much influenced by the behaviour of other materials in places we inhabit as they are by our intentional or unintentional actions. (Gough, 2015, p. 160)

Previously we sought to demonstrate how a move from a metaphysics of transcendence, to a metaphysics of immanence in environmental education practice can help overcome the limitations of, and possible damage resultant from, pointillist (i.e., emphasizing subjects and objects which are then *connected*) theory and practice, suggesting the need for a praxis of participation and performativity that moves beyond these essentialist notions (Clarke & Mcphie, 2014).

Here we seek to continue the critique of pointillist environmental education approaches by arguing that phenomena such as plants, trees, stones, clouds, rainbows, humans, plastic bags, and smart phones are not *objects* or *subjects* that interact, relate, or even *connect* with each other. Rather they are transient, enactive *physical processes* continuously taking place and always *becoming* as *intra* agencies; better described as *haecceities* (a thing's thisness) rather than *quiddities* (a thing's whatness). Perception of these entities as *objects* is resultant of an anthropocentric, perceptual, and temporal discrepancy that has arisen from concepts that have been passed along ecological lines of (predominantly) Western culture (such as binary bias, essentialism, platonic idealist/logocentric discourse, transcendentalism, Cartesian duality, and Newtonian science). The material turn's philosophy of intra-relational process materialism counters these ontologies and offers a new direction for thought, one that is partly exemplified through both historical and current (even *new*) animistic practices. This potential paradigm shift also has implications for pragmatic changes to existing pedagogies to support a relatively empathetic and sustainable present/future for the planet. Ultimately, we are concerned with helping learners, and ourselves, to continue to wonder at the becoming of the world.

In this article, we take the reader on a walk in a local park with some of our students to help explore the process-relational world *becoming* in contrast to more prevalent and dominant conceptions of the human relationship to the environment. As with any good lesson, we shall learn *with* (rather than *about*) the world as we go.

BACKGROUND READING TO THE LESSON: PROCESS-RELATIONAL THOUGHT

Adrian Ivakhiv (2013, p. 43) suggests that process-relational thought focuses on "the dynamism by which things are perpetually moving forward, interacting, and creating new conditions in the world" and on the "world-making creativity of things: on how things become rather than what they are, on emergence rather than structure." He goes on to state that this process-relational reality "is constituted, at its core, not by objects, permanent structures, material substances, cognitive representations, or Platonic ideas or essences, but by relational encounters or events" (Ivakhiv, 2013, p. 43). This ontology has been adopted by new materialist authors such as Barad (2007), Bennett (2010), Connolly, (2011), and Coole and Frost (2010), who have taken various process-relational approaches and have reflected on the subtleties, differences, and broader implications of this *material turn*.

However, this ontology is not new. The pre-Socratic philosopher Heraclitus (535–475 BCE) purported that a person cannot put his foot in the same river twice (Poster, 1996) and the Buddhist philosopher Nagarjuna's (150–250 CE) "middle way" demonstrated interconnectedness within his "central concept of the 'emptiness (sunyata) of all things (dharmas),' which pointed to the incessantly changing and so never fixed nature of all phenomena" as well as a "lack of autonomous existence (nihsvabhava)." (Berger, 2003, para. 1).

A not-too-dissimilar ontology is also understood and enacted in many animist traditions around the world, such as First Nation cultures in the Americas, Maori culture, Aboriginal Australian culture, and eco-paganism (Harvey, 2006). Similar to much animistic thought and practice, continental philosophers Deleuze and Guattari (2004) advise us "to regard the animal as a going on: not as a living thing of a certain kind but as the manifestation of a process of becoming, of continuous creation, or simply of *being alive*" (in Ingold, 2011, p. 174). For example, they suggest *wolfing* as an alternative to wolf. This perspective supports a philosophy of immanence and bares a strong resemblance to non-romanticized/spiritualized[1] animistic practices throughout the world both past and present. Ingold (2011, p. 170) states, "We ourselves might speak of having seen an owl, or several owls but the Koyukon name does not really refer to the owl as an object, but to what we might call the activity of 'owling.'"

> In the west we are accustomed to thinking of animals as "living things," as though life were an interior property of a class of objects deemed "animate" and that causes them to act in particular ways. In Koyukon ontology, by contrast, each animal is the instantiation of a particular way of being alive—a concentration of potential and a locus of growth in that entire field of relations that is life itself (Ingold 2000a: 95–98). The names of animals, then, do not refer to classes of objects, for in the Koyukon world there are no objects as such to classify. They refer, rather, to ways of living. (Ingold, 2011, p. 170)

Paraphrasing the archetypal psychologist James Hillman, Harding (2006, p. 27) suggests that "any phenomenon has the capacity to come alive and to deeply inform us through our interaction with it, as long as we are free of an overly objectifying attitude." This is not the same as the common colonialist misconception of animism as a "projection of human feelings onto inanimate matter" (Harding, 2006, p. 27). Advocated by philosophers such as Spinoza, Leibniz, and Whitehead, one view of animism has been described by Harding (2006, p. 28) as recognizing "that the material world around us has always been a dimension of sensation and feelings—albeit sensations that may be very different from our own—and that each entity must be treated with respect for its own kind of experience." However, a "new animism" may also be described as "learning how to be a good person in respectful relationships with other persons ... only some of whom are human." (Harvey, 2006, p. xi). The recent publication of Graham Harvey's *The Handbook of Contemporary Animism* (2013), reflects a (re)newed scholarly interest in animist ontologies. Harvey is joined by such renowned company as Bird-David, Descola, Abram, Ingold, and Plumwood, to name just a few (41 authors tackle the 40 chapters of the book), in advocating an increased engagement with animism in order to (re)imagine a more animated human relationship with a world becoming.

This animistic worldview runs counter to the majority of current unsustainable conceptual processes and practices that stem from the Western mind/worldview (Ingold, 2011), a mechanized mode of thinking that has a long history incorporating various landmarks of change. In his book, *The Participatory Mind* (1994), Henryk Skolimowski described four stages of Western thought: Mechanos (after the Enlightenment), Theos (after the Roman invasions), Logos (post-Socratic thought), and Mythos (pre-Socratic thought). These stages all denote important changes in conception, perception, and behavior. We would also include the agricultural revolution as a fundamental change in Western thought due to changes in social and environmental equity as well as a more static understanding of the world compared to the mobile nomadic view (Mcphie, 2014a). Of particular interest to us is the change from animistic Celtic perceptions and practices to Roman and Roman Christian ones. The Greeks and Romans had become urban cultures (further developing the alphabetized written language we use in the modern Western world) whereas the Celts comprised predominantly pastoral cultures. As the Celts had an oral tradition, the Romans translated and interpreted many Celtic conceptions, a practice called *interpretatio romana* (Green, 1997), in a static, essentialized and transcendent manner.

> In her book *Exploring the World of the Druids*, archaeologist Miranda Green (1997) emphasises that the Celtic spirit/god "Taranis" name indicates not that he was the god of thunder: he *was* thunder; Sequana was the River Seine at its spring source; Sulis was the hot spring at Bath, not simply its guardian or possessor" (p. 24). This suggests that whilst the animistic Celtic belief system was still very much of the land, the Roman introduction of a monotheistic Christian belief in a transcendent God began to cultivate a belief, in the West, of separation and division (although it could be argued that this belief of separation had already begun with the agricultural revolution). (Mcphie, 2015, p. 228)

Through this attempt at translation, meaning was changed or lost. We emphasize Green's (1997) point again: Taranis was not the god of thunder; he *was* thunder. This nuanced understanding is the difference between two wildly conflicting worldviews and has significant ramifications for the modern globalized world. It is the difference between an immanent worldview and a transcendent worldview; a world of presenting and unfolding perception-and-life, and a world of dead things and human representation. It is the difference between a *flat* ecological perspective (see de Vega, n.d.) and both a shallow ecological *and* deep ecological perspective. It is the difference between understanding ourselves as *of* the world, as opposed to *in* or *on* the world.

Process-relational thought/process metaphysics has also partly matured from a variety of similar ontologies that have emerged from/through a number of Western and Eastern philosophers. It has arisen and progressed at different moments throughout history[2] and is written/recorded in the philosophies of Heraclitus, Nagarjuna, Zhuang Zhu, Spinoza, Leibniz, Schelling, Bergson, Peirce, James, Dewey, Whitehead, Hartshorne, Simondon, Bateson, Deleuze, Guattari, Rescher, Weber, Faber, Connolly, Stengers, Massumi, Latour and in certain respects Hegel, Marx, Nietzsche, and Heidegger (list taken from Ivakhiv, 2013, pp. 42–43).

In addition, General Systems theories (developed as systems biology by von Bertalanffy in 1928) played an increasingly important role in process-relational thought from the 1970s onward from Lovelock's *Gaia* (Lovelock, 1972; Lovelock & Margulis, 1974) to Maturana and Varela's *autopoiesis* (1972), thus informing Abram's *The Spell of the Sensuous* (1996), Capra's *Web of*

Life (1996), and Harding's *Animate Earth* (2006). Gregory Bateson's *Steps to an Ecology of Mind* (1972) is an obvious link between systems thinking, process-relational thought, and theories of extended cognition as he has been influential in all of these areas of study.

From the initial feelers tentatively extended within externalist philosophy in the 1980s, a number of new theoretical frameworks have arisen, such as *extended cognition* (Clark, 1997, 2001, 2008; Manzotti, 2006; Menary, 2006, 2010; Rowlands, 2009, 2010; Wheeler, 2005); *embodied cognition* (Anderson, 2003; Chemero, 2009; Chiel & Beer, 1997; Johnson, 1987; Lakoff & Johnson, 1980; Rowlands, 1999; Shapiro, 2010); and *enactive cognition* (di Paolo, 2009; Maturana & Varela, 1980; Noë, 2009; Stewart, Gappene, & di Paolo, 2010; Thompson, 2007; Thompson & Stapelton, 2009; Varela, Thompson, & Rosch, 1991;) (list taken from Malafouris, 2013, pp. 57–58). Clark and Chalmers' (1998) "The Extended Mind" (where cognition is conceived as a *transcranial* process) and Varela, Thompson, and Rosch's (1991) *The Embodied Mind* (where *the body* is seen as a lived, experiential structure as well as the context of cognitive mechanisms) seem to have had significant and lasting impacts on theories of mind.

Such is the potential of emerging theories (and science) of mind that a recent edition of *New Scientist* featured an article (Spinney, 2014) discussing the possibilities that extended theories of mind bring to the *hard problem* of consciousness—*where is the mind*? Indeed, this novel topological conception of the mind is now spilling into other areas of study, including anthropology (Hutchins, 2010; Ingold, 2011), archaeology (Tilley, 1994; Wylie, 2002) and mental health and well-being (Fuchs, Sattel, & Henningsen, 2010; Mcphie, 2013, 2014a, 2014c), even encouraging Mcphie (2013, 2014c) to suggest that if *mental health is a transcranial process,* then more haecceitically apt questions to ask would perhaps be *where* or *when* is mental health as opposed to what, why, or how questions often found in normative mental health research.

The opposition to Cartesian duality is a prominent feature of these various approaches to process-relational paradigms. Gilbert Ryle coined the phrase, "Ghost in the Machine" in his book *The Concept of Mind* (1949) to describe the absurdity of Rene Descartes mind-body dualism. Ryle (1949) suggests that it is a *category mistake* to subject the mind to the same logical categorization as either idealist arguments (reducing physical reality to the same ontological status as mental reality) or materialist arguments (reducing mental reality to the same ontological status as physical reality) (Roger, 2008). However, a new materialist comprehension of the world would differ from either of these descriptions as in many cases it takes an *intra* over an *inter* understanding of reality.

> Barad (2003) coined the term "intra-action" to replace "inter-action" in order to highlight that agencies do not precede encounters, but rather that agency emerges from the relationships between components [. . .] Barad (2003, p. 817) also points out that, "[a]gential intraactions are specific causal material enactments that may or may not involve humans." (Poole, 2014, p. 6)

If we are *of* the world, as opposed to *in* or *on* it, then we may place both mind and material in the same arena yet at the same time realize that mind is *haecceitically* different and that it is useful in its existence to aid discussions that try to clarify a more nuanced grasp of reality. Rather than attempting to break down meanings into categories, essentializing and atomizing through taxonomies, rules, and regulations, we may think in terms of stories that use metaphor and analogy to explore different understandings of the world.

Therefore, instead of performing an extended literature review on this emerging worldview (see Clark and Mcphie (2014) for an initial exploration of process-relational philosophy in outdoor environmental education for sustainability) we shall attempt to explain this alternative ontological paradigm through a pragmatic approach that focuses on a single outdoor learning session of encounters in a park. Each encounter has a story to tell about our embodied material intra-relation with/of the world. The first part of this session is a ghost story. You (the facilitator) may wish to build a campfire for this part of the session, or begin in a cave (it is a ghost story after all!).

THE OUTDOOR LEARNING SESSION

9 a.m.: Ghost in the Machine

Good morning, everyone. Before we begin, we want you to imagine a ghost rattling around in your brain—in your pineal gland, to be precise. It has no material quality—no physical substance—and so is similar to a ghost. Descartes knew dogs had pineal glands, but did not believe they had this extra quality of mind that humans had, and so thought them soulless, as he did every other creature (justifying vivisection among the *enlightened* scientists). This perception is still very evident in the modern Western world. For example, "does anyone here believe in ghosts?" A few students raise their hands. "What about ghost blades of grass?" One student replies, "Of course not; they're just plants." This student believes humans are special and have souls that after death would transcend the human body (or brain, if you believe it resides there, as Descartes did). Many *scientists* have a similar anthropocentric, Cartesian understanding of the world. Many may not admit that they believe in ghosts, although we know some that do!

It may be argued that we should do away with the concept of the mind altogether (in the same manner Morton (2007) calls for the abandonment of *Nature* in his *dark ecology*) as it is problematic in terms of binary bias and a transcendent conception of the world. However, by keeping the term and putting it under ~~erasure~~ (a method called *sous rature* that Derrida borrowed from Heidegger to denote certain concepts as inadequate, yet necessary), or changing its literary definition/existence to exemplify immanence rather than transcendence, it could promote a deeper understanding of the immanent physical nature of the mind as opposed to the Cartesian non-physical, Westernised spiritual mind of transcendence.

This transcendent thinking has led to certain ecological conceptions, prompting one student to say we need to be *reconnected* to ~~Nature~~ if we are to overcome the current environmental crisis. Indeed, some recent academic conferences are now dedicated to this concept, such as "Nature Connections: An Interdisciplinary Conference to Examine Routes to Nature Connectedness" (Nature Connections, 2015). Elsewhere, we argue that a literal disconnection is impossible as we are of the same materials, forces, and energies of Earth (Clarke & Mcphie, 2014). Therefore, a re-connection is also impossible. However, there may be a *conceptual* (mis)understanding that influences our perception and behavior so we come to *believe* there is a disconnection. If this is so, the perception and belief that we are not (or no longer) part of our environments may have unintended behavioral outcomes that influence and further encourage Cartesian thinking. Such thinking may add to destructive climatic and mass extinction events, as well as encouraging social inequities (such as discrimination and intolerance). Bai (2009) demonstrates this understanding in her call for a re-animation of the universe through environmental education, arguing, as we do, that Cartesian dualism and logocentric platonicism be, at the least, complemented by other forms of knowledge. On the part of positivists/reductionists/essentialists/realists, etc., this has obvious ramifications due to believing we may change our environments without it affecting *us* too much, leading to environmental degradation. On the part of constructivists/idealists/humanists/deep ecologists, etc., the belief that we may be, or are, *disconnected* still encourages a Cartesian dualism and therefore propagates a perception that humans *can* be separate (possibly leading to further destructive or unsustainable behaviors). These perceptions and beliefs have filtered through Western society, influencing schooling, health care, politics, finance, etc. This outdoor learning session/story is just one practical example of how we may deterritorialize this unhealthy (if we accept that a mass extinction would be *unhealthy*) situation.

David Abram (2011, p. 4) asks,

> What if thought is not born in the human skull, but is a creativity proper to the body as a whole, arising spontaneously from the slippage between the organism and the folding terrain that it wanders? What if the curious curve of thought is engendered by the difficult eros and tension between our flesh and the flesh of the earth?

Let us now take a walk around the park to see if we can explore the alternative paradigm that Abram suggests.

9:30 a.m.: The Secret Life of Plants

So, we're walking along with our students when we come across a *Rhododendron ponticum*. One student, a middle-class Westerner, perceives it as beautiful. This view, possibly an aesthetic conception culturally constructed and passed on from the Romantic period, is a way of *seeing* that John Urry (1990) would term a *romantic gaze*. However, when asked if the Rhododendron thinks *itself* beautiful, the student replies, "You're joking aren't you? Plants can't think!"

Michael Marder (2013, p. 2) complains, "If animals have suffered marginalization throughout the history of Western thought, then non-human, non-animal living beings, such as plants, have populated the margin of the margin, the zone of absolute obscurity undetectable on the radars of our conceptualities." Yet Marder (2013, p. 152) believes that vegetal life has a "non-conscious intentionality" that "amounts to an essentialism-free way of thinking that is fluid, receptive, dispersed, non-oppositional, non-representational, immanent, and material-practical . . ."; in other words, they think!

Now let us look at the rhododendron from the point of view of classical science, which has influenced ecology (evident in most Western education systems[3], including environmental education). The teacher might say it is a genus of flora in the kingdom of plants, separate but also a *part* of its surrounding environment. This derives from the Linnaeus tree of knowledge and taxonomy—that we made up! Let us deconstruct it for a moment: Kingdom (gender inequality), subkingdom (reductionist), superdivision (hierarchical), division (Cartesian binary bias), and so on. In fact, the term *ecological* is itself problematic due to its Greek etymology of *logos*; ways of thinking that privilege *reasoned* Western hierarchical thought over any other.

However, the explanation we give the student could hint at the existence of the plant's mind as described by Li, Clark, and Winchester (2010, pp. 407–408):

> The way the plant knows about the environment is through its interaction with the environment it lives in. Hence the plant's knowledge of its world depends on the environment it lives in and the

actions the plant is capable of (Reid, 1995). The plant neither determines its world, nor is determined by it, but co-emerges with the world. It is important to note that there is no dichotomy (i.e. the plant and the environment) because any system and its context are inseparable (Fenwick, 2000).

The ecologist may perceive the rhododendron as a threat to the ecosystem if it is intruding as an unwanted alien invader originating from a place where it evolved over a longer period, where it had time to *fit in* with its environment in a more sustainable manner. One student asks, "But this idea could also be used as an argument that sees Europeans as *pests,* couldn't it?' We agree! Due to the fairly rapid colonization period of the Americas and Australasia, for example, the ecosystems/environments that suffered (including processes from the biosphere, troposphere, hydrosphere, and lithosphere) could not adapt fast enough to compete and so became obsolete or *less* than they once were (in number or in health). First Nation people are good examples of human processes who have been (are being) *weeded* or *sprayed* by the European monoculture gardeners and whose ancestors are still suffering from the hierarchical hegemonic power relations that unsustainable gardeners have over *their* biotic and abiotic communities.

For example, many First Nation people were treated as unwanted pests when the Europeans needed a picturesque or sublime view when they *fenced off* Yellowstone Park to create America's first national park in 1872. The area was preserved "for the benefit and enjoyment of the people" (inscribed on the Roosevelt Arch at the North entrance to the park as part of the *organic act* legislation), yet the indigenous populations who were either from this region or were forced to pass through this area (for example, the Shoshone Sheep Eaters and the Nez Perce) did not seem to *fit* into the Romantic ideal of the Eurocentric concept of *wilderness* and so were *removed*. Although they were seen as *man*, they were not seen as *human*, at least not humans of the same equality or civility as humans of European descent (see Callicott (2000) for an in-depth discussion of wilderness as an androcentric, colonial, racist, and genocidal concept). These wildernesses are still heavily contested, as is the Western post-colonial perception of *indigenous* people around the world and the social and environmental inequalities this perception (re-)enforces. (For an in-depth discussion of green postcolonialism, see Huggan and Tiffin, 2007.)

"But hark, what's that I hear," asks Dave. "The beautiful trill of a songbird? The flutter of beating wings?"

9:45 a.m.: Birds and Columns

"Look students; there's a lapwing over there." And by naming it so, we've just sucked the life out of it! Some call it a peewit due to its call. But that's not all a lapwing *is*, a sound. Just as the Celts personified their environments, even old English (Anglo-Saxon) names for animals seem to support an immanent understanding of the world that advocates bringing the world to life. For example, the animated Old English verbal name for the modern English static noun lapwing is *hlēapewince*, meaning to dance or leap (hlēapan) and wink (wincian) (Clark-Hall, 2011). Now we breathe life back into it.

For the Koyukon of Alaska,

The spotted sandpiper's name is "flutters around the shore,", the osprey's is "stares into the water," the boreal owl's is "perches in the lower part of spruce trees," and the savanna sparrow's is "sits on a stalk of grass" (Ingold, 2011, p. 169)

These relational verbs seem to encourage a sort of sympathy and respect of/for things from animals to buildings.

> When we see the bird moving, we feel its motion; with the column, we see it standing still but also feel its motion and activity. The bird lives in an aesthetic relation with the air, as the column lives-with its adjacent partners; a difference only occurs at the point where aesthetics becomes a profession: the making of beautiful things. In short, aesthetics is something that existed long before humans did, exchanged between objects, but we use it to make those objects. When we see-feel a bird in flight, the aesthetics originates in the intensification of an extensive motion, but when we design a column, to make it aesthetic we must draw it in the realm of correspondence, and therefore as a product of motion. (Spuybroek, 2011, p. 183)

So, the act of architecture is a relational performance between emerging events. I think we'll come back to this point later in the day . . . you never know, we might even see some architects!

Let us continue our walk because some students seem to be distracted by a faint buzzing sound nearby.

10 a.m.: Wasps and Orchids

Now we come across a wasp on an orchid; the wasp, an organism of fauna, of the order Hymenoptera; the orchid, an organism of flora. The students conceive the wasp and orchid to be separate entities, but continuing along the same vein of disruption, the wasp and the orchid together may be seen as a *multiplicity* or an *assemblage*. In Deleuze and Guattari's (2004) famous description, the wasp becomes part of the orchid's reproductive apparatus (a mobile sexual appendage) and the orchid becomes the sexual organ of the wasp (or an orgasm). The orchid does not try to attract other orchids; it flirts with the wasp! As Dema (2007, para. 5) notes, "this forms the wasp-orchid assemblage which operates via inorganic, rather than organic, life." Our students watch the wasp-orchids for a while until one mentions how amazing it is to see organisms *in* their environments. Another student says, "Where is the environment, or the organism, if the two constitute each other? Are there two?" Varela, Thompson, and Rosch (1991, p. 217) offer some insight here when they say, "organism and environment enfold into each other and unfold from one another in the fundamental circularity that is life itself."

As a group, we start walking toward a nearby group of trees, wondering about our assumptions of orgasms, organisms, and environments.

10:30 a.m.: Trees

Jamie asks the students what they think a tree is. They give him funny looks! Trees are collectively perceived in various ways from copse to jungle, each having differing meanings and associations. They are a symbol of environmentalism (tree huggers) and health (green therapies). However, most of the lessons about trees are as objects of varying species (as in the books *I-Spy Trees* and *I-Spy Nature*). Why not try Tim Ingold's (2008, p. 4) example instead:

> Where does the tree end and the rest of the world begin? . . . Is the bark, for example, part of the tree? If I break off a piece in my hand and observe it closely, I will doubtless find that it is inhabited by a great many tiny creatures that have burrowed beneath it and made their homes there. Are they part of the tree? . . . If we consider, too, that the character of this particular tree lies just as much in the way

it responds to the currents of wind, in the swaying of its branches and the rustling of its leaves, then we might wonder whether the tree can be anything other than a tree-in-the-air. These considerations lead me to conclude that the tree is not an object at all, but a certain gathering together of the threads of life. That is what I mean by a thing.

Alternatively, even this account by Spuybroek (2011, pp. 182–183):

The tree feels the wind, and as the tree feels, it takes on form, and as the tree takes on form, we start to feel it too—not physical wind but rage—and then we take on form by adjusting our position or posture. If I were to map out such relations in a diagram, with dots indicating forms and arrows indicating forces and feelings, we would not even be able to see the difference between animate and inanimate things . . . sympathy only appears when the dualism disappears, at the point where things become feelings and feelings things.

Even if we dismiss all anthropocentric subjectivity (as a tree is perceived differently to each person, at every age, in every class, from each culture, throughout history), a tree is still not *a tree* for a dog! It is an *affordance*. For example, it may be a message board to display its *Tag* (an extended self?). What is a tree to a jellyfish, bacteria, or cell (are we not bacteria and cell too)? A tree as we understand it is simply an anthropocentric account, one that has changed and is still changing historically, geographically, and culturally over time.

Then, there is the anthropocentric account of taxonomical knowledge, often depicted and symbolized as a tree; separating, essentializing, reducing, hierarchicalizing, homogenizing. This overuse of the tree led Deleuze and Guattari (1987, p. 15) to consider the world in a different way:

We're tired of trees. We should stop believing in trees, roots, and radicals. They've made us suffer too much. All of arborescent culture is founded on them, from biology to linguistics. Nothing is beautiful or loving or political aside from underground stems and aerial roots, adventitious growths and rhizomes.

Deleuze and Guattari's (1987) critique of the Western tree metaphor has been influential across diverse educational disciplines in recent years (Cousin, 2005; Johnson, 2014; Masny, 2013; Semetsky & Masny, 2013). Whereas the majority of this work looks to disrupt stagnant and neo-liberal practices in research and the management of education, we look to use Deleuze and Guattari (1987) as a means to help students disrupt their own assumptions about trees, and other organisms they perceive to be *in* environments. To do this we must be careful how we word our ecological explanations and assumptions to our students. We must look for ways to move our discourse with students beyond tree metaphors and we must be mindful of our anthropocentricity. For example, pollution is one thing for humans but is another thing entirely for some forms of bacteria who thrive on it (such as desulfitobacteria).

Research, such as *the human microbiome project* (Turnbaugh et al., 2007) suggests that humans are supraorganisms being 90% microbes. Are we simply a carrying vessel for them or is this just another example of sub-systems (bacteria) within larger systems, very similar to how Gregory Bateson describes *minds*, as there is always "a larger Mind of which the individual mind is only a subsystem" (Bateson, 2000, p. 467)? Of course, if we keep working our way up the systems, we get to the minds of forests (Kohn, 2013) and eventually what James Lovelock describes as Gaia, an interplay of the Earth's biosphere, lithosphere, hydrosphere, and troposphere. However, there is no need to stop at our atmosphere. The Universe, simply put, is a very large ~~Mind~~ of which humans are just a process.

Beneath the tree the students gaze about, considering where they end and the tree begins. "There are certainly plenty of humans *in* this park" notes one of the students.

11 a.m.: Humans

Merleau-Ponty (1964) suggested that humans were *of* the world rather than *in* or *on* it! We are made *of* the materials, forces, and energies of the Earth, not a separate entity that dwells *on* or *in* it, implying a certain literal disconnection. Harris (2008) notes that there is an assumption that the mind-brain-body remains somehow detached or isolated from the wider environment, but as we learned from Varela, Thompson, and Rosch (1991) earlier, the organism is not *in* the environment and so the mind is not *in* the head. For instance Manzotti and Pepperell (2013, p. 3) claim that nearly 30 years of intensive study have failed to discover any "mental content or phenomenal experience" inside the human head and that continued claims that the brain is where the mind is located amount to a conceptual bias in the scientific community.

"So, to reference a Pixies song," says one confused looking student, "where *is* my ~~mind~~?"
Break time *(please, can everyone search around for this student's ~~mind~~?)*

11:15 a.m.: Where *Is* My ~~Mind~~?

Bateson concurred with Merleau-Ponty that mind is immanent in the world. Andy Clark follows Bateson in concluding that what we normally accept as *mental processes* extend beyond the *skin bag* into the local environment (Clark, 1997). "In other words, the mind does not inhabit the body; rather, the body inhabits the mind" (Malafouris, 2013, p. 60). Writing in agreement, Preston (2003) develops this discussion further by claiming that *we think with place*, and this has a fundamental impact on our being-in-the-world.

Yet a similar type of thinking/worldview already exists within animist cultures. As Ingold states:

> For the Ojibwa, knowledge is grounded in experience, understood as a coupling of the movement of one's awareness to the movement of aspects of the world. Experience, in this sense, does not mediate between mind and nature, since these are not separated in the first place. (Ingold, 2000, p. 11)

Therefore, the eco~~system~~ that is the human is also a process of the eco~~systems~~ we generally think of as our external environments. This has great implications for the manner in which we conceive of education for, as Spuybroek (2011, p. 182) notes, "we are not recipients but participants." There is great potential, then, in exploring animistic ways of seeing in environmental education (Clarke, 2014; Clarke & Mcphie, 2014, 2015).

11:30 a.m.: Haecceity

Perceiving humans as quiddities (a thing's *whatness*) rather than haecceities (a thing's *thisness*) alters our perception of (and behavior of) the world, influencing us to think of ourselves as separate from the processes of materiality that we are ultimately of (not a *part* of). The idea of an essential form and substance that makes us *what* we are—humans—partly stems from platonic idealism. This has important ramifications for how we perceive and treat each other, as well as the world that we are part of. For example, the idea that we have a static, unchangeable identity (an essential *me* to me), which has come from this essentialist mode of thinking (and links to binary bias), could have racist, sexist (Mcphie, 2014a) and speciesist implications. Arguments that education for sustainability must include social and economic aspects, as well as environmental, can be answered in part, by understanding that a move to immanence is required for not only our conceptions of the environment, but also of our social and economic ~~systems~~. The Cartesian notion of human supremacy works across what dominant thinking would perceive as separate entities—the environmental, the social, the economic—leading to social and ecological inequity such as vivisection and class politics justifying the oppression of some humans over others, humans over animals, animals over plants, plants over rocks, etc.

Therefore, there seems to be much disentangling to be done regarding distinctions between life and non-life, or species. Yet Spuybroek (2011, p. 331), examining the aesthetic ideas of John Ruskin, suggests that:

> we do not need to disentangle anything; on the contrary, the earth veil is all about entangling ... Life is not something stored in biological creatures; hybrids or bastards can be more alive than the purified versions, naturally, because they are imperfect, wild and radically picturesque.

However, if we thought of ourselves instead as haecceities (as championed by Deleuze and Guattari, 2004) or as Ingold (2011) explains, *Knots*, where we focused on a positive characteristic of an individual that caused him to be *this* individual and no other, we may begin to realize the complex intra-connected nature of humans as *of* the environment. This is opposed to focusing on commonalities of certain things, which automatically induces a binary perception, thereby separating groups of things and individual things from the environments. In turn, this fragmentation leads to destructive environmental behavior as we've argued elsewhere (Clarke & Mcphie, 2014; Mcphie, 2014a).

> ... the organism is that which life sets against itself in order to limit itself, and there is a life all the more intense, all the more powerful for being inorganic. (Deleuze & Guattari, 1987, p. 503)

Dema (2007) directs us to the implications of Deleuze and Guattari's (1987) conception of *inorganic* life: "It is not so much that organisms are not alive, but that life can be articulated in all things." (para. 1). It is a reimagining of life that is variable in intensity, rather than a property that is either *exclusively* present or absent (Dema, 2007).

As a haecceity, we can no longer *measure* ourselves as if objects of the same genetic species. So instead of describing *what* a human is (as a quiddity), an explanation for the students in the park may instead go something like this:

> The organism is no longer the paradigmatic unit of life, nor is the cell, the genetic code, the population, the species, or the ecosystem. The authors of *A Thousand Plateaus* are proposing an ontological theory in which everything is inorganically alive, everything is assembled. When a person walks into a room, when a new fabric touches a finger, when a star wobbles, when a molecule falls apart, when a mayor feels threatened, when a recipe approaches a critical threshold: in all cases the laws of assembling are operating and are universally applied. If we want to know more about how inorganic life works, the next step is to learn more about the mechanisms of assembling. (Dema, 2007, para. 20)

In this paradigm we no longer have to think of ourselves as organisms. Perhaps we could be assemblages, haecceities, or multiplicities (Deleuze & Guattari, 2004); meshworks or knots (Ingold, 2011); cat's cradles (Haraway, 1994); or even Mr. Messys (Mcphie, 2014a). If this is so, the hierarchical tree of taxonomy begins to shake. For example, human intention and design is highly regarded in the world of flora and fauna. Hierarchically, we are at the top of the tree (and even trees are above stones!)! We marvel at our invention and artistry. Just look at Gaudi's fantastical cathedral or the skyscrapers of modern civilization with their air conditioning . . . a human invention come about through sheer intentional intellectual cognitive brilliance! Really? We wonder if something that is usually considered as insignificant compared to humans in the world of cognitive functioning could also produce something similar? What about something really small . . . that we don't have to speculate on . . . as they already exist—incredibly small architects?

12 p.m.: Termites

"Oh look class . . . there's a termite . . . or more accurately, a colony of termites. And what's that they've built? Wow! They also build fantastical Gaudiesque Cathedrals and skyscrapers. They also have aesthetic artistic design and air conditioning too? Hmmm, we'll have to go back to the drawing board on this one for now!"

So, if we suggest that flora and fauna are not objects but processes, what about things that we usually perceive as static objects (at least things that are not able to move of their own accord . . . such as stones)?

12:30 p.m.: Stones

"But surely," one student asks, "stones are just stones . . . aren't they?' Ingolda (2010a, p. 5) tells us:

> A rolling stone, the proverb says, gathers no moss, yet in the very process of gathering moss, the stone that is wedged in place becomes a thing, while on the other hand the stone that rolls —like a pebble washed by a running river—becomes a thing in its very rolling. Just as the tree, responding in its movements to the currents of wind, is a tree-in-the-air, so the stone, rolling in the river current, is a stone-in-the-water.

"Okay" says a student, "so a stone isn't just an object separate from everything else; I get that. But it's still not conscious like a human. I mean, it doesn't have *agency* does it?" Rautio (2013, p. 11) suggests stones have (intra-)agency: stones do things to us and with us:

> They have us pick them up, feel them, close them in our fist (if particularly smooth and rounded) or hold them between our thumb and forefinger (if small and edgy). They condition our walking . . . we exist as a consequence of stones: the event of carrying stones makes us in the moment . . . we become stone-carrying with carrying stones.

Some stones have been discovered to walk, slide, or sail! A number of stones at Racetrack Playa, Death Valley, California, have been documented (Reid et al., 1995) as *sailing* across the desert floor, leaving trails like snails behind them, criss-crossing in varying directions depending on their destination. Rather like plants creeping around when played back on video at high speed, rocks also begin to become more overtly animated and slither around. The illusion of time deceives us all.

We suggest that instead of introducing stones to students as inert geological objects made of porous limestone or igneous granite, you might try starting the students off by conversing with the stone through more creative means. We have found that a reading of *Conversation with a Stone* (1997 [1962]), by Wislawa Szymborska gets students talking about stones in very different ways. It begins, "I knock at the stone's front door . . ." and continues to question the nature of Western perception, the impossibility of *knowing*.

A student calls out from the back of the group, "What about larger stones then? What about mountains?"

1 p.m.: Mountains

Once again, we may see them as static, immovable objects in our relatively short life spans. However, if we were to fix a video recorder in place to view the mountains over a few million years and then play it back on a very fast speed, we would see that they flow and ebb just as a river or ocean. In the 1800s, John Ruskin began to see the world in this way, in two contrasting, yet still romanticized empathies; the *feeling* of impressionism (as in Turner's sublime landscapes) and the semi-scientific intricacies of *detail* (as in the Pre-Raphaelites' depictions of the environment). From his nuanced grasp of *a sympathy of things* (Spuybroek, 2011) and while living at Brantwood (with a view of the Old Man of Coniston, a mountain in the Lake District in England), Ruskin consequently saw the beginnings of human influence over the climate. He "foresaw climate change in The Storm-Cloud of the Nineteenth Century – both as a physical threat, in industrial pollution, and a metaphysical one, as a 'plague cloud made of dead men's souls.'" (Hoare, 2014, para. 9).

"Look up students; can you see the blue sky in contrast with the plague clouds brewing in the distance?"

2 p.m.: Kites, Plastic Bags, and Weather

"So, now that we have discussed the biosphere and lithosphere (if you want to reduce and separate them in that way), what about the troposphere or hydrosphere?" Jamie asks the students. Merleau-Ponty (1962, p. 249) may provide an answer.

> As I contemplate the blue of the sky . . . I abandon myself to it and plunge into this mystery, it "thinks itself within me," I am the sky itself as it is drawn together and unified, and as it begins to exist for itself; my consciousness is saturated with this limitless blue.

Tim Ingold (2010b) suggests kite flying as a way to *know* our weather world: "A kite-in-the-air behaves very much like a living being. It seems to possess an agency of its own" (pp. 132–133).

We advise getting students to make their own kites and then fly them while *feeling* the pull and push of the intra-relational processes of the wind-kite-human as they flow through the string *into* the body.

the weather is not so much what we perceive, as what we perceive in. We see in sunlight whose shades and colours reveal more about the composition and textures of the ground surface than about the shapes of objects, we hear these textures in the rain from the sounds of drops falling on diverse materials, and we touch and smell in the keen wind that—piercing the body—opens it up and sharpens its haptic and olfactory responses. Indeed a strong wind can so overwhelm the senses as virtually to drown out the perception of contact with the ground. (Ingold, 2011, p. 131)

The film *American Beauty* (Mendes, 1999) has a short section demonstrating exquisitely the flow of materialism that is usually reserved for the anthropocentric concept of *life*. A plastic bag is animated in loops of *aliveness*, captured on video. However, it is not merely the wind that *causes* the bag to move in a linear cause-and-effect sequence essentialized under a Newtonian *law*. Rather, a play has co-emerged with the distributed agential intra-actions of vital materiality (a combination of Barad's (2007) *intra-actions* and Bennett's (2010) *vital materiality*). For many, this aliveness is obvious in a murmuration of starlings, for example, yet agential qualities of inertly conceived matter are rarely discussed in a serious manner in the more accepted halls of academe. Coole and Frost (2010, p. 1) ask, "How could we ignore the power of matter and the ways it materializes in our ordinary experiences or fail to acknowledge the primacy of matter in our theories?"

However, a challenge to the anthropocentric conception of agency is not new. *Narratives*, developed out of animal fables and oriental tales (Lamb, n.d.), were in circulation in the eighteenth and nineteenth centuries. *The Golden Spy* (1709) by Charles Gildon, *Adventures of a Shilling* (1710) by Joseph Addison, *The Adventures of a Guinea* (1760) by Charles Johnstone, *Adventures of a Hackney Coach* (1783) anonymously written, and *The Adventures of a Three Guinea Watch* (1893) by Talbot Baines Reed, are examples of stories about material circulation (rather than production) that transformed objects into subjects (Green, 2013; Lamb, n.d.). Although not particularly engaging in more nuanced discussions of agential distribution, the stories certainly *attempt* to steer away from anthropocentrism (although they are still from an anthropocentric perspective of a non-human perspective). Arjun Appadurai's (1986) *The Social Life of Things* was a more recent attempt at socializing materiality that sparked a (re)newed interest in "challenging the deeply entrenched anthropocentric idea of agency" (Malafouris, 2013, p. 122) and has culminated in Coole and Frost's *New Materialisms* (2010), a collection of posthumanist discussions about matter exhibiting agency and aliveness.

Litter, waste, smart phones, and other human produce are just as alive, becoming, and ~~natural~~ as the more traditional and romantic conceptions of ~~nature~~ as our examples in this article have suggested. Although also ~~natural,~~ themes of homogenization, hierarchy, staticization, and pointillism as unsustainable concepts and practices may be more rewarding than one-dimensional discussions supporting ~~re-connections to nature~~. The demolition of the nature/culture binary may appear troublesome to environmentalists, especially when post-structuralism appears to attack the sacred borders of nature reserves or national parks (Mcphie, 2014b). However, the cost of retaining a distinct—and ultimately false—~~nature~~ may be much higher, as we have explored in previous work (Mcphie & Clarke, 2014).

As the kites and plastic bags dance of the air, one student spots a rainbow; "Who's going to find the pot of gold at the end?"

3 p.m.: Rainbows

Western intellectuals have been criticized by post-colonial theorists for depreciating non-Western forms of knowing, by re-formulating or reducing them to folklore or myth (Said, 1978; Sharp, 2008; Spivak, 1988). Richard Dawkins (2011) does this (a lot) in his book, *The Magic of Reality*. After recounting the non-scientific stories such as Vikings seeing rainbows as bridges to Asgard, Dawkins states that they are *merely* myth and, therefore, not factual—whereas the Western scientific perspective derived from Newton is the *only* true model (pp. 140–155).

However, in our facilitation to undergraduate students, we have often used this next illustration of the rainbow as an example of process externalism as it exemplifies a paradigmatic shift in thinking that often has dramatic consequences for the students.

Manzotti (2011, para. 8) begins . . .

> Consider a physical phenomenon like the rainbow . . . a rainbow is a process that requires a further physical system in order to take place. Where is the rainbow? Where is the experience of the rainbow? Is there a rainbow without an observer? Is there a rainbow-observer without a rainbow in the cloud? . . . it is impossible, from a physical perspective, to disentangle the rainbow from its observer . . . Processes are necessarily private and yet physical. Secondarily, the rainbow is something that takes place. It is not a static entity. The rainbow takes place and it is extended in time and in space.

The rainbow is far from an objective or subjective phenomena. However, it could be said to be intersubjective-interobjective or possibly even *intra-relational* (Mcphie, 2015).

Plato said, "We must carve nature at its joints" (Phaedrus 265d–266a, in Hutchins, 2010, p. 705) but where are its joints? If we try to cut phenomena into illusory *parts*, what monsters may emerge? To categorize, cut, split, border, separate, partition, disconnect, connect, territorialize, hierarchicalize, homogenize, etc., would seem to place us where we are today, the sixth mass extinction. Gregory Bateson (2000) said that a blind man walking with a stick perceives through his arm, his hand, his stick, and the ground before him (*tap, tap, tap*)—to break these points apart is to place the human at the center of a world much more than human.

> If what you are trying to explain is a given piece of behavior, such as the locomotion of the blind man, then for this purpose, you will need the street, the stick, the man, the street, the stick, and so on, round and round. (Bateson, 1972, p. 459)

4 p.m.: Session Review

Prevailing educational approaches based on objectivist understandings of the world are problematic on two obvious levels. First, they are simplistic in the way they describe the nature of the world, attempting to define without questioning inherent assumptions and biases; education of this type is indoctrination. This in itself would not be overly problematic if it were not that the perpetuation of this way of seeing is ultimately damaging and oppressing. It is our contention that our modes of conceptualizing the essence of our relationships to our sociomaterial world have a direct influence on, or are co-emergent with, our modes of acting and behaving—our modes of valuing, decision making, and moving. If we ontologically understand the world to be essential, transcendent, objective, and eternal in its form (or in the various forms we are used to considering it: nature, forest, mind, tuna, culture)—then our modes of valuing, decision making, and moving can in no way conceive the end of these forms, either through morphogenesis, or the more pressing extinction event we are perpetuating. More than this, in a world of eternal transcendent forms, we have no interest beyond the instrumental.

Environmental Education is limited if it relies on moralistic calls to care for "the" environment—as if it were an object we can reach out and touch. This is why scholars call for a *reconnection*, so that caring might spring from an almost spiritual union *between* people and nature. However, a paradox emerges here, as the term reconnection implies separation—or distinct entities—the existence of which remain in our metaphysical conceptualization of the world even when we might think we are *reconnecting*, and thus will always leak through to our choices and behavior, resultantly justifying oppressions. We propose a dissolving of *connection = care* ideas in environmental education, instead (re)placing both moralistic and connection narratives with a narrative of a relationally underpinned metaphysics of immanence.

As Li, Clark, and Winchester (2010, p. 413) state, a more open, creative, process-oriented mode of education:

> offers a dynamic new vision for examining learning and performance, and enables us to see this field in a new light. It claims that our mind, body, and the world are inseparable. Learning is through the learners' acts and is acted upon by the world and understanding is embedded in doing.

The outdoor learning session we describe is not a carefully planned pedagogical endeavor; rather, it is a description of the wanderings of past students and ourselves as we have considered new materialist, poststructuralist, and relevant philosophical and artistic accomplishments as we have engaged with our environments. However, this experimentation in teaching and learning is a critical one, as it is through these exploratory practices that dominant, oppressive narratives of the nature of the human-environment condition can begin to be overcome.

In the film, *An Ecology of Mind* (Bateson, 2011), Nora Bateson, recollecting Krishnamurti's words, said, "You might think you're thinking your own thoughts. You're not. You're thinking your culture's thoughts." However, the body is not merely a passive surface onto which societal meaning is inscribed (Thrift, 1997). Our cultures thoughts *are* our own thoughts, which in turn *are* our environments thoughts for they cannot be disentangled. *They become.*

Class dismissed. Have a nice day.

ACKNOWLEDGMENTS

An earlier version of this article was presented at the conference, *Under Western Skies 3: Intersections of Environments, Technologies and Communities* at Mount Royal University, Calgary, Canada (September 9–12, 2014).

NOTES

1. We understand a transcendent Westernized spirituality to differ from a more contemporary animistic physicalist spirituality of immanence, which is partly how our session would take shape. The difference that we are advocating is the immanent material aliveness of things as opposed to a transcendent non-material spirit/soul.

2. This buildup and generation of ideas acts rather like the notion of a "palimpsest," a layering of rhizomatic conceptions that overwrite previous philosophies/landscapes/cultures and yet the ancestral remains may still be traced, although only faintly as a shadow or apparition to be historically romanticized.
3. ~~System~~ appears under erasure as the common conception of a system is a group of interdependent components or parts. While a philosophy of immanence supports the notion of ~~self~~[4]-sustaining processes, this process would not be constructed of independently existing "parts."
4. ~~Self~~ is under erasure as the notion of a self-contained being is problematized in a philosophy of immanence.

REFERENCES

Abram, D. (2004). Earth stories. *Resurgence, 222*, 20–22.

Abram, D. (2011). *Becoming animal: An earthly cosmology*. New York, NY: Random House.

Anderson, M. L. (2003). Embodied cognition: A field guide. *Artificial Intelligence, 149*, 91–130.

Appadurai, A. (Ed.). (1986). *The social lives of things: Commodities in cultural perspective*. Cambridge, UK: Cambridge University Press.

Bai, H. (2009). Re-animating the universe: Environmental education and philosophical animism. In M. McKenzie, H. Bai, P. Hart, & B. Jickling (Eds.), *Fields of green: Restorying culture, environment, and education* (n.p.). Cresskill, NJ: Hampton Press.

Barad, K. (2007). *Meeting the universe halfway: Quantum physics and the entanglement of matter and meaning*. Durham, NC: Duke University Press.

Bateson, G. (2000). [1972] *Steps to an ecology of mind*. Chicago, IL: The University of Chicago Press.

Bateson, N. (Director). (2011). *An ecology of mind* [DVD]. Reading, PA: Bullfrog Films.

Bennett, J. (2010). *Vibrant matter: A political ecology of things*. Durham, NC: Duke University Press.

Berger, D. (2005). Nagarjuna (c. 150—c. 250). *Internet Encyclopaedia of Philosophy*. Retrieved from http://www.iep.utm.edu/nagarjun/

Callicott, J. B. (2000). Contemporary criticisms of the received wilderness idea. In D. N. Cole, S. F. McCool, W. A. Freimund, J. O'Loughlin (Eds.), *Wilderness science in a time of change*, Vol 1: Changing Perspectives and Future Directions (pp. 24–31). Ogden, UT: U. S. Department of Agriculture, Forest Service, Rocky Mountain Research Station.

Capra, F. (1996). *The web of life*. London, UK: HarperCollins.

Chemero, A. (2009). *Radical embodied cognitive science*. Cambridge, MA: MIT Press.

Chiel, H. J., & Beer, R. D. (1997). The brain has a body: Adaptive behaviour emerges from interactions of nervous system, body and environment. *Trends in Neurosciences, 20*, 553–557.

Clark, A. (1997). *Being there: Putting brain, body and world together again*. Cambridge, MA: MIT Press.

Clark, A. (2001). Reasons, robots and the extended mind. *Mind & Language, 16*(2), 121–145.

Clark, A. (2008). *Supersizing the mind: Embodiment, action, and cognitive extension*. Oxford, UK: Oxford University Press.

Clark, A., & Chalmers, D. (1998). The extended mind. *Analysis, 58*, 10–23.

Clarke, D. A. G. (2014). The potential of animism: Experiential outdoor education in the ecological education paradigm. *Pathways: Ontario Journal of Outdoor Education, 26*(2), 13–17.

Clarke, D. A. G., & Mcphie, J. (2014). Becoming animate in education: Immanent materiality and outdoor learning for sustainability. *Journal of Adventure Education & Outdoor Learning, 14*(3), 198–216.

Clarke, D. A. G., & Mcphie, J. (2015) From places to paths: Learning for sustainability, teacher education and a philosophy of becoming. *Environmental Education Research*. doi: 10.1080/13504622.2015.1057554

Clark-Hall, J. R. (2011). *A concise Anglo-Saxon dictionary*. Radford, VA: Wilder Publications.

Connolly, W. E. (2011). *A world of becoming*. Durham, NC: Duke University Press.

Coole, D., & Frost, S. (Eds.) (2010). *New materialisms: Ontology, agency, and politics*. Durham, NC: Duke University Press.

Cousin, G. (2005). Learning from cyberspace. In R. Land & S. Bayne (Eds.), *Education in cyberspace* (pp. 117–129). Abingdon, UK: RoutledgeFalmer.

Dawkins, R. (2011). *The magic of reality: How we know what's really true*. London, England: Bantam Press.

Deleuze, G., & Guattari, F. (2004/1980). *A thousand plateaus: Capitalism and schizophrenia*. (Trans. B. Massumi). London, UK: Continuum.

Deleuze, G., & Guattari, F. (1987/1980). *A thousand plateaus: Capitalism and schizophrenia*. (Trans. B. Massumi). Minneapolis, MN: University of Minnesota Press.

Dema, L. (2007). "Inorganic, yet alive": How can Deleuze and Guattari deal with the accusation of vitalism? *Rhizomes*, *15*. Retrieved from:http://www.rhizomes.net/issues15dema.html

de Vega, E. P. (n.d.). *Thinking the ecological present*. Retrieved from http://www.academia.edu/2964186/Thinking_The_Ecological_Present

di Paolo, E. (2009). Extended life. *Topoi*, *28*(1), 9–21.

Fenwick, T. (2000). Expanding conceptions of experiential learning: A review of the five contemporary perspectives on cognition. *Adult Education Quarterly*, *50*(4), 243–273.

Fuchs, T., Sattel, H. C., & Henningsen, P. (Eds.). (2010). *The embodied self: Dimensions, coherence and disorders*. Stuttgart, Germany: Schattauer.

Gough, N. (2015). Undoing anthropocentrism in educational inquiry: A Phildickian space odyssey? In N. Snaza & J. A. Weaver (Eds.), *Posthumanism and educational research* (pp. 151–166). New York, NY: Routledge.

Green, E. H. (2013). Memoirs of a musical object, supposedly written by itself: It–narrative and eighteenth-century marketing. *Current Musicology*, *95*, 193–213.

Green, M. J. (1997). *Exploring the world of the Druids*. London, England: Thames and Hudson.

Haraway, D. J. (1994). A game of cat's cradle: Science studies, feminist theory, cultural studies. *Configurations*, *2*(1), 59–71.

Harding, S. (2006). *Animate earth: Science, intuition and Gaia*. Cambridge, UK: Green Books.

Harris, A. P. (2008). *The wisdom of the body: Embodied knowing in eco-paganism* (Doctoral dissertation). University of Winchester, Winchester, UK.

Harvey, G. (2006). *Animism: Respecting the living world*. New York, NY: Columbia University Press.

Harvey, G. (Ed.). (2013). *The handbook of contemporary animism*. Handbooks on Contemporary Religion. Durham, NC: Acumen Publishing.

Hoare, P. (2014). *John Ruskin: Mike Leigh and Emma Thompson have got him all wrong*. Retrieved from http://www.theguardian.com/artanddesign/2014/oct/07/john-ruskin-emma-thompson-mike-leigh-film-art

Huggan, G., & Tiffin, H. (2007). Green postcolonialism. *Interventions: International Journal of Postcolonial Studies*, *9*(1), 1–11.

Hutchins, E. (2010). Cognitive ecology. *Topics in Cognitive Science*, *2*, 705–715.

Ingold, T. (2000). *The perception of the environment: Essays on livelihood, dwelling and skill*. Oxon, UK: Routledge.

Ingold, T. (2008). Bindings against boundaries: Entanglements of life in an open world. *Environment and Planning A*, *40*(8), 1796–1810.

Ingold, T. (2010a). *Bringing things to life: Creative entanglements in a world of materials* (Realities, Working Paper #15). Retrieved from: http://citeseerx.ist.psu.edu/viewdoc/download?doi=10.1.1.188.7076&rep=rep1&type=pdf

Ingold, T. (2010b) Footprints through the weather-world: Walking, breathing, knowing. *Journal of the Royal Anthropological Institute* (n. s.). 121–139.

Ingold, T. (2011). *Being alive: Essays on movement, knowledge and description*. Oxon, UK: Routledge.

Ivakhiv, A. (2013). *Ecologies of the moving image: Cinema, affect, nature*. Waterloo, Ontario, Canada: Wilfrid Laurier University Press.

Ivakhiv, A. (2014). *On matters of concern: Ontological politics, ecology, and the anthropo(s)cene* (UC Davis Environments and Societies Paper). University of California at Davis.

Johnson, M. (1987). *The body in the mind: The bodily basis of meaning, imagination, and reason*. Chicago, IL: University of Chicago Press.

Johnson, S. (2014). Deleuze's philosophy of difference and its implications for ALL practice. *Journal of Academic Language and Learning*, *8*(1), A62–A69.

Kohn, E. (2013). *How forests think: Toward an anthropology beyond the human*. Berkeley, California: University of California Press.

Lakoff, G., & Johnson, M. (1980). *Metaphors we live by*. Chicago, IL: University of Chicago Press.

Lamb, J. (n.d.). *The implacability of things*. Retrieved from http://publicdomainreview.org/2012/10/03/the-implacability-of-things/

Li, Q., Clark, B., & Winchester, I. (2010). Instructional design and technology grounded in enactivism: A paradigm shift? *British Journal of Educational Technology, 41*(3), 403–419.

Lovelock, J. E. (1972). Gaia as seen through the atmosphere. *Atmospheric Environment, 6*(8), 579–580.

Lovelock, J. E., & Margulis, L. (1974). Atmospheric homeostasis by and for the biosphere: The Gaia hypothesis. *Tellus.* Series A (Stockholm: International Meteorological Institute), 26(1/2), 2–10.

Malafouris, L. (2013). *How things shape the mind: A theory of material engagement.* Cambridge, MA: MIT Press.

Mannion, G., Fenwick, A., & Lynch, J. (2013). Place-responsive pedagogy: Learning from teachers' experiences of excursions in nature. *Environmental Education Research, 19*(6), 792–809.

Manzotti, R. (2006). Consciousness and existence as a process. *Mind and Matter, 4*(1), 115–119.

Manzotti, R. (2011). The spread mind: Seven steps to situated consciousness. *Journal of Cosmology, 14*, 1–22.

Manzotti, R., & Pepperell, R. (2013). Denying the content–vehicle distinction: A response to "The New Mind Revisited." *Ai and Society, 28*(2), 1–4.

Marder, M. (2013). *Plant-thinking: A philosophy of vegetal life.* New York, NY: Columbia University Press.

Masny, D. (Ed.). (2013). *Cartographies of becoming in education.* Rotterdam, Netherlands: Sense Publishers.

Maturana, H. R., & Varela, F. J. (1972). *De Maquinas y Seres Vivos (Machines and Living Beings),* Santiago, Chile: Editorial Universitaria S.A.

Maturana, H. R., & Varela, F. J. (1980). *Autopoiesis and cognition: The realization of the living.* Dordrecht, Netherlands: Reidel.

Mcphie, J. (2013, July 24). *Distributed well-being: Creativity in therapeutic environments.* Paper presented at University of Cumbria & Brathay Trust Wellbeing Conference, Ambleside, Cumbria, UK.

Mcphie, J. (2014a). Mr Messy and the ghost in the machine: A tale of becoming … a working-class academic (Researching environ(mental) health). *Rhizomes.net, 27.* Retrieved from http://rhizomes.net/issue27/mcphie.html

Mcphie, J. (2014b, February 12). *Access 'vs' environment: Where do you draw the line? There is no line!* Paper presented at the Access vs Environment debate 2014. University of Central Lancashire, Preston, UK. Retrieved from http://breeze01.uclan.ac.uk/p4bytfh9mnz/

Mcphie, J. (2014c, September 9–12). *Walking in circles? Exploring environ(mental) health creatively.* Paper presented at Under Western Skies Conference, Mount Royal University, Calgary, Alberta, Canada.

Mcphie, J. (2015). A Last Wolf in England: The Wolfd's Tale. In D. Hine and P. Kingsnorth (Eds.) *Dark Mountain* (Vol. 7, pp. 223–229). UK: The Dark Mountain Project.

Menary, R. (2006). Attacking the bounds of cognition. *Philosophical Psychology, 19*, 329–344.

Menary, R. (Ed.). (2010). *The extended mind.* Cambridge, MA: MIT Press.

Mendes, S. (Director). (1999). *American Beauty* [Film] Universal City, CA: DreamWorks.

Merleau-Ponty, M. (1964). *The primacy of perception: and other essays on phenomenological psychology, the philosophy of art, history, and politics.* Evanston, IL: Northwestern University Press.

Morton, T. (2007). *Ecology without nature: Rethinking environmental aesthetics.* London, UK: Harvard University Press.

Nature Connections. (2015, March 26). *Nature Connections 2015: An interdisciplinary conference to examine routes to nature connectedness.* College of Life and Natural Sciences, University of Derby, UK. Retrieved from http://www.derby.ac.uk/enterprisecentre/events/nature-connections/

Noë, A. (2009). *Out of our heads: Why you are not your brain, and other lessons from the biology of consciousness.* New York, NY: Hill and Wang.

Poole, K. (2014). The contextual cat: Human–animal relations and social meaning in Anglo-Saxon England. *Journal of Archaeological Method and Theory,* (n.p.). doi: 10.1007/s10816-014-9208-9

Poster, C. (1996). Being and becoming: Rhetorical ontology in early Greek thought. *Philosophy & Rhetoric, 29*(1), 1–14.

Preston, C. J. (2003). *Grounding knowledge: Environmental philosophy, epistemology, and place.* Athens, GA: The University of Georgia Press.

Rautio, P. (2013). Children who carry stones in their pockets: On autotelic material practices in everyday life. *Children's Geographies.* doi:10.1080/14733285.2013.812278

Reid, D. (1995). *Enactivism.* Retrieved from http://www.acadiau.ca/~dreid/enactivism/EnactivismDef.html

Reid, J. B., Bucklin, E. P., Copenagle, L., Kidder, J., Pack, S. M., Polissar, P. J., & Williams, M. L. (1995). Sliding rocks at the Racetrack, Death Valley: What makes them move? *Geology, 23*(9), 819–822.

Roger, J. (2008). *Philosophy of mind.* Retrieved from http://www.philosopher.org.uk/mind.htm

Rowlands, M. (1999). *The body in mind.* Cambridge, UK: Cambridge University Press.

Rowlands, M. (2009). Extended cognition and the mark of the cognitive. *Philosophical Psychology, 22*, 1–19.

Rowlands, M. (2010). *The new science of the mind*. Cambridge, MA: MIT Press.

Ryle, G. (1949). *The concept of mind*. London, England: Hutchinson.

Said, E. W. (1978). *Orientalism*. New York, NY: Pantheon.

Semetsky, I., & Masny, D. (Eds.). (2013). *Deleuze and education*. Edinburgh, Scotland: Edinburgh University Press.

Shapiro, L. (2010). *Embodied cognition (New problems of philosophy)*. Oxon, UK: Routledge.

Sharp, J. P. (2008). *Geographies of postcolonialism*. London, England: Sage.

Skolimowski, H. (1994). *The participatory mind: A new theory of knowledge and of the universe*. London, England: Penguin/Arkana.

Spinney, L. (2014). Upside-down world: The goggles that remake reality. *New Scientist*. Issue 2990. Retrieved from https://www.newscientist.com/article/mg22429901-300-upside-down-world-the-goggles-that-remake-reality/

Spivak, G. C. (1988). Can the subaltern speak? In C. Nelson & L. Grossberg Eds., *Marxism and the interpretation of culture* (pp. 271–313). Urbana, IL: University of Illinois Press.

Spuybroek, L. (2011). *Sympathy of things: Ruskin and the ecology of design*. Rotterdam, Netherlands: V2 Publishing.

Stewart, J. O., Gappene, O., & di Paolo, E. (Eds.). (2010). *Enaction: Towards a new paradigm in cognitive science*. Cambridge, MA: MIT Press.

St. Pierre, E. A. (2004). Deleuzian concepts for education. *Educational Philosophy and Theory, 36*(3), 283–296.

Szymborska, W. (1997/1962). Conversation with a stone. In *Nothing twice: Selected poems* (p. 54).(Stanisław Barafczak & Clare Cavanagh, Trans.) Kraków, Poland: Wydawnictwo Literackie.

Thompson, E., & Stapelton, M. (2009). Making sense of sense-making: Reflections on enactive and extended mind theories. *Topoi, 28*, 23–30.

Thrift, N. (1997). The still point: Resistance, expressive embodiment and dance. In S. Pile & M. Keith (Eds.), *Geographies of resistance* (pp. 124–152). London, England: Routledge.

Tilley, C. (1994). *A phenomenology of landscape: Places, paths and monuments*. Oxford, UK: Berg.

Turnbaugh, P. J., Ley, R. E., Hamady, M., Fraser-Liggett, C., Knight, R. & Gordon, J. I. (2007). The human microbiome project: Exploring the microbial part of ourselves in a changing world. *Nature, 449*(7164), 804–810.

Urry, J. (1990). *The tourist gaze: Leisure and travel in contemporary societies*. London, England: Sage Publications Ltd.

Varela, F. J., Thompson, E., & Rosch, E. (1991). *The embodied mind: Cognitive science and human experience*. Cambridge, MA: MIT Press.

von Bertalanffy, L. (1928). Kritische Theorie der Formbildung. Gebrüder Borntraeger; Berlin, Germany. Abhandlungen zur theoretischen Biologie, 27. Trans. 1933, J. H. Woodger as *Modern theories of development: An introduction to theoretical biology.* Oxford, UK: Clarendon Press.

Wheeler, M. (2005). *Reconstructing the cognitive world: The next step*. Cambridge, MA: MIT Press.

Wylie, A. (2002). *Thinking from things: Essays in the philosophy of archaeology*. Oakland, CA: University of California Press.

Index

Aboriginal Australian cultures 150
About Face Theatre Company 105
Abram, D. 151, 154
abuse 111, 118, 120
actants 6–7, 9, 50, 53, 66, 73, 78, 113, 119, 121
activism 11, 39, 43
Addison, J. 162
advertising 67, 73, 112
aesthetics 39, 43–4, 64, 95, 97, 102–3, 154, 156, 159–60
affect 2–9, 11–13, 18, 32, 36–46; and common world pedagogy 132, 141; and embodied classroom practices 50, 57, 59; and new materialist imaginaries 105, 107; and school absence registration 90; and teen digital sexuality assemblages 112–16, 120–1
Affect Theory Reader 39
affordances 113–15, 121, 125–6, 157
agency 1–2, 7–9, 31–2, 37, 49; agential cuts 6, 11–12, 22, 36, 48, 50–3, 56–7, 59–60; agential realism 4–6, 11, 20, 100, 148; agential separability 100–1; agentic assemblage 16–24; agentic force 21, 33–4, 48; and common world pedagogy 126, 128–33, 141, 144; distributed agency 17–20, 162; and embodied classroom practices 54–5; and neo-liberal teaching practices 72–3; and new materialist imaginaries 95, 97–8, 106–7; and outdoor environmental education 149, 152, 160–2; and teen digital sexuality assemblages 112–13, 115, 119–21
agricultural revolution 151
Ahmed, S. 28, 30
Alaimo, S. 107
alienation 103–4
Allen, L. 49
American Reputation Aid Society (ARAS) 38
androcentrism 155
animism 149–51, 158
Anthropocene 2, 9–10, 125–47
anthropocentrism 5, 11, 25, 91, 112, 149, 153, 157, 162
anthropology 39, 57, 152
anthropomorphisation 54, 130–1
ants 10–11, 125–47
Appadurai, A. 162
archaeology 152
architecture 156, 160

Aristotle 134
Artists' Soup Kitchen 5, 36–46
arts 5, 8, 36–46, 90, 94–6, 98–101, 103, 105, 107, 164
Åsberg, C. 44
assemblages 1, 3–6, 8–9, 12, 16–24; and artists' soup kitchen 37, 42–3; collective-body-assemblages 33; collective-researcher-assemblages 26; and common world pedagogy 127; and embodied classroom practices 48, 51–6, 58, 60; and new materialist imaginaries 100; and outdoor environmental education 156, 159–60; research assemblages 4–5, 8; and researcher subjectivities 26, 33; teen digital sexuality assemblages 111–24
atomisation 152
attunement 4–5, 12, 36–8, 43–4, 132
autonomy 11, 18, 58, 133–4, 149–50
autopoiesis 151

bacteria 10, 130–1, 135, 157
Bai, H. 153
Bakhtin, M. 59
Barad, K. 1–2, 4–9, 11–12, 16–17, 20–2, 37, 47–50, 52–3, 56, 60, 72, 97–8, 100, 150, 152, 162
Barrett, E. 99
Bateson, G. 151–2, 157–8, 163
Bateson, N. 164
BBM 114, 119
Bellacasa, M.P. 135
Bennett, J. 4, 12, 16–21, 53, 55, 150, 162
Bergson, J. 151
Berlant, L. 112
Bertalanffy, L. von 151
bias 149, 153–4, 158–9, 163
binaries/binary logic 26–7, 31, 54, 73, 90, 107, 113, 119–21, 149, 153–4, 159
biodiversity 127
biosphere 127–8, 155, 157, 161
Bird-David, N. 150
birds 155–6, 162
Blackman, L. 98, 113–14
Bodén, L. 7, 83–93
bodies 6, 47–62
body language 51, 53
Bohr, N. 5
Bonta, M. 20

eating as art 5, 12, 38–9, 41–4
ecology 5, 10, 13, 37, 44, 127, 129, 148–9, 151–5, 157, 159, 164
ecopaganism 150
ecosystems 135, 140, 155, 158–9
educational research 1–15; and diffractive pedagogies 94–110; and embodied practices of mattering 6, 47–62, 103; and images of thinking 25–35; and learning to be affected 36–46; and multispecies vulnerability 125–47; and outdoor environmental education 148–68; research assemblages 4–5; and researcher subjectivities 25–35; role of 11–13; and school absence registration 83–93; and space-time-matterings 5–8; and Teachers Pay Teachers 63–82
Ellsworth, E. 98
embodied practices 6, 47–62, 103
emergence 1, 3, 7, 10, 18, 20–2; and artists' soup kitchen 43; and embodied classroom practices 48–9, 58, 60; and neo-liberal teaching practices 77; and new materialist imaginaries 99, 101–2; and outdoor environmental education 149, 163; and voice 20–2
empiricism 3–4, 6, 36, 43, 47–8, 51, 56, 59–60, 84–5, 87, 89–91, 120
enfolding 6, 100, 156
Enlightenment 58, 60, 151, 153
entanglement 1–7, 9–13, 16–17, 20–2, 37–8; and artists' soup kitchen 43; and common world pedagogy 127–30, 132–4, 143; and embodied classroom practices 48, 51–3, 57–60; and neo-liberal teaching practices 65, 72–3; and new materialist imaginaries 99–101, 107; and outdoor environmental education 159, 163; and school absence registration 83, 91; and teen digital sexuality assemblages 111, 113–14, 117, 120
entrepreneurs 69, 77
environment 10, 47, 100, 104–5, 107–8; and common world pedagogy 126, 128–31, 134, 136, 140, 144; environmental education 2, 148–68
epistemology 2–3, 5–6, 8, 11, 13; and common world pedagogy 128; and embodied classroom practices 49, 59–60; and neo-liberal teaching practices 73; and new materialist imaginaries 98, 100; and researcher subjectivities 26–8; voice 17, 22
erotophobia 119
essentialism 10–11, 40–1, 54, 148–9, 151–2, 154, 157–9, 163
ethics 1, 3, 7–8, 10, 43–4; and common world pedagogy 126–9, 131, 134, 136, 142, 144; and embodied classroom practices 48–9, 51, 56, 59–60; ethico-onto-epistemology 2, 5–6, 11, 13; and neo-liberal teaching practices 73, 79; and new materialist imaginaries 105; planetary ethics 2
ethnicity 30, 105
ethnography 6, 10, 39, 47, 49–50, 126, 131–4, 148
Etsy 70
etymology 154
Eurocentrism 8–9, 155
exceptionalism 9, 11, 126, 128–30, 133
extinction 9, 127, 153–4, 163–4

Facebook 9, 67–8, 112–16, 119
fascicular root-thinking 26–34
fear 7, 40, 94, 111
felfies 116, 119
Feminist Posthumanisms 1–15; conflict in 25–7; core conceptual starting points in 2–4; and diffractive pedagogies 94–110; and embodied practices of mattering 6, 47–62, 103; fem-inal theorists 2, 4, 8; feminist capacities/possibilities 1; and images of thinking 25–35; and immanence 8–10; and learning to be affected 36–46; and micro-ontologies 8–10; and multispecies vulnerability 125–47; and outdoor environmental education 148–68; posthuman participations 8–10; and renewed feminist materialisms 25–6, 28–30, 34; and research assemblages 4–5; and researcher subjectivities 25–35; role of 11–13; and school absence registration 83–93; and space-time-matterings 5–8; and Teachers Pay Teachers 63–82; and teen digital sexuality 111–24
fetishisation 111
figuration 2, 41, 44
First Nation cultures 150, 155
firsthand perspectives 28, 34
food as art 5, 12, 38–9, 41–4
force relations 1, 10–12, 112–13, 115, 117, 121
fossil fuels 126
Foucault, M. 7, 9, 49, 52, 56, 71, 73, 119
Francis, B. 59
Freud, S. 112
Frontlinedance 105
Frost, S. 150, 162
Fuller, A. 49
further research 21–3, 59, 65, 70, 73, 79, 85, 104–5
future generations 127, 138

Gaia 151, 157
Gallop, J. 98
Galton, M. 49
gardening 155
Gatens, M. 98
Gaudi, A. 160
gender 2, 4, 6, 11, 19–22; and embodied practices of mattering 47–62; and neo-liberal teaching practices 65–6, 77–9; and new materialist imaginaries 95, 104, 106; and outdoor environmental education 154; and researcher subjectivities 28, 30, 33; and school absence registration 85; and teen digital sexuality assemblages 112–14, 116–17, 120
Gender and Education 3, 37
General Systems Theory (GST) 151–2
genocide 155
genome 33
geology 161
Gildon, C. 162
Gill, R. 65
global warming 143
globalisation 112, 151
Goodings, L. 73
Google 67